# National Symposium on Family Issues

Volume 9



**Series editors**
Susan M. McHale
Valarie King
Jennifer Van Hook

More information about this series at http://www.springer.com/series/8381

Jennifer Van Hook • Susan M. McHale
Valarie King
Editors

# Families and Technology

Springer

*Editors*
Jennifer Van Hook
Department of Sociology
Pennsylvania State University
University Park, PA, USA

Susan M. McHale
Social Science Research Institute
Pennsylvania State University
University Park, PA, USA

Valarie King
Department of Sociology
Pennsylvania State University
University Park, PA, USA

ISSN 2192-9157 ISSN 2192-9165 (electronic)
National Symposium on Family Issues
ISBN 978-3-030-07054-0 ISBN 978-3-319-95540-7 (eBook)
https://doi.org/10.1007/978-3-319-95540-7



This Springer imprint is published by the registered company Springer Nature Switzerland AG
The registered company address is: Gewerbestrasse 11, 6330 Cham, Switzerland

# Preface

New communication technologies such as smartphones and social media are rapidly diffusing across the globe among both children and adults. American teens spend an average of 9 h a day engaged in social media such as online videos or music and half feel they are addicted to their smartphones. Fifteen percent of US adults have used an online dating site. Ninety-one percent of US adults own a cell phone, as do 89% of adults in Nigeria, 83% in Ghana, 76% in Bangladesh, and 65% in Uganda. As of the first quarter of 2018, Facebook had 2.19 billion monthly active users worldwide. Technological changes such as these are rapidly changing how parents raise their children, how couples meet and form relationships, and how family members remain connected across long distances. The 2017 National Symposium on Family Issues focused on how these dramatic changes are shaping and changing families and family life in both positive and negative ways and aimed at identifying novel directions for population and family research.

The chapters in this volume represent the work that was presented at the Symposium. Together, they advance research on how families use and monitor the use of technology among family members. As highlighted in Part I of this volume, children are often the first in their families to pick up new technologies, turning the tables on parent-child lines of authority and expertise and widening the generational divide. Part II focuses on how technologies, including online dating apps, affect couple relationships. While dating apps may alter how and how quickly couples find each other, these technologies may not fundamentally change the number of partners people have or the duration or quality of their long-term relationships. Nevertheless, social media and other technologies provide opportunities for surveillance, which can erode trust within couple relationships. Finally, Part III explores how the global spread of communication technology, such as cell phones, has the potential to help families remain connected across long distances and even act as conduits for the transmission of new ideas about family roles, yet also appears to foster feelings of isolation and depression.

Overall, research on how communication technologies are shaping families and family relationships is in its nascent stage. Technology evolves quickly, making it difficult for research to keep up. Additionally, the nearly universal saturation of some technologies, such as television, makes it difficult to disentangle cause and effect. As highlighted throughout the volume and in the concluding chapter, there remain many unanswered questions and many opportunities for future researchers to explore the role of technologies in how families form and function.

Jennifer Van Hook
Susan M. McHale
Valarie King

# Acknowledgments

The editors are grateful to the organizations at Penn State that sponsored the 2017 Family Symposium and this resulting volume, including Penn State's Social Science Research Institute (SSRI); Population Research Institute (PRI); the departments of Sociology and Criminology, Human Development and Family Studies, Psychology, Communication Arts and Sciences; and the Child Study Center. The editors also gratefully acknowledge essential core financial support in the form of a five-year grant from the Eunice Kennedy Shriver National Institute of Child Health and Human Development (NICHD; R13-HD048150), as well as ongoing advice from Regina Bures at NICHD. The support of our partners enabled us to attract outstanding scholars from a range of backgrounds and disciplines from the community of researchers, practitioners, and policy-makers on whom the quality of the series depends.

The efforts of many individuals went into planning the 2017 symposium and producing this volume. Our internal advisory board, consisting of Dawn Witherspoon, Greg Fosco, Nancy Luke, Patricia Miranda, Doug Teti, Kevin Thomas, Sarah Damaske, and Mayra Bamaca, were helpful from the early stages of brainstorming for the 2017 symposium. In addition, we are very grateful to Diane Felmlee and Scott Yabiku for moderating symposium sessions and Jennifer Glick for providing welcoming remarks. We also thank the administrative staff in the Population Research Institute and the Social Science Research Institute at Penn State including Sherry Yocum, Angela Jordan, Diane Diviney, Jackie Jacobs, and Li Ge. Finally, the Symposium and book would not have been possible without Carolyn Scott's organizational skills, commitment, and attention to the many details that go into developing an engaging conference and producing a scholarly volume.

Jennifer Van Hook
Susan M. McHale
Valarie King

# Contents

# Contributors

**Meghan Bisbey** Center for Research on Media, Technology, and Health, University of Pittsburgh, Pittsburgh, PA, USA

**Nicholas Bowman** Department of Communication, University of West Virginia, Morgantown, WV, USA

**Lynn Schofield Clark** Department of Media, Film & Journalism Studies, University of Denver, Denver, CO, USA

**Jason B. Colditz** Center for Research on Media, Technology, and Health, University of Pittsburgh, Pittsburgh, PA, USA

**Jodi Dworkin** Department of Family Social Science, University of Minnesota, St. Paul, MN, USA

**Cesar G. Escobar-Viera** Department of Medicine, University of Pittsburgh, Pittsburgh, PA, USA

**Zoya Gubernskaya** Department of Sociology, University at Albany, SUNY, Albany, NY, USA

**Katherine M. Hertlein** Marriage and Family Therapy Program, University of Nevada, Las Vegas, NV, USA

**Rukmalie Jayakody** Department of Human Development and Family Studies, Penn State, PA, USA

**Sabrina A. Karim** University of Pittsburgh School of Medicine, Pittsburgh, PA, USA

**Jennifer Knight** Department of Communication, University of West Virginia, Morgantown, WV, USA

**Cassie McMillan** Department of Sociology and Criminology, Penn State, PA, USA

**Amy I. Nathanson** School of Communication, Ohio State University, Columbus, OH, USA

**Brian A. Primack** University Honors College, University of Pittsburgh, Pittsburgh, PA, USA

**Michael Rosenfeld** Department of Sociology, Stanford University, Stanford, CA, USA

**Pepper Schwartz** Department of Sociology, University of Washington, Seattle, WA, USA

**Ariel Shensa** Department of Medicine, University of Pittsburgh, Pittsburgh, PA, USA

**Jaime E. Sidani** Department of Medicine, University of Pittsburgh, Pittsburgh, PA, USA

**Xiaoran Sun** Department of Human Development and Family Studies, Penn State, PA, USA

**Judith Treas** Department of Sociology, University of California, Irvine, CA, USA

**Nicholas Velotta** Department of Sociology, University of Washington, Seattle, WA, USA

**Michelle S. Woods** Department of Medicine, University of Pittsburgh, Pittsburgh, PA, USA

# About the Editors

**Jennifer Van Hook, Ph.D.** is Roy C. Buck Professor of Sociology and Demography and Director of the Graduate Program in Sociology at Penn State and nonresident fellow at the Migration Policy Institute.

**Susan M. McHale, Ph.D.** is Director of the Social Science Research Institute and Distinguished Professor of Human Development and Family Studies and Professor of Demography at Penn State.

**Valarie King, Ph.D.** is Professor of Sociology, Demography, and Human Development and Family Studies at Penn State and Director of the Family Demography Training Program at the Population Research Institute.

# Part I
# Parents' Role in Children's Screen Time

# Chapter 1
# How Parents Manage Young Children's Mobile Media Use

**Amy I. Nathanson**

For decades, researchers have studied how parents manage their children's media use, including whether and how they discuss content with children, restrict access to media, and co-use media. These activities are known in the communication literature as "parental mediation" (Nathanson, 2001). The vast majority of research on parental mediation has focused on television. Today's children still watch a lot of television. However, the way in which content is consumed has evolved. Increasingly, children are using media on mobile devices, such as tablets or smartphones. Even if they are watching the same material, the experience is different. Mobile devices can be used just about anywhere, and their small screen size typically limits the number of people who can view the content. As a result, children are increasingly using media by themselves in spaces that are outside of the home.

The purpose of this chapter is to discuss parental mediation of young children's media use within the context of today's media environment. Beginning with the concept of parental mediation, I discuss how it has been applied in the past and how we might revise its conceptualization. I then discuss the research on parental mediation, which has focused primarily on its predictors and outcomes. I then consider parental mediation within the new media landscape in which children's media consumption is increasingly private and mobile. In conclusion, trade-offs of engaging in parental mediation are considered and suggestions for future research are provided.

A. I. Nathanson (✉)
School of Communication, Ohio State University, Columbus, OH, USA
e-mail: nathanson.7@osu.edu

 
J. Van Hook et al. (eds.), *Families and Technology*, National Symposium on Family Issues 9, https://doi.org/10.1007/978-3-319-95540-7_1

## Parental Mediation

Parental mediation is a construct that is commonly used in the communication discipline to refer to a variety of parental behaviors concerning children's media use. This multidimensional construct is typically used to describe three subcategories of behaviors: active mediation (parent–child communication about media content), restrictive mediation (parent-initiated rules for children's media access and use), and co-viewing or co-use (simultaneous parent–child consumption of media; Nathanson, 2001). In other disciplines, scholars use the term parental media monitoring to refer to many of the same behaviors (Padilla-Walker & Coyne, 2011).

### *Active Mediation*

Active mediation (sometimes called evaluative guidance or instructive mediation; Bybee, Robinson, & Turow, 1982; Valkenburg, Krcmar, Peeters, & Marseille, 1999) is itself a multidimensional construct since there can be great variety in the types of conversations parents and children have about media. Conversations can be negative in tone, such as when parents make disparaging remarks about characters or media content, or positive in nature, such as when parents express admiration for characters or enjoyment of the storyline. Sometimes, parental comments are neutral in valence, such as when parents offer additional information about storylines, explain how special effects work, or ask children questions about story content (Nathanson, 2001).

In fact, active mediation can be considered a very broad concept so as to encompass any comment parents make to children about media. However, it is important to explicitly articulate our definition of this subdimension of parental mediation in order to maximize its utility. To do so requires us to consider a few key questions that can lead to development of a common understanding of active mediation. First, we must ask *what intentions underlie parental comments about children's media use?* Parents may offer a variety of comments, but only some of the comments are motivated by a desire to shape children's responses to media content. Offhand remarks or other spontaneous comments (e.g., "Wow, that's cool!") may impact children's viewing experience and reactions to shared media content. But, should these types of comments count as a form of active parental mediation or should they be considered something else? In my prior thinking (e.g., Nathanson, 2001), I adopted a very liberal definition of parental active mediation and indeed, considered any form of parental commentary—regardless of its motivation—to count as active mediation. However, I now question the utility of a very broad conceptualization of active mediation and recommend that the term be restricted to comments intended to somehow shape children's understanding of or reaction to media content. Without this restriction, the labels active and mediation do not seem appropriate.

Second, to aid our identification of active mediation behaviors, we should ask *when do active mediation behaviors occur?* That is, must active mediation occur while children are consuming media content, or can it occur before or after exposure? Most active mediation research, as evidenced by the conceptualization and/or measurement of the term, appears to assume that active mediation occurs only while, or sometimes after, parents and children co-experience media content (Rasmussen, 2014). Questions assessing active mediation often ask parents to report the frequency with which they comment "when [their] child is watching TV," for example. This assumption makes co-use a necessary condition for active mediation. However, I believe this is an unnecessary and ultimately counterproductive assumption that should be dismantled. Parental comments aimed at tempering or enhancing media effects can occur in advance of exposure, such as when parents warn their children that the movie they are about to view contains some bad language that should not be repeated, or after exposure, such as when parents discuss over dinner a movie they both watched. In fact, parental active mediation can occur even if parents have not seen the content at all. For example, parents may learn that their child watched a movie at a sleepover party and later engage their child in a discussion of the content. These examples highlight the importance of the first question regarding the parents' motives for making media-related comments. Regardless of when the comments are made, if parents wish to shape their children's reaction to media exposure, then we should consider those comments as active mediation. Thus, I believe that the boundary conditions concerning the timing of active mediation should be generous.

Provided that parents intend to influence their children's interpretation of media content in some way, active mediation can encompass a variety of content. One of the more commonly studied types of active mediation is evaluative comments, such as when parents express a positive or negative judgment about media content. Since much of parental mediation research has examined the methods parents use to prevent negative media effects, much of the prior work in this area has focused on negative evaluative comments and the impact on children. Negative evaluative comments can include expressions of the parent's own distaste for the content (e.g., "I don't like this show") or comments that are more directly aimed at the child (e.g., "The hero is using bad language–don't copy him"). Parents can also make factual comments about media content, such as providing information that is designed to enhance comprehension. For example, parents can tell their child that what they are seeing on television is not real or explain that the characters are actors playing a part. Factual comments might be considered parents' attempts to enhance children's media literacy.

In Clark's (2011) theorizing on parental mediation, she noted that most parental mediation research ignores the potential for parents to learn with and from their children by engaging in dialogue surrounding the child's media use. She advised mediation scholars to consider participatory learning as an additional category of parental mediation in order to capture collaborative parent–child interactions in which parents and children co-share teacher and learner roles. This form of mediation becomes particularly important as children mature into adolescence and become relative experts (compared to parents) in newer forms of technology and applications, including those used by parents (e.g., mobile phones, and social networks). Likewise, the concept of child-initiated support is intended to describe parent–child interactions that originate from the child's curiosity or desire to learn, rather than from the parent's desire to instruct or protect the child (Livingstone et al., 2017).

In addition to the type of content parents discuss with children, active mediation can vary according to the form or style it takes. Parents may offer direct statements or commands that do not necessarily invite additional discussion (e.g., "I don't want you to act like that character"). Alternatively, parents may ask children questions or otherwise signal a desire to process the material together (e.g., "What do you think about how the hero behaved in that scene?"; Nathanson & Yang, 2003). Using self-determination theory as a guide, a measure of parental mediation that captures the way in which parents discuss media with children was introduced (Valkenburg, Piotrowski, Hermanns, & de Leeuw, 2013). The argument is that youngsters' acceptance of parental values and rules is most effective when parents engage in autonomy-supportive behaviors, such as validating children's perspectives and being responsive to children's needs. Parents who engage in autonomy-supportive active mediation behaviors would consider the child's opinions and offer comments that are sensitive to the child's viewpoint (e.g., "I can understand why you like the hero a lot, but I think he could find other ways to solve problems"). Parents at the other end of this continuum engage in controlling active mediation behaviors, such as communicating an opinion or expectation without allowing the child to disagree or by threating punishment if the child does (e.g., "That character is bad—if you ever act like he does, you'll be grounded"). Controlling behaviors limit children's opportunities to express themselves and rely on the child's submission to parental authority to gain compliance.

By considering the style with which parents discuss media with their children, the connection between parental mediation and parenting styles and strategies in general becomes evident. Parents' behaviors surrounding media may reflect broader beliefs about parenting and parent–child relationships that vary according to family socioeconomic status (SES; Clark, 2013). These nuances remind us that parental mediation may have more to do with parenting and the unique circumstances surrounding families than with specific beliefs about media.

Active mediation, because it is a form of parenting and parental communication, is a complex term that requires careful conceptualization. It is useful to identify the range of active mediation behaviors, both in terms of content and style, to gain a fuller understanding of the concept and to make predictions about its effectiveness.

## *Restrictive Mediation*

Restrictive mediation, or gatekeeping activities (Jiow, Lim, & Lin, 2017), refers to the rules parents place on children's media use. The conceptualization of restrictive mediation is relatively straightforward, compared with active mediation's conceptualization, but has become more complicated in the Internet age. Nevertheless, it is important to define how restrictive mediation varies in both its content and form.

Parents can institute a variety of types of media rules, but most of the rules fall under one of three categories. First, parents regulate the *amount and timing* of media exposure. For example, parents may allow no more than 2 h of media use per day, enact a "no screens" rule past 8 pm on school-nights, or forbid smartphones at the dinner table. Second, parents create rules pertaining to *media content.* Parents may forbid exposure to R-rated movies or restrict the amount of time spent playing violent video games, for example. Relatedly, parents may regulate the type of content they permit their children to create, such as forbidding children from sharing photos or personal information online (e.g., through chat features on video games, via social media). Technical features or technical restrictions, such as filtering software, may enable parents to restrict children's access to certain content (Livingstone & Helsper, 2008). Third, in regulating online exposure, parents may have rules about their children's privacy and online interactions, or interaction restrictions, such as insisting that children share passwords, mandating that parents be "friends" with children on social media sites, or forbidding online interactions entirely (Livingstone & Helsper, 2008). These rules are designed to enable parents to oversee and regulate their children's behaviors online.

Like active mediation, parents can implement rules using different styles or forms. In their paper connecting self-determination theory to parental mediation work, Valkenburg et al. (2013) argued that compliance with rules is most likely when parents engage in autonomy-supportive restrictive mediation, such as when they discuss media rules with their children and negotiate boundaries that demonstrate sensitivity and respect for the child's viewpoint. Compliance is least likely, they argue, and rebellion quite possible, when parents use controlling forms of restrictive mediation, such as when parents institute rules without entertaining children's perspective, questions, or protests.

## *Co–Use*

Co-use refers to parents and children using the same media together. Originally, the concept was called co-viewing because of the research community's focus on television. Co-viewing may still be used to describe joint television viewing by parents and children, but a more accurate term is co-use which encompasses not only shared television viewing but also shared video game playing and Internet use.

There is some debate in the parental mediation literature concerning whether co-use should be considered a form of mediation. Parents may share media use with their children for a variety of reasons, including common media interests or the coincidence of being co-present in the room while a media form is in use. Because co-use can embody the coincidence of being co-present, it has been called unfocused guidance (Bybee et al., 1982) to denote its unintentional nature. Co-use can be intentional, however, such as when parents monitor their children's Internet activities or observe the content of a favored television program (Jiow et al., 2017). In these cases, parents co-use with the goal of possibly altering the children's media consumption, for example, to offer clarifying comments, to condemn problematic portrayals, or to end media exposure if it is deemed inappropriate.

The co-use concept presents a tricky dilemma for the conceptualization of parental mediation. Although we can distinguish between intentional and happenstance instances of co-use, it appears that intentional co-use would usually lead to active mediation and might inform restrictive mediation. For example, co-playing video games may aid parents in guiding their active and restrictive mediation behaviors. For this reason, co-play is conceptualized as a form of investigative activities (Jiow et al., 2017). The presence of a parent while a child is online is considered a form of active co-use, a concept that also encompasses parent–child conversations about their Internet use, along with rules about online activity (Livingstone & Helsper, 2008). However, it then becomes questionable whether the co-use concept—in the context of parental mediation work—becomes unnecessary due to its redundancy with active or restrictive mediation. Although I have argued that the mere presence of a parent during media consumption can alter a child's experience—and there is evidence to support this claim (Nathanson, 2001), the observation of co-use effects should not itself serve as a criterion for identifying it as a form of parental mediation.

It is difficult to entirely remove co-use from our discussion of parental mediation given that it has historically been considered a key component of the larger construct. This chapter acknowledges work on co-use and considers its significance. However, because of its overlap with other forms of mediation (particularly active mediation), I recommend that future work consider co-use as a separate form of behavior from parental mediation.

## Central Questions Surrounding Parental Mediation

Research on parental mediation has concentrated on two primary questions: (1) What characteristics predict whether parents provide mediation? and (2) How does parental mediation affect children? Because of the obvious practical applicability of parental mediation work, it is understandable that scholars have been most concerned with who uses mediation and with what impact, so that effective interventions can be developed to help parents manage children's media use. Perhaps because of its practical applicability, less work has been devoted to developing or using theory in this area. This is an unfortunate oversight, as it has limited the body of work's connection to other relevant literatures and disciplines (e.g., on family studies, parenting, and developmental psychology) which could ultimately aid in meeting the goal of providing informed advice to parents. The next section will review the research on the predictors and outcomes of parental mediation.

## *Predictors of Parental Mediation*

Research investigating the precursors to parental mediation has revealed a largely unsurprising collection of results. One of the most consistent predictors of parental mediation is beliefs about the impact of media on children. In the case of restrictive mediation, parental concern about harmful media effects on children is a strong predictor (Bybee et al., 1982; Van der Voort, Nikken, & Van Lil, 1992). In contrast, active mediation and co-use are predicted by both concern over negative effects (Warren, 2003) and beliefs that media exposure can benefit children (Bybee et al., 1982; Van der Voort et al., 1992).

Among the other parent demographic variables that are typically explored, research has found that parent education is positively associated with both active mediation (Valkenburg et al., 1999) and restrictive mediation (Van der Voort et al., 1992). In addition, mediation of all kinds is more likely to be provided by mothers than by fathers (Valkenburg et al., 1999; Van der Voort et al., 1992).

In an exploration of the role of parental availability and involvement in predicting parental mediation of preschoolers' media use, mediation was more likely among parents who were otherwise more involved with and available to their children, in part due to their employment conditions (Warren, 2003, 2005). The work reminds us that parental mediation may be less about parental choice and more about parental opportunity instead.

Some research on the predictors of parental mediation has examined the role of child factors. Although the results have varied, a few trends are worth noting. Parents are more likely to use restrictive mediation and, to some extent active mediation, with younger children (Van der Voort et al., 1992). In the case of media rules in particular, parents may sense that their children become increasingly resistant to accepting parental involvement as they age. Research on social domain theory, applied to parenting, has found that as children move toward adolescence, they develop beliefs about the domains in which parents have legitimate authority (e.g., moral issues; Smetana, Crean, & Campione-Barr, 2005). Teenagers typically regard media rules to belong to the "personal domain" in which parents do not have legitimate authority in dictating exposure patterns. Social domain theory provides a sensible account of why parents may become less involved in their children's media use as they get older.

## *Effects of Parental Mediation*

Research has explored whether and how parental mediation is associated with various child outcomes. Among children (and not adolescents), most parental mediation appears to be effective. In particular, active mediation is related to a number of positive outcomes among children. Correlational research has shown that children whose parents talk with them about media tend to have less media exposure, better comprehension of television programs (Desmond, Singer, Singer, Calam, & Colimore, 1985), less positive evaluations of aggressive television characters, and less aggressive attitudes (Nathanson, 1999). Experimental work has found that a variety of types of comments parents make during media exposure is linked with enhanced understanding of educational content (Valkenburg, Krcmar, & de Roos, 1998), increased empathy (Rasmussen et al., 2016), less endorsement of gender stereotypes (Nathanson, Wilson, McGee, & Sebastian, 2002), and less aggressive feelings among boys (Nathanson & Cantor, 2000).

Not all comments are equally effective though, and some types of active mediation can backfire and increase unwanted outcomes from media exposure. We suggested that older children may resent or tune out when confronted with direct statements about media violence but that more indirect methods, such as asking questions, may motivate them to engage in critical viewing of media violence. In contrast, younger children, who may be less certain about social conduct norms, may require more blatant condemnations of media violence in order to view aggressive characters and events as undesirable (Nathanson & Yang, 2003). Asking young children (ages 5–7) questions about violent perpetrators while viewing cartoon violence led children to report more liking of the aggressor and more tolerance of aggression (Nathanson & Yang, 2003). However, making direct, evaluative statements to young children about the perpetrator (e.g., "That guy in the mask is not cool") was associated with more prosocial responses after viewing. The opposite pattern of results was found among older children (ages 9–11). Older children had less liking of violent characters and less tolerance for aggression when they were asked questions, but they reported more liking of violent characters and more tolerance of aggression when provided with statements.

In another study (Nathanson, 2004), evaluative statements were found to be superior to statements teaching facts (e.g., "that show is not real") in reducing children's acceptance of violent characters and actions. Throughout childhood, youngsters may benefit from hearing condemnations of media violence, but parents may need to adapt the way in which they deliver this content (from direct statements to asking questions) as children mature.

Research on the consequences of parental mediation for preschoolers is relatively rare. Active mediation was related to a less healthy diet among preschoolers in one study, raising the possibility that there may be a minimum age at which active mediation can be effective (Harrison & Liechy, 2012). However, since preschoolers' diets are determined mostly by caregivers, this finding may suggest something more about parents instead of children. Moreover, correlational work cannot rule out the possibility that child behaviors predict parent behaviors, such that parents are more likely to talk with children about media when they suspect their child has been negatively affected by exposure. Longitudinal work is needed to address this question.

The effectiveness of restrictive mediation is more questionable than active mediation, particularly as children mature. A recent meta-analysis found that restrictive mediation is largely unrelated to a host of child outcomes (Collier et al., 2016). Other work has found that parental media rules are related to less media exposure among younger children and some correlational work also shows that restrictive mediation is associated with better comprehension of television stories (Desmond et al., 1985), less perceived importance of television, and less aggression (Nathanson, 1999). While the association between restrictive mediation and media exposure is logical, it is unclear why restrictive mediation would be related to outcomes like aggression and comprehension, assuming media exposure is controlled in statistical analyses. Perhaps media rules socialize children to adopt a more skeptical view of media, which then manifests in less vulnerability to media effects. Or, perhaps restrictive mediation is a reflection of a parenting style that is also related to the child outcomes studied in parental mediation research. I also found that media rules were related to fewer aggressive attitudes among second through sixth graders, but only when media rules were not very strict (Nathanson, 1999). This finding echoes the possibility discussed earlier in this chapter, that the way in which rules are implemented may be important in their overall effectiveness.

Relatedly, the interactive effects of active and restrictive mediation may be important to understand. Most work on parental mediation examines mediation types separately. This practice ignores the near certainty that parents use more than one form of mediation in parenting and that a combination may produce unique outcomes. For example, in a study of teenagers, restrictive mediation was more effective when parents also engaged in high levels of active mediation (Nathanson, 2002).; Research on younger children should also consider the multiplicative effect of using more than one form of parental mediation.

Research on pure media co-use (e.g., ignoring the influence of active mediation that may occur while co-using) is practically absent from the literature on parental mediation. Certainly, co-use paired with comments should help children understand educational material better (e.g., research on *Sesame Street*). There is also some indication that co-use in the form of sheer presence of a parent signals to children that particular media are important and worth attending to, leading to an intensification of media effects. Hence, pure co-use of educational media is associated with greater learning (Salomon, 1977) and pure co-use of violent media is related to more aggressive outcomes among children (Nathanson & Cantor, 2000).

Overall, parental mediation research indicates that active mediation may be the best strategy for preventing unwanted media exposure effects among children. Media rules (as in restrictive mediation) are helpful in limiting exposure among young children, but the quality of rule implementation may be important in shaping restrictive mediation's overall effectiveness.

## Changed Media Landscape and Parental Mediation

Most of the work reviewed thus far was conducted prior to the emergence and rapid adoption of mobile media forms. However, since that time, the media landscape has undergone considerable change. The nature of this change, from mostly shared, stationary media platforms to private, mobile ones, may have significant implications for how parents regard media and mediate it. Some parental mediation work has explored how parents manage the mobile technologies (e.g., Clark, 2011; Livingstone et al., 2017), leading to important insights, which this chapter builds upon. In addition, the combination of both increased availability of educational media and positive public perceptions of the value of media results in a changed environment in which it is expected that children will devote time to media for both entertainment and learning.

## *Mobile Media Exposure*

Based on a report of media use in the UK, most children's media time is dominated by online exposure and television exposure (Ofcom, 2016). Younger children are still exposed to more television compared with online material, but among 8–11-year-olds, about equal time is devoted to both methods of delivery.

More specifically, young children today not only consume media on television sets and stationery video game systems, but also increasingly through tablets and smartphones (Pearson, 2014). Tablet use among children is particularly widespread and begins at young ages. In a study of parents and children in the UK by the Office of Communications, television and tablets were the most widespread forms of media used among children ages 3–11 (Ofcom, 2016). According to their report, tablets are used by 55% of 3–4-year-olds (with 16% owning tablets; use is up from 28% in 2013), 67% of 5–7-year-olds (32% ownership; use is up from 39% in 2013), and 80% for 8–11-year-olds (49% ownership; use is up from 44% in 2013). Both tablets and smartphones experienced increases in ownership among 5–15-year-olds (44% in 2016 vs. 40% in 2015 for tablets; 41% in 2016 compared with 35% in 2015 for smartphones), with a corresponding decrease in use of desktop and laptop computers (from 74% to 67%) and game consoles (from 72% to 66%). Although the increase in smartphone ownership is mostly due to 8–15-year-olds (with 32% of 8–11-year-olds and 79% 12–15-year-olds owning a smartphone in 2016), the increase in tablet ownership was not due to any particular age group. To place these statistics in context, it is useful to note that television remains a nearly universally used medium (ranging from 92 to 98% use among 3–11-year-olds, reflecting no change since 2015), while between 34 and 37% of children report regularly reading books, magazines, or comics.

According to some recent reports, children from lower SES groups are not less likely to have tablets or smartphones and are more likely to have a traditional television set than children from higher SES groups (Ofcom, 2016; Pearson, 2014). In a survey of lower-income parents of 0–4-year-olds, nearly all children had household access to mobile devices and were using them daily by 2 years of age (Kabali et al., 2015). In addition, two-thirds of 4-year-olds owned their own tablet device. However, Common Sense Media's report revealed that whereas 91% of households with higher incomes had a household computer, only 48% of lower-income families owned a computer (Rideout, 2011). Similarly, gaps were found between high- and low-SES teens in their mobile internet use (79% vs. 66%) as were differences between Caucasian, African American, and Hispanic teens' mobile internet use (77%, 74%, and 63%, respectively; Madden, Lenhart, Duggan, Cortesi, & Gasser, 2013). Among American parents of young children, significantly fewer lower-income parents understood the meaning of "apps" or had downloaded apps for their children compared with higher-income parents (Rideout, 2011). Common Sense Media's report highlighted that children from less advantaged households may become further disadvantaged if schools expect children to have computer and Internet access in order to complete assignments.

Mobile media has expanded the number and types of settings within which media can be used. Media time is no longer confined to the household, a setting in which parental supervision is possible. Children can and do consume media in a variety of settings outside of the home, including when parents are not present. Although I am not aware of any data illustrating the proportion of media time spent outside of the home versus within the home, it is worth considering the implications of media exposure that occurs beyond the home environment. This is important because the environment in which children consume media can shape their responses to the material they view.

In particular, it is worth considering: (1) the stimulation level in the environment (e.g., noisy vs. quiet), and (2) the duration of children's exposure. The first factor is important since it appears that parents provide mobile devices to their children to keep them occupied in otherwise challenging situations, such as at a restaurant, in the grocery store line, or at the airport. As a result, a portion of children's media consumption may be consumed in rather intense environments. What effect do media have on children who may already be overstimulated by a high-stress environment? Also, do children become accustomed to adapting to these environments with the help of media, and are they therefore deprived of opportunities to practice important self-regulation skills? Radesky, an expert on young children's self-regulation, has written about the possible consequences of children relying on media, rather than developing their own self-soothing strategies, to cope with difficult situations. She has asked whether this practice may ultimately hinder children in developing important self-regulatory strategies (Radesky, Schumacher, & Zuckerman, 2015).

Second, when children consume media outside of the home, especially when parents provide tablets or smartphones to occupy or distract children, their exposure may be frequently interrupted and reduced to short periods of time initiated by and terminated by parents. It would be difficult for children to benefit from educational content during these time periods. More concerning, though, is the ultimate effect of this pattern of exposure on children's attention regulation and processing skills. Research indicates that parents should avoid directing their children's attention too frequently and should instead follow their children's lead, allowing them to devote attention to things that interest them and changing focus when they are ready (Conway & Stifter, 2012). According to this work, children who are allowed to devote attention to what interests them should develop superior executive function skills. Applying the concept to media use, it is worth investigating whether children who frequently engage with mobile devices in parent-controlled short bursts (e.g., when exposure is permitted because parents benefit from having children occupied for brief periods of time) experience similar deficits in executive function.

## *Private Media Exposure*

Increasingly, children of all ages are consuming media in private. Even before the rise of mobile media, an increasing number of parents were installing televisions in their children's bedrooms at younger and younger ages. According to a 2006 Kaiser Family Foundation report, 33% of 0–6-year-olds had a television in their bedroom. Specifically, 19% of infants had bedroom televisions, 29% of 2–3-year-olds had bedroom televisions, and 43% of 4–6-year-olds had bedroom televisions (Rideout & Hamel, 2006). Common Sense Media's report includes even higher percentages, with 30% of 0–1-year-olds having a bedroom television (Rideout, 2011). Other surveys have found a decrease in bedroom televisions over time, however. For example, in a survey of parents in the UK, 20% of 3–4-year-olds and 48% of 5–15-year-olds had a television set in their bedroom, although these numbers reflect a decrease compared to 2007 when 69% of 5–15-year-olds had a bedroom television (Ofcom, 2016). Similarly, there appears to have been a decline in the presence of game consoles and desktop or laptop computers in children's bedrooms between 2007 and 2016, a trend that Ofcom (2016) notes is likely due to the rise of mobile media which can be transported throughout the house.

It is not clear why sizeable percentages of parents install televisions in their young children's bedrooms, but several explanations are possible. Newer generations of parents, having grown up with television themselves, may have more positive attitudes toward the medium and therefore less reluctance to providing bedroom televisions to their young children. And, with the increase in children's television programs marketed as educational (including programs aimed at infants), parents today may feel that there is an educational benefit from media exposure. Another possibility is that parents today may feel busier, more stressed, and less able to find down time. As a result, today's parents may be more inclined to send their children to their rooms to watch television so that the parents can relax and recharge.

An even bigger contributor to the increase in children's private media use is the rise of mobile media, discussed earlier. Today, both parents and children attend to their own private screens, enjoying their own content. Co-viewing may be less frequent, thereby reducing opportunities for active mediation. In addition, parents may be less aware of the content their children are consuming, and with what frequency. According to Ofcom (2016), young children are still watching television content but are increasingly consuming it via tablet computers.

## *Increased Educational Content*

Media content aimed at infants and young children is prevalent, is on the rise (Shuler, 2012), and is now a billion-dollar industry (Haughton, Aiken, & Cheevers, 2015), with a majority of offerings asserting some kind of educational benefit for users (Fenstermacher et al., 2010; Garrison & Christakis, 2005). As a result, parents may find themselves overwhelmed by the number of options available to them, particularly when it comes to educational apps for mobile devices (Hirsh-Pasek et al., 2015). Although parents may be unsure which apps are best for learning, their frequent exposure to educational media options may nevertheless convince them that educational media benefits children. In fact, parents of diverse incomes are unified in their belief that educational apps are valuable enhancements to children's learning (McClure, Vaala, & Toub, 2017). Given this media environment, scholars may wish to consider whether parents feel less motivated to provide mediation, believing that media use should be encouraged and will be beneficial.

## *Technology and Education*

Relatedly, schools have embraced various media forms as a means of transmitting educational lessons to students. In fact, it is common today for students not only to access desktop or laptop computers for schoolwork but also to bring their own personal devices, such as tablets and smartphones, to school with them. Twenty-one percent of elementary school children use tablets at schools on a daily basis. In addition, 61% of elementary school students say they need Internet access either several times a week or every day in order to complete their homework (Pearson, 2014).

Students report positive attitudes toward using mobile media for schoolwork. In an online poll of students between 4th and 12th grades, the majority of students reported that tablets help them do better in school (82%) and make learning more fun (90%; Pearson, 2014). Using tablets and smartphones for schoolwork is common, although Hispanic and African American students are more likely than Caucasian students to report that they "ever" use a smartphone or tablet for this purpose. Teachers from disadvantaged schools are more likely to express concern about the reliance of technology for schoolwork. For example, only a very small percentage of teachers in high-poverty schools (3%) report that their students have the necessary digital tools to complete their homework compared with teachers from low-poverty schools (52%; Darling-Hammond, Zielezinski, & Goldman, 2014).

Although children from minority or disadvantaged groups are not inherently less likely to have access to mobile devices (and may be more likely to own them; Pearson, 2014), there is some evidence that banning mobile devices like smartphones from schools benefits disadvantaged and underperforming high school students (Beland & Murphy, 2016). In contrast, bans on smartphones in high schools had no impact on other students' academic performance. These results suggest that lower performing or disadvantaged students are more distracted by smartphones. As a result, schools that require smartphones in the classroom may inadvertently widen achievement gaps between advantaged and disadvantaged students.

When media use becomes expected in educational settings, parents' attitudes toward media may shift and become more positive. As a result, parents may be less likely to provide certain types of mediation. In fact, parents may encourage their children to use media at young ages in order to be successful in school. Thus, changes in educational practices may have implications for parental mediation practices.

## *Changed Parent Media Habits*

As children's media habits have evolved, so have those of parents (and adults more generally). Parents are heavy users of social media (Duggan, Lenhart, Lampe, & Ellison, 2015) and more likely to download apps (Lenhart, 2012) compared with other adults. Research suggests that adults have become more and more dependent on mobile devices, especially their smartphones, with large percentages reporting that they always have their phones with them and cannot imagine living without them (Rainey & Zickuhr, 2015; Smith, 2015). Research is now investigating the concept of *technoference*, or technology interference, that occurs when media use causes disruptions in family functioning, such as co-parenting, (McDaniel & Coyne, 2016b) and managing romantic relationships (McDaniel & Coyne, 2016a), or leads to undesirable outcomes, such as child behavior problems (McDaniel & Radesky, 2017). Observations of caregivers and children in fast-food restaurants showed that the majority of caregivers used their smartphone during the meals, many being more absorbed with their phones than with their children (Radesky et al., 2014).

It is worth considering whether adults' apparent preoccupation with their own mobile devices changes the way in which they manage their children's screen time. We might expect that this new reality will result in increased screen exposure for children, but there may be disparate reasons why this might occur. The association between parent and child screen time may occur because children model their parents' behaviors, or because parents hold generally positive attitudes toward media which translates into parents providing their children with easy access to media. Alternatively, increased screen time may result from parents who seek to preserve their own media time by occupying their children with media. In this scenario, increasing children's screen time is a method by which parents are able to maintain their desired media habits.

## Implications for Parents and Children in the Changed Media Landscape

Earlier generations of parents worried about their children's access to undesirable or age-inappropriate content (e.g., violence, sex, and profanity). Today's parents have the same concerns but may have even more difficulty addressing them due to children's increasing use of mobile media, often in private spaces. More generally, parents today are faced with new struggles, including whether and how to regulate media use that occurs outside of the home. In addition, they may feel increasingly conflicted about the role of media in their children's lives, given their own affinity for mobile devices and awareness of the presence of technology in education and learning.

The new media environment appears to present several new risks and opportunities for parents and children. One risk is the possibility that private, mobile media use among both parents and children contributes to *increased separation between parents and children*. The television set, often featured prominently in household living rooms, can bring families together to share media content. Today, parents and children can watch their own television programs separately—either in the same room or in separate spaces in the household. Second, and relatedly, our current media environment may contribute to *decreases in parent–child interaction* due to both parties' absorption in their own screens. Research on the presence of background television has shown that parent–child communication decreases when household televisions are on (Kirkorian, Pempek, Murphy, Schmidt, & Anderson, 2009). When parents and/or children carry media devices with them throughout the house, is parent–child interaction further diminished? Third, *technoference may alter parenting*, possibly resulting in undesirable child outcomes. For example, prior research has found that infants learn a tremendous amount through nonverbal interactions with caregivers and that infant bids for attention that are met with an unresponsive "still face" cause distress, among other unwanted outcomes (Adamson & Frick, 2003). Researchers have found that the still face effect does indeed occur when parents focus their visual attention on their smartphones rather than their children (Kildare, 2017). Older children also notice when their parents are distracted by phones. When this happens, undesirable child outcomes can follow, such as weaker task performance or acting out to regain parent attention (Kildare & Middlemiss, 2017).

Yet, the new media environment may present opportunities for both parents and young children in terms of their relationships, learning, and well-being. Today, children can *more easily stay connected* with distant family through the use of video communication. As children mature, there are opportunities for increased contact with parents through the use of mobile phones. Second, new media may provide children with unique opportunities to serve as authorities and *teach their parents about media*. This role reversal could strengthen parent–child bonds. Third, both parents and children (especially as children mature and move into adolescence) may *find support* from various online communities that they cannot as easily locate in their immediate environments.

For parents, the decision to engage in parental mediation may involve a weighing of its trade-offs. To engage in mediation, parents must invest time and energy. In today's world of mobile media, it is difficult to know exactly what children are watching and for how long they are using it. Parents are busy and may not have time available to engage in mediation. Parental mediation is linked, in part, to resources, including parental availability (Warren, 2003, 2005). Technological advancements have provided more options for parents in terms of monitoring their children's media use (e.g., apps that track children's use), but knowing about, locating, and using these tools also requires resources. Parents who also recognize the advantages of their children's media use may feel less inclined to mediate. For them, the benefits of their children using media (and possibly the benefits of not needing to monitor it) could outweigh the costs involved in mediation. With limited resources, parents must decide which activities are most likely to benefit their family and will consider the costs and rewards accordingly (Warren, 2005). From this perspective, it is understandable why parental mediation is not used by all parents.

## Future Directions

There is a long tradition of scholarship that tracks children's media use. It is important for future work to continue this trend and to pay particular attention to whether and how mobile media are changing children's media use. Scholars should be mindful of some of the key differences inherent in mobile media—that mobile media provide increased opportunities for private media use in practically any location. Future work should consider whether this form of media use alters family dynamics and if parents are increasingly relying on media as a reward, punishment, and/or soothing strategy. In addition, it will be important to understand whether and how parents' own mobile media use shapes family norms and interactions.

Future research on parental mediation should consider whether and how parenting practices surrounding children's media use substantially differ from more general parenting practices. To this end, media scholars are encouraged to consult the literatures in developmental psychology, family studies, and other related disciplines to inform their work. It is important for scholarship on parents and children to build on a common base of knowledge to permit ideas to advance. Research on parental mediation should incorporate the insights, concepts, and theories from disciplines that are devoted to the study of parents and children. An additional benefit of doing so is the inclusion of much-needed theory to the area of parental mediation.

With the rise of mobile media, scholars should acknowledge the increasing difficulty caretakers face in providing parental mediation. To engage in parental mediation requires the resources of time, energy, knowledge, and sometimes money. Parents' decision-making regarding parental mediation may center around questions of trade-offs and priorities. With an awareness of the benefits of media exposure (combined with sometimes inflated claims about the educational benefits of the so-called educational media) and faced with other parenting challenges, many parents may decide that mediation is simply not worth it in the grand scheme of things. Continued work is needed to engage with these issues in more depth and further our understanding of how parents manage young children's media use in today's media environment.

## References


Adamson, L. B., & Frick, J. E. (2003). The still face: A history of a shared experimental paradigm. *Infancy, 4*(4), 451–473. Retrieved from. https://doi.org/10.1207/S15327078IN0404_01

Beland, L.-P., & Murphy, R. (2016). Ill communication: Technology, distraction & student performance. *Labour Economics, 41*, 61–76. Retrieved from. https://doi.org/10.1016/j.labeco.2016.04.004

Bybee, C. R., Robinson, D., & Turow, J. (1982). Determinants of parental guidance of children's television viewing for a special subgroup: Mass media scholars. *Journal of Broadcasting & Electronic Media, 26*(3), 697–710. https://doi.org/10.1080/08838158209364038

Clark, L. S. (2011). Parental mediation theory for the digital age. *Communication Theory, 21*(4), 323–343. https://doi.org/10.1111/j.1468-2885.2011.01391.x

Clark, L. S. (2013). *The parent app: Understanding families in the digital age*. New York: Oxford University Press.

Collier, K. M., Coyne, S. M., Rasmussen, E. E., Hawkins, A. J., Padilla-Walker, L. M., Erickson, S. E., & Memmott-Elison, M. K. (2016). Does parental mediation of media influence child outcomes? A meta-analysis on media time, aggression, substance use, and sexual behavior. *Developmental Psychology, 52*(5), 798–812. https://doi.org/10.1037/dev0000108

Conway, A., & Stifter, C. A. (2012). Longitudinal antecedents of executive function in preschoolers. *Child Development, 83*(3), 1022–1036. https://doi.org/10.1111/j.1467-8624.2012.01756.x

Darling-Hammond, L., Zielezinski, M. B., & Goldman, S. (2014). *Using technology to support at-risk students' learning*. Stanford Center for Opportunity Policy in Education. Retrieved from https://edpolicy.stanford.edu/sites/default/files/scope-pub-using-technology-report.pdf.

Desmond, R. J., Singer, J. L., Singer, D. G., Calam, R., & Colimore, K. (1985). Family mediation patterns and television viewing: Young children's use and grasp of the medium. *Human Communication Research, 11*(4), 461–480. https://doi.org/10.1111/j.1468-2958.1985.tb00056.x

Duggan, M., Lenhart, A., Lampe, C., & Ellison, N. (2015). Parents and social media: Mothers are especially likely to give and receive support on social media. Pew Research Center, *Internet and Technology*. Retrieved August 2017, from http://www.pewinternet.org/2015/07/16/parents-and-social-media/

Fenstermacher, S. K., Barr, R., Salerno, K., Garcia, A., Shwery, C. E., Calvert, S. L., & Linebarger, D. L. (2010). Infant-directed media: An analysis of product information and claims. *Infant and Child Development, 19*(6), 557–556. https://doi.org/10.1002/icd.718

Garrison, M. M., & Christakis, D. A. (2005). *Teacher in the living room? Educational media for babies, toddlers, and preschoolers*. Retrieved August 2017, from https://kaiserfamilyfoundation.files.wordpress.com/2013/01/7427.pdf

Harrison, K., & Liechy, J. M. (2012). US preschoolers' media exposure and dietary habits: The primacy of television and the limits of parental mediation. *Journal of Children and Media, 6*(1), 18–36. https://doi.org/10.1080/17482798.2011.633402

Haughton, C., Aiken, M., & Cheevers, C. (2015). Cyber babies: The impact of emerging technology on the developing infant. *Psychology Research, 5*(9), 504–518. https://doi.org/10.17265/2159-5542/2015.09.002

Hirsh-Pasek, K., Zosh, J. M., Golinkoff, R. M., Gray, J. H., Robb, M. B., & Kaufman, J. (2015). Putting education in "educational" apps: Lessons from the science of learning. *Psychological Science in the Public Interest, 16*(1), 3–34. https://doi.org/10.1177/1529100615569721

Jiow, H. J., Lim, S. S., & Lin, J. (2017). Level up! Refreshing parental mediation theory for our digital media landscape: Parental mediation of video gaming. *Communication Theory, 27*(3), 309–328. https://doi.org/10.1111/comt.12109

Kabali, H. K., Irigoyen, M. M., Nunez-Davis, R., Budacki, J. G., Mohanty, S. H., Leister, K. P., & Bonner, R. L., Jr. (2015). Exposure and use of mobile media devices by young children. *Pediatrics, 136*(6), 1044–1050. https://doi.org/10.1542/peds.2015-2151

Kildare, C. A. (2017). *Infants' perceptions of mothers' phone use: Is mothers' phone use generating the still face effect?* (Doctoral dissertation). Retrieved August 2017, from https://digital.library.unt.edu/ark:/67531/metadc984229/m2/1/high_res_d/KILDARE-DISSERTATION-2017.pdf

Kildare, C. A., & Middlemiss, W. (2017). Impact of parents mobile device use on parent-child interaction: A literature review. *Computers in Human Behavior, 75*, 579–593. https://doi.org/10.1016/j.chb.2017.06.003

Kirkorian, H. L., Pempek, T. A., Murphy, L. A., Schmidt, M. E., & Anderson, D. R. (2009). The impact of background television on parent-child interaction. *Child Development, 80*(5), 1350–1359. https://doi.org/10.1111/j.1467-8624.2009.01337.x

Lenhart, A. (2012). Downloading apps for children. *Pew Research Center, Internet & Technology*. Retrieved from: http://www.pewinternet.org/2012/05/15/downloading-apps-for-children/ Accessed Aug 2017.

Livingstone, S., & Helsper, E. J. (2008). Parental mediation of children's internet use. *Journal of Broadcasting & Electronic Media, 52*(4), 581–599. https://doi.org/10.1080/08838150802437396

Livingstone, S., Ólafsson, K., Helsper, E. J., Lupiáñez-Villanueva, F., Veltri, G. A., & Folkvord, F. (2017). Maximizing opportunities and minimizing risks for children online: The role of digital skills in emerging strategies of parental mediation. *Journal of Communication, 67*(1), 82–105. https://doi.org/10.1111/jcom.12277

Madden, M., Lenhart, A., Duggan, M., Cortesi, S., & Gasser, U. (2013). Teens and technology 2013. *Pew Research Center, Internet & Technology*. Retrieved August 2017, from http://www.pewinternet.org/2013/03/13/teens-and-technology-2013/

McClure, E., Vaala, S., & Toub, T. S. (2017). *Discovering kids' apps: Do family strategies vary by income?* The Joan Ganz Cooney Center at Sesame Workshop. Retrieved August 2017, from http://www.joanganzcooneycenter.org/wpcontent/uploads/2017/06/jgcc_discoveringkidsapps.pdf.

McDaniel, B. T., & Coyne, S. M. (2016a). "Technoference": The interference of technology in couple relationships and implications for women's personal and relational well-being. *Psychology of Popular Media Culture, 5*(1), 85–98. https://doi.org/10.1037/ppm0000065

McDaniel, B. T., & Coyne, S. M. (2016b). Technology interference in the parenting of young children: Implications for mothers' perceptions of coparenting. *The Social Science Journal, 53*(4), 435–443. https://doi.org/10.1016/j.soscij.2016.04.010

McDaniel, B. T., & Radesky, J. S. (2017). Technoference: Parent distraction with technology and associations with child behavior problems. *Child Development, 89*(1), 100–109. https://doi.org/10.1111/cdev.12822

Nathanson, A. I. (1999). Identifying and explaining the relationship between parental mediation and children's aggression. *Communication Research, 26*(2), 124–143. https://doi.org/10.1177/009365099026002002

Nathanson, A. I. (2001). Mediation of children's television viewing: Working toward conceptual clarity and common understanding. In W. B. Gudykunst (Ed.), *Communication yearbook* (Vol.

25, No. 1, pp. 115–151). Mahwah, NJ: Lawrence Erlbaum Associates. doi:https://doi.org/10.1080/23808985.2001.11679002

Nathanson, A. I. (2002). The unintended effects of parental mediation of television on adolescents. *Media Psychology, 4*(3), 207–230. https://doi.org/10.1207/S1532785XMEP0403_01

Nathanson, A. I. (2004). Factual and evaluative approaches to modifying children's responses to violent television. *Journal of Communication, 54*(2), 321–336. https://doi.org/10.1111/j.1460-2466.2004.tb02631.x

Nathanson, A. I., & Cantor, J. (2000). Reducing the aggression-promoting effect of violent cartoons by increasing children's fictional involvement with the victim: A study of active mediation. *Journal of Broadcasting & Electronic Media, 44*(1), 125–142. https://doi.org/10.1207/s15506878jobem4401_9

Nathanson, A. I., Wilson, B. J., McGee, J., & Sebastian, M. (2002). Counteracting the effects of female stereotypes on television via active mediation. *Journal of Communication, 52*(4), 922–937. https://doi.org/10.1111/j.1460-2466.2002.tb02581.x

Nathanson, A. I., & Yang, M. (2003). The effect of mediation content and form on children's responses to violent television. *Human Communication Research, 29*(1), 111–134. https://doi.org/10.1111/j.1468-2958.2003.tb00833.x

Ofcom. (2016). *Children and parents: Media use and attitudes report*. Retrieved August 2017, from https://www.ofcom.org.uk/__data/assets/pdf_file/0034/93976/Children-Parents-Media-Use-Attitudes-Report-2016.pdf

Padilla-Walker, L. M., & Coyne, S. M. (2011). "Turn that thing off!" Parent and adolescent predictors of proactive media monitoring. *Journal of Adolescence, 34*(4), 705–715. https://doi.org/10.1016/j.adolescence.2010.09.002

Pearson (2014). *Pearson student mobile device survey 2014: National report: Students in grades 4–12*. Retrieved August 2017, from http://www.pearsoned.com/wp-content/uploads/Pearson-K12-Student-Mobile-Device-Survey-050914-PUBLIC-Report.pdf

Radesky, J. S., Kistin, C. J., Zuckerman, B., Nitzberg, K., Gross, J., Kaplan-Sanoff, M., & Silverstein, M. (2014). Patterns of mobile device use by caregivers and children during meals in fast food restaurants. *Pediatrics, 133*(4), e843–e849. https://doi.org/10.1542/peds.2013-3703

Radesky, J. S., Schumacher, J., & Zuckerman, B. (2015). Mobile and interactive media use by young children: The good, the bad, and the unknown. *Pediatrics, 135*(1), 1–3. https://doi.org/10.1542/peds.2014-2251

Rainey, L., & Zickuhr, K. (2015). Americans' views on mobile etiquette. *Pew Research Center, Internet & Technology*. Retrieved August 2017, from http://www.pewinternet.org/2015/08/26/americans-views-on-mobile-etiquette/

Rasmussen, E. E. (2014). Proactive vs. retroactive mediation: Effect of mediation's timing on children's reactions to popular cartoon violence. *Human Communication Research, 40*(3), 396–413. https://doi.org/10.1111/hcre.12030

Rasmussen, E. E., Shafer, A., Colwell, M. J., White, S., Punyanunt-Carter, N., Densley, R. L., & Wright, H. (2016). Relation between active mediation, exposure to *Daniel Tiger's Neighborhood*, and US preschoolers' social and emotional development. *Journal of Children and Media, 10*(4), 443–461. https://doi.org/10.1080/17482798.2016.1203806

Rideout, V. (2011). *Zero to eight: Children's media use in America*. Retrieved August 2017, from https://www.commonsensemedia.org/file/zerotoeightfinal2011pdf-0/download

Rideout, V., & Hamel, E. (2006). *The media family: Electronic media in the lives of infants, toddlers, preschoolers, and their parents*. Menlo Park, CA: Henry J. Kaiser Family Foundation. Retrieved August 2017, from https://kaiserfamilyfoundation.files.wordpress.com/2013/01/7500.pdf

Salomon, G. (1977). Effects of encouraging Israeli mothers to co-observe *Sesame Street* with their five-year-olds. *Child Development, 48*(3), 1146–1151. https://doi.org/10.2307/1128378

Shuler, C. (2012). *iLearn II: An analysis of the education category of Apple's app store*. New York: The Joan Ganz Cooney Center at Sesame Workshop. Retrieved August 2017, from http://www.joanganzcooneycenter.org/wp-content/uploads/2012/01/ilearnii.pdf

Smetana, J., Crean, H. F., & Campione-Barr, N. (2005). Adolescents' and parents' changing conceptions of parental authority. *New Directions for Child and Adolescent Development, 2005*(108), 31–46. https://doi.org/10.1002/cd.126

Smith, A. (2015). *U.S. smartphone use in 2015. Pew Research Center, Internet & Technology*. Retrieved August 2017, from http://www.pewinternet.org/2015/04/01/us-smartphone-use-in-2015/

Valkenburg, P. M., Krcmar, M., & de Roos, S. (1998). The impact of a cultural children's program and adult mediation on children's knowledge of and attitudes toward opera. *Journal of Broadcasting & Electronic Media, 42*(3), 315–326. https://doi.org/10.1080/08838159809364452

Valkenburg, P. M., Krcmar, M., Peeters, A. L., & Marseille, N. M. (1999). Developing a scale to assess three styles of television mediation: "Instructive mediation," "restrictive mediation," and "social coviewing". *Journal of Broadcasting & Electronic Media, 43*(1), 52–66. https://doi.org/10.1080/08838159909364474

Valkenburg, P. M., Piotrowski, J. T., Hermanns, J., & de Leeuw, R. (2013). Developing and validating the perceived parental media mediation scale: A self-determination perspective. *Human Communication Research, 39*(4), 445–469. https://doi.org/10.1111/hcre.12010

Van der Voort, T. H., Nikken, P., & Van Lil, J. E. (1992). Determinants of parental guidance of children's media use: A Dutch replication study. *Journal of Broadcasting & Electronic Media, 36*(1), 61–74. https://doi.org/10.1080/08838159209364154

Warren, R. (2003). Parental mediation of preschool children's television viewing. *Journal of Broadcasting & Electronic Media, 47*(3), 394–417. https://doi.org/10.1207/s15506878jobem4703_5

Warren, R. (2005). Parental mediation of children's television viewing in low-income families. *Journal of Communication, 55*(4), 847–863. https://doi.org/10.1111/j.1460-2466.2005.tb03026.x

# Chapter 2
# Adolescents as the Family Technology Innovators

**Jodi Dworkin**

Communication during the adolescent years can be a significant challenge for parents and children due to development and changes in the adolescent's role in the family (Collins, Gleason, & Sesma, 1995). Specifically, adolescents and their parents are renegotiating the parent–child relationship and shifting communication patterns to adapt to adolescents' increased maturity and desire for autonomy (Steinberg & Silk, 2002). This shift occurs at a time when adolescents are beginning to own and use their own technology (e.g., smartphones, tablets, etc.; Lenhart, Madden, & Hitlin, 2005). Adolescents have more control than younger children over how, with whom, and when they communicate, and parents must adjust to these changes. With young people spending an increasing amount of time away from parents, it is harder for parents to keep track of what they are doing. To help maintain communication at a distance, parents need to learn to use the technologies their children are using.

As young people enter adolescence, they begin to use technology for social reasons, in particular to connect with peers and friends they already have. In 2015, only 12% of teens did not have a cell phone; 73% of teens had access to a smartphone with access to the Internet (Lenhart, 2015). These numbers have likely continued to rise: in 2018, 100% of young adults aged 18–29 owned a cell phone, and 94% owned a smartphone (Pew Research Center, 2018). Parents need to balance the growing autonomy of adolescents and the necessity to set boundaries on technology use (Hertlein & Blumer, 2014). A critical look at parental mediation and specifically the role of parental mediation in young children's use of technology is presented by Nathanson (Chap. 3).

National samples have provided a glimpse into the ways parent technology use changes with child age (Rudi, Dworkin, Walker, & Doty, 2015a). Large differences emerged between parents of children of different ages and whether parents were

J. Dworkin (✉)
Department of Family Social Science, University of Minnesota, St. Paul, MN, USA
e-mail: jdworkin@umn.edu

 
J. Van Hook et al. (eds.), *Families and Technology*, National Symposium on Family Issues 9, https://doi.org/10.1007/978-3-319-95540-7_2

likely to use a specific technology to communicate with their children. Parents of adolescents were significantly more likely than parents of school-aged children to use text messages, email, social networking sites (SNSs), and Skype to communicate with their child. Parents of preschool-aged children were significantly less likely than parents of school-aged children to use text messages, email, and SNS to communicate with their child (Rudi, Walkner, & Dworkin, 2015b). The differences found between parents of school-aged and adolescent children and parents of preschool-aged children are not surprising, given that very young children are not yet using technologies independently for intentional communication.

Parents' greater use of technologies to connect with adolescents aligns with other research suggesting that children's technology use increases with child's age (Lenhart et al., 2011; Mascheroni & Ólafsson, 2014; Subrahmanyam & Greenfield, 2008) and with increases in reciprocal child-rearing, which is the idea that parents alter their behavior to meet their children's developmental needs (Belsky, 1984). For adolescents, technology is a way to maintain relationships when not physically with someone. When young people are spending significantly more time away from home, and then no longer living at home, communication technologies become a necessary tool for communication.

Socialization theory and a child effects perspective, along with diffusion of innovation, suggests that not only are adolescents emerging as active users of technology, they are also introducing innovations and technologies into the family and teaching parents to use new technologies. I will consider the role of technologies in families with adolescents, the ways that family relationships impact technology use, and the ways in which technology use impacts family relationships. Next, a case will be made to recognize a flip in the family's power dynamic, as youth are the drivers and innovators. Last, future directions for research and implications for practice will be considered.

## Technology Use and Family Relationships

Considering rates of technology use by adolescents does not provide a complete picture of the ways in which use impacts and is impacted by family relationships. Family access to the Internet, how other family members use the Internet in the home, as well as pre-existing values and norms within the family are theorized to influence why and how frequently youth go online (Hertlein, 2012). One motivation of youth for using the Internet is to enhance communication with family (i.e., to make plans with and stay connected to family; Subrahmanyam & Greenfield, 2008). Adolescents are rapidly adopting new technologies as they emerge. Despite the lack of existing research that considers the bidirectional relationships between technology use and family relationships, it is reasonable to expect that family relationships impact, in complex ways, how youth and parents use online media.

In this chapter, empirical data are presented from large, quantitative, national survey studies conducted by Dworkin and colleagues. Data are from both parents and young people. The data reflect their general technology use, technology use specifically for parenting, and the associations between technology use and quality of family relationships.

## *Parents' Use of Technology*

Technology provides parents with social support and information about parenting and their own needs (e.g., Doty & Dworkin, 2014; Jang & Dworkin, 2014; Jang, Dworkin, & Hessel, 2015). Parents of adolescents in particular are active users of technology. In a national study of parents, 35.6% were identified as highly active, using a variety of devices and performing a range of activities daily, while only 20% were identified as limited technology users (Walker, Dworkin, & Connell, 2011). A comprehensive literature review of parents' online behavior examined the purpose for their Internet use (Dworkin, Connell, & Doty, 2013). The literature revealed that parents go online to search for parenting information and receive social support. They are generally satisfied with the resources found on the Internet. Parents express hesitation in trusting various online resources though, and desire greater education in Internet searching and deciphering the credibility of online information (Dworkin et al., 2013). Despite concerns about the credibility of information and advice, parents report receiving social support online and value the convenience and anonymity of online resources (Doty & Dworkin, 2014).

In a more focused look at parents of adolescents, differences in frequency of communication methods by family communication patterns were found (Rudi, Dworkin, et al., 2015a). Family Communication Patterns Theory (Koerner & Fitzpatrick, 2002) is based on the assumption that families need to create a shared reality and they do that through conversation and conformity. Unique patterns in families based on the capabilities of the chosen communication method (e.g., voice versus text), as well as on differences between communication with mothers and fathers were demonstrated (Rudi, Dworkin, et al., 2015a). Specifically, talking in person was the most frequent form of communication with both parents, followed by talking on the phone and text messaging, then emailing. Overall, adolescents reported communicating with their mother more frequently than with their father. On average, adolescents reported talking to their mother on the phone three to 5 days per week, and texting one to 2 days per week. On average, adolescents reported talking to their father on the phone one to 2 days a week, and texting every few weeks (Rudi, Dworkin, et al., 2015a).

To extend our understanding of the role of technology in family relationships to understanding the role of social media specifically, we examined parents' use of technology for communication and connection with their extended personal networks (i.e., family members they do not live with, parents of their children's friends, and others outside the immediate family who care for their child; Dworkin, Walker, Rudi, & Doty, 2015). Among mothers of adolescents, positive attitudes toward technology increased both the frequency of using SNSs for parenting and the number of SNS activities (e.g., staying in touch with friends, meeting new people, joining interest groups, and posting photos, videos, or music) mothers engaged in.

Feeling comfortable using technology was also positively associated with the number of SNS activities (Jang & Dworkin, 2014). For mothers of adolescents, frequency of using SNSs for parenting was positively associated with both bonding social capital and bridging social capital. Bonding social capital is the close-knit relationships that provide social and emotional supports (Lin, 2001); bridging social capital is the social relationships that cut across diverse groups and acquaintances (Harpham, Grant, & Thomas, 2002; Narayan, 1999), and provides access to new information (Putnam, 2000).

Mothers' online experiences stand in stark contrast to fathers' online experiences. For example, despite fathers being highly comfortable using technology, they are only neutral toward online parenting information; while fathers are frequently online, they are rarely searching for parenting information. Being comfortable using technology and attitudes toward online parenting information were positively correlated. Fathers reported frequently using emails to communicate with nonresident family, friends, and children, text messages to communicate with children and the other parent, and SNSs to communicate with friends, nonresident family, and children. Fathers also go online to identify problems, confirm that what they are doing or believe as a parent is right, and to explore different parenting perspectives (He & Dworkin, 2015/2016).

Beyond parent gender, there are also demographic differences in how parents are using technology. Parents with lower incomes and parents of color reported engaging in online classes and sending videos more frequently. They were using email and sending text messages less frequently, reporting daily to weekly use. The finding that low-income parents were more likely to use discussion boards/chat rooms, share video files, and create blogs frequently corroborates earlier findings that low-income parents may gravitate toward social media (Doty, Dworkin, & Connell, 2012). Similarly, parents on discussion boards tended to have lower than average incomes (Sarkadi & Bremberg, 2004). In contrast, those with a higher level of education and with higher incomes were more likely to use email than parents with lower incomes and lower levels of education (Dworkin et al., 2015).

Data suggest that lower income parents and parents of color may seek out a greater range of devices and engage in different activities than white or higher income parents (Dworkin et al., 2015). For example, parents of color reported more frequent use than white parents of a variety of communication activities, such as using Skype, sharing audio and video files, using a webcam, and creating and maintaining a website. This is consistent with other studies (Smith, 2010; Zickhur & Smith, 2012) that found African Americans and Latinos were somewhat less likely than whites to access the Internet but more likely to have mobile devices that provided the potential to access a range of activities. Texting and email, activities easily done with handheld devices such as smartphones and tablets but also done with less mobile devices such as computers, appear to be more frequently used by parents who are older, with higher income and more education. Social activities like discussion boards and chat rooms are popular among mothers, lower income parents, and parents living in urban areas (Dworkin et al., 2015).

## *Technology Use in Support of Parent–Child Relationships*

There is an emerging literature from Dworkin and colleagues on how parents use technology for communication with their children, for parenting more broadly, and to maintain other family relationships (e.g., with co-parents). In these studies, parenting was defined as *all things you do to take care of your children and support their growth and development.. . things that help you in your role as a parent* (Dworkin et al., 2015; Walker et al., 2011). Parents are actively using technology to seek information, advice, and support about parenting; resolve conflicting parenting information; explore different parenting perspectives; and to confirm that what they are doing or believe as a parent is right. They use the same online tools for parenting that they used in general—email, text messaging, and social networking sites.

Parents use multiple technologies to communicate and connect with their children; a process known as media multiplexity (Haythornthwaite, 2005). Parents were significantly more likely to text, use instant messaging, use Skype, and share audio files for communicating with children than for communicating with other family members, co-parents, parents of children's friends, and others who care for their child (Dworkin et al., 2015). Data from a national sample of parents of 13- to 22-year-old children revealed that of parents who reported using technology weekly, 54% reported using email to communicate with children, 70.4% reported using text messaging, 46.6% reported using SNSs, 60.1% reported using instant messaging, and 23.7% reported using microblogs. Of those parents who reported using technology monthly, 40.6% shared video files, 56.8% made phone calls/used Skype, 38.9% used a webcam, and 46.0% shared audio files; in addition, 47.1% ever sent or received photos (Dworkin et al., 2015).

Guided by a uses and gratification perspective, Doty and Dworkin (2014) examined parents' of adolescents' use of SNSs to connect with their children. Analyses revealed that parents of adolescents used SNSs for parenting more often than other online communication technologies such as instant messaging, Skype, chat rooms, or blogging. The top two reasons for using SNSs were to communicate with children and to communicate with extended family. Hierarchical logistic regression results indicated that parents of adolescents who performed a greater number of SNS activities were more likely to use SNSs to communicate with their children, their children's friends, and the parents of their children's friends. Those parents who had positive attitudes toward technology were more likely to use SNSs to communicate with their children's friends (Doty & Dworkin, 2014).

**Parental Monitoring of Adolescent Behavior Via Technology** Parents influence their adolescent's use of technology often by reacting, responding to, and engaging with what the young person initiates. For instance, parents may monitor their adolescent's use of technology and their online behavior, as well as make decisions about adolescents' access to technology. This could include setting rules about the age at which adolescents can have a cell phone and setting guidelines about use of that cell phone, based on family environment and values and the adolescent's past behavior.

Technology provides a quick and presumably less invasive way for parents to monitor their adolescents (e.g., by checking in with their adolescent) and for the adolescent to disclose information to the parent. With the emergence of technology, parents have new tools for checking in, such as email and instant messaging. In a study using multinomial ordered logit models with a national sample of youth, parental monitoring and mother–child relationship satisfaction were significant predictors of whether or not youth were frequent users of email and instant messaging (Rudi & Dworkin, 2014). Youth whose parents *try a lot* to monitor their activities by focusing on five aspects of their lives (*Where you go at night*; *What you do with your free time*; *Who your friends are*; *How things are going at school or work*; and *Who you are dating*) and youth who reported lower relationship satisfaction with their mother were more likely to be in the high technology user group than youth whose parents *try a little* or *don't try* to monitor their activities and youth who reported higher relationship satisfaction with their mother. In contrast, youth whose parents *know a lot* about their activities were significantly less likely to be in the high technology user group than youth whose parents *know a little* or *don't know* about their activities (Rudi & Dworkin, 2014). Parents reported that they were more likely to communicate with and monitor older children's activities via mobile phone than younger children's activities (Devitt & Roker, 2009; Razorfish & CafeMom, 2009).

These findings suggest that when parents are working to stay engaged via technology in the lives of their youth and try to know a lot about their activities, the youth are also engaged with technology more frequently. Perhaps parents feel the need to work particularly hard to stay connected to a young person who is online so frequently. Evidence of this is seen as youth who reported lower relationship satisfaction with their mother were more likely to be in the high user group for communication and information-seeking. When parents are not only trying to stay connected but are actually successful at doing so, it may be because the young person is simply online less frequently and is more engaged in in-person interactions with parents. Interestingly, youth–father relationship quality was not significant in any of these models (Rudi & Dworkin, 2014). These data undoubtedly suggest that additional research on the relationship between parent–child relationship quality and youth technology use is needed.

The ways in which fathers use technology with their adolescents has been further considered (Hessel, He, & Dworkin, 2017). Fathers use of technology to monitor their teen's behavior, specifically through online solicitation of information from adolescents' friends, was negatively correlated with parental control and youths' prosocial behaviors, and positively correlated with youth internalizing and externalizing behaviors. Based on social domain theory, young people may see the online context as a personal domain, providing an opportunity to establish communication rules on their own terms; online solicitation would violate that expectation. In contrast, online disclosure was positively associated with internalizing behavior but was not associated with externalizing or prosocial behavior. The differences between disclosure and solicitation suggest that when youth initiate communication, the experience for young people is very different from when fathers initiate communication; when youth feel a sense of control they may be more likely to disclose

(Hessel et al., 2017). Further, youth perceive parents' online behaviors differently than parents' in-person behaviors. In-person solicitation was negatively correlated with internalizing and externalizing behaviors and positively associated with prosocial behaviors. Thus, these parenting behaviors have different outcomes for youth (Hessel et al., 2017). However, we are just beginning to understand what happens to the parent–child relationship when parents enter online spaces that youth consider part of their domain and perhaps even a space that young people believe parents should not be actively engaged with. The boundaries of parents' role as new technologies continue to emerge are blurry.

## Youth as Socializing Agents and Innovators

Socialization theory describes how children internalize rules and norms from their parents, siblings, other family members, teachers, media, and others. Consistent with this perspective, most studies on the uses and effects of media and communication by parents and children have focused on how parents influence their children's use of media. Socialization, however, is a bidirectional and reciprocal process in which not only are children socialized by their parents, but children also actively socialize their parents. They are equal influencers in the system (Nelissen & Van den Bulck, 2018). Children socialize their parents in the use of media, including devices such as tablets, as well as applications and tools such as texting and Instagram. The reciprocal nature of socialization is part of the trajectory of normal adolescent development. For example, youth often introduce music or fashion into the family system. Despite this, researchers have lagged behind in our exploration of the dynamic. Children are active agents in the family, who can both intentionally and unintentionally influence parents (Crouter & Booth, 2003; Kuczynski, 2003). For example, children not only introduce digital media to their parents and influence the purchase of new innovations in the family (Götze, Prange, & Uhrovska, 2009), but also teach and guide parents how to use and interact with new digital media.

Children's influence on parents in relation to technology mirrors the general literature on parenting that suggests much of parenting is a reaction to child behavior (e.g., Crouter & Booth, 2003; Kuczynski, 2003). Parenting around technology use is often a reaction to children's interest in and use of emerging technologies. This also parallels the emergence of previous innovations such as radio, television, and even the Internet. Youth are the ones introducing technology and social media into the family system. For instance, the tools youth are using in their daily lives are the same tools they want to use with family. If a child primarily uses text messages to communicate with friends, the parent may start texting to communicate with the child. The fact that youth are learning to use social media and new technologies before their parents do impacts and has the potential to disrupt the traditional power structure in the family system. For today's parents of adolescents, technology changes very quickly; parents cannot anticipate what new technologies youth will use or how they will use them. This is complicated by the fact that parents of today's teens did not grow up with technology; future generations will undoubtedly have a different experience. It is unchartered territory for most parents of adolescents, and thus hard for parents to stay ahead of their adolescent.

New technologies that are introduced into the family system are a source of social change, the effects of which are mediated by the ways in which the media are processed by individual family members. Family stability will be determined by how the family system responds to these changes that are brought into the system by youth (Rudi, Dworkin, et al., 2015a). However, the literature is lacking theoretical and conceptual frameworks for understanding the complex role of technology in family systems (Dworkin et al., 2013). Next, I will consider how diffusion of innovation and a child effects perspective might help us better understand the role of technology in families with adolescents.

## *Diffusion of Innovation*

When the balance of power shifts in the family and children are the drivers of innovation, one way to understand this transfer of power within the family system related to technology use specifically is to consider the diffusion of innovation (Rogers, 1983; Rogers & Shoemaker, 1971). Diffusion research examines how ideas spread among groups of people. Diffusion is focused on the conditions that increase or decrease the likelihood that an innovation, a new idea, or product will be adopted by group members. More specifically, in multi-step diffusion, the opinion leader influences the behavior of individuals, or adopters; intermediaries would exist between, in this situation, the technology and the audience's decision-making. One intermediary is the change agent, someone who encourages an opinion leader to adopt or reject an innovation (Infante, Rancer, & Womack, 1997). As considered in this chapter, the young person is the adopter initially and then becomes the intermediary or change agent who may encourage, support, or teach a parent in order to influence the parent's adoption of a new technology.

The short-term goal of most change agents is the adoption of an innovation; adoption happens through personal relationships (Rogers, 1983; Rogers & Shoemaker, 1971). Innovations are not adopted by all individuals in a social system at the same time. Instead, they are adopted in a sequence, and individuals can be classified into adopter categories based upon how long it takes them to adopt the innovation. The diffusion of innovation theory would suggest that every market has groups who differ in their readiness and willingness to adopt a new product or in this case, device, application, or tool. Innovation reaches different groups at different times. Most populations show the following pattern in adoption: innovators (2% of population), early adopters (14%), early majority (34%), late majority (34%), and laggards (16%; Rogers, 1983). In this scenario, young people would be the innovators and parents could fall into any of the other categories. Parents may be quick to pick up what their child is offering (early adopter), resistant (laggard), or fall somewhere in between.

Using diffusion of innovation theory, the child becomes an intermediary or change agent who encourages parents to adopt or reject a technology device or application. It is assumed that the child's goal is to facilitate the adoption of an innovation. Parents can then become adopters who might pass the innovation along to their peers or perhaps their own parents. In a rather simple example, an adolescent might teach a parent to use Facebook, and the parent then teaches the grandparent to view posts from their grandchildren. The child is the leader and motivated to stay connected to family and friends via Facebook, The parent and grandparent are somewhat willing learners and adopters.

## Child Effects on the Family

The *child-effect* (Bell, 1968), or the idea that youth have an impact on the family system and much of parenting is a reaction to that impact, is a perspective that has been largely ignored in the social science literature in general, and in media research in particular. Given recent changes in the media landscape (such as the introduction of smartphones and tablets), it has been argued that scholars need to consider this perspective now more than ever (Van den Bulck, Custers, & Nelissen, 2016; Van den Bulck & Van den Bergh, 2016). Research questions previously considered must be reversed to advance the field. Understanding technology use is not just about the ways parents control communication, but the role youth play in how technology is being used in the family and in support of family relationships. Children can passively impact parenting behavior, for example, when a parent perceives that a tablet will benefit the child in school and therefore purchases a tablet. Children can also be active influencers, for example, when a teen works to persuade a parent to buy them the newest iPhone.

Building on the premise that children are active agents who influence their parents' media use, Nelissen and Van den Bulck (2018) investigated the guidance children provide to parents around digital media. They investigated whether children providing digital media guidance to parents was associated with whether parents and children had arguments about different media. A cross-sectional survey was conducted with 187 parent–child dyads in Belgium. Analyses revealed that both children and parents reported that children do in fact guide their parents regarding how to use digital media, and this is especially true for newer media such as smartphones, tablets, and apps. Families who reported more child guidance of parent digital media use, perhaps not surprisingly, also reported more conflicts about media. These relationships were similar for both parent and child reports.

In-depth interviews with 14 parent–child dyads and surveys with 242 dyads revealed that youth influenced their parents use of all the technologies studied (computer, mobile Internet, social networking), challenging the traditional patterns of influence found in families (Correa, 2014). However, children reported more influence on parents than parents reported their children have on them, suggesting that while parents might recognize some influence of their children on their technology use, either parents do not recognize the full extent of that influence or youth overestimate their influence on parents. The bottom-up influence of children on parents was more likely to occur with mothers and in families with lower socioeconomic status. Digital media represents a new environment for lower socioeconomic families; children in these families were more likely to learn about technology from school and friends than directly from family. This further supports the bottom-up influence whereby children become systematically prepared and equipped to teach their parents. The process is similar to what happens among low-income immigrant families in which children may act as language and culture brokers between the family and the new environment. Children become technology brokers between parents and new media (Correa, 2014). For further discussion see Clark (Chap. 3).

The extent to which sons and daughters influenced their parents' adoption of digital media, particularly the Internet, as compared to other sources of potential influence has been investigated (Correa, Straubhaar, Chen, & Spence, 2015). Relationships between structural factors (such as education, income, age, and gender), parents' internet self-efficacy, and the bottom-up influence previously discussed were also explored. Drawing from socialization and diffusion of innovation research, Correa et al. (2015) found that children play a role in engaging their parents in the digital environment. Again, this was particularly true for mothers, parents who were age 35 years and older, and parents of lower socioeconomic status. For some families, children's social networks provide opportunities to access technology and digital media. However, this bottom-up influence of technology use was somewhat negatively associated with parents' internet self-efficacy. Whether parents who need help from their children are likely to have lower internet self-efficacy is unclear, as is whether children teaching their parents about technology negatively impacts parents' internet self-efficacy.

## Implications and Future Directions

We are only beginning to understand the ways in which young people are introducing technologies into the family system and the ways in which family relationships are impacted. At this stage in research, what seems clear is that the face-to-face relationship does not translate directly to the online context, and online communication is not completely replacing in-person family relationships. Youth and parents continue to report frequent in-person and phone communication. One finding that emerges consistently from my lab is that despite high rates of technology use, when youth and parents want to discuss a problem or communicate about something important (beyond just checking in), they want to do it face-to-face or by phone and not via text or other technology (Connell & Dworkin, 2012). With all of our data sets that have been collected via online data collection methods, anecdotal rhetoric that technology and text-based communication is the dominant form of family communication is not supported.

Despite this critical finding, parents need to continue to expand the ways in which they use technology to engage with their adolescent children, as that is the way young people are communicating with others around them and is generally a medium they are comfortable using. A trajectory of parent–child relationships would suggest that mid-adolescence would be the hardest time for families to negotiate this, and parent–child relationships would then stabilize after that. For example, parents may initially require a young adolescent to accept their friend request on Facebook, and then perhaps youth move into more comfort with that role and their evolving relationship. Young adults are willing to accept their parents' Facebook friend requests without setting up additional privacy settings (Child & Westermann, 2013). Technology provides parents with more ways to stay connected and perhaps better engaged with their child's day-to-day life, which is likely to help set the stage for a positive and engaged parent–child relationship.

To continue to advance the field, we need a complex and deeper understanding of family relationships in the context of changing communication technologies. One way to advance the field is through the intentional and dynamic integration of theory into technology research. Lack of theory has been a tremendous gap in the literature (Valkenburg & Peter, 2013). Diffusion of innovation and child effects are two complementary perspectives that begin to provide a lens into the complexity of technology use in family systems. Further, the perspectives elucidate the ways in which behaviors around technology in families may follow less traditional and nonlinear patterns of influence.

As the technology landscape continues to rapidly change, researchers must begin to ask different research questions using different methodologies. When children are often the media or technology brokers in the family, the balance of power shifts and they become the experts in the family system. It seems likely that youth will always be the innovators and using technologies in different ways. As a result, youth bear the responsibility for influencing family adoption of technologies as well as integrating these into the family system. However, parents who are having children now will have grown up with technologies themselves. As the technology landscape changes, it is unclear how the balance of power will continue to shift.

For parent education and prevention programming, there are also important implications of understanding the ways in which youth impact the family system. Research suggests that parents need skills for monitoring and supporting their children's technology use, for using technology in support of their own parenting and in support of their own development, and for using technology to maintain and enhance family relationships. To most effectively support parents, parent education must be comprehensive, recognizing and supporting these unique but complementary uses of technology by parents.

## References

Bell, R. Q. (1968). A reinterpretation of the direction of effects in studies of socialization. *Psychological Review, 75*(2), 81–95.

Belsky, J. (1984). The determinants of parenting: A process model. *Child Development, 55*(1), 83–96.

Child, J. T., & Westermann, D. A. (2013). Let's be Facebook friends: Exploring parental Facebook friend requests from a communication privacy management (CPM) perspective. *Journal of Family Communication, 13*(1), 46–59.

Collins, W. A., Gleason, T., & Sesma, A. (1995). Internalization, autonomy, and relationships: Development during adolescence. In J. E. Grusec & L. Kuczynski (Eds.), *Parenting and children's internalization of values: A handbook of contemporary theory* (pp. 78–99). New York: Wiley.

Connell, J., & Dworkin, J. (2012). College students' information and communications technology (ICT) use with parents. *Journal of the Association of Higher Education Parent/Family Program Professionals, 2*(2), 2–17.

Correa, T. (2014). Bottom-up technology transmission within families: Exploring how youths influence their parents' digital media use with dyadic data. *Journal of Communication, 64*(1), 103–124.

Correa, T., Straubhaar, J. D., Chen, W., & Spence, J. (2015). Brokering new technologies: The role of children in their parents' usage of the internet. *New Media & Society, 17*(4), 483–500.

Crouter, A. C., & Booth, A. (2003). *Children's influence on family dynamics: The neglected side of family relationships*. Mahwah, NJ: Lawrence Erlbaum.

Devitt, K., & Roker, D. (2009). The role of mobile phones in family communication. *Children & Society, 23*(3), 189–202.

Doty, J. L., & Dworkin, J. (2014). Online social support for parents: A critical review. *Marriage & Family Review, 50*(2), 174–198.

Doty, J. L., Dworkin, J., & Connell, J. (2012). Examining digital differences: Parents' online activities. *Family Science Review, 17*(2), 18–39.

Dworkin, J., Connell, J., & Doty, J. (2013). A literature review of parents' online behavior. *Cyberpsychology: Journal of Psychosocial Research on Cyberspace, 7*(2). https://doi.org/10.5817/CP2013-2-2

Dworkin, J., Walker, S., Rudi, J., & Doty, J. (2015). Parents' use of new media for communication: A consideration of demographic differences. In C. J. Bruess (Ed.), *Family communication in the age of digital and social media* (pp. 408–425). New York: Peter Lang Publishing.

Götze, E., Prange, C., & Uhrovska, I. (2009). Children's impact on innovation decision making: A diary study. *European Journal of Marketing, 43*(1/2), 264–295.

Harpham, T., Grant, E., & Thomas, E. (2002). Measuring social capital within health surveys: Key issues. *Health Policy and Planning, 17*(1), 106–111.

Haythornthwaite, C. (2005). Social networks and internet connectivity effects. *Information, Communication and Society, 8*(2), 125–147.

He, Y., & Dworkin, J. (2015/2016 Winter). Cyber dads: What are fathers doing online? *Fathering, 13*(3), 219–230.

Hertlein, K. M. (2012). Digital dwelling: Technology in couple and family relationships. *Family Relations, 61*(3), 374–387.

Hertlein, K. M., & Blumer, M. L. C. (2014). *The couple and technology framework: Intimate relationships in a digital age*. New York: Routledge.

Hessel, H., He, Y., & Dworkin, J. (2017). Paternal monitoring: The relationship between online and in-person solicitation and youth outcomes. *Journal of Youth & Adolescence, 46*(2), 288–299.

Infante, D. A., Rancer, A. S., & Womack, D. F. (1997). *Building communication theory* (3rd ed.). Prospect Heights, IL: Waveland Press.

Jang, J., & Dworkin, J. (2014). Does social network site use matter for mothers? Implications for bonding and bridging capital. *Computers in Human Behavior, 35*, 489–495.

Jang, J., Dworkin, J., & Hessel, H. (2015). Mothers' use of information and communication technologies for information seeking. *Cyberpsychology, Behavior and Social Networking, 18*(4), 221–227.

Koerner, A. F., & Fitzpatrick, M. A. (2002). Toward a theory of family communication. *Communication Theory, 12*, 70–91.

Kuczynski, L. (2003). Beyond bidirectionality: Bilateral conceptual frameworks for understanding dynamics in parent-child relations. In L. Kuczynski (Ed.), *Handbook of dynamics in parent-child relations* (pp. 1–24). Thousand Oaks, CA: Sage.

Lenhart, A. (2015). *Teens, social media & technology overview*. Pew Research Center, Internet and Technology. Retrieved from http://www.pewinternet.org/2015/04/09/teens-social-media-technology-2015/

Lenhart, A., Madden, M., & Hitlin, P. (2005). *Teens and technology: Youth are leading the transition to a fully wired and mobile nation*. Washington, DC: Pew Internet & American Life Project Retrieved from http://www.pewinternet.org/~/media//Files/Reports/2005/PIP_Teens_Tech_July2005web.pdf.pdf

Lenhart, A., Madden, M., Smith, A., Purcell, K., Zickuhr, K., & Rainie, L. (2011). *Teens, kindness and cruelty on social network sites*. Washington, DC: Pew Internet & American Life Project Retrieved from http://pewinternet.org/~/media//Files/Reports/2011/PIP_Teens_Kindness_Cruelty_SNS_Report_Nov_2011_FINAL_110711.pdf

Lin, N. (2001). *Social capital: A theory of social structure and action*. Cambridge, MA: Cambridge University Press.

Mascheroni, G., & Ólafsson, K. (2014). *Net children go mobile: Risks and opportunities* (Second ed.). Milano: Educatt Retrieved from http://netchildrengomobile.eu/reports/

Narayan, D. (1999). Bonds and bridges: Social capital and poverty. Washington, DC: Poverty Group of the World Bank. Retri8eved from https://pdfs.semanticscholar.org/c89d/23d6943303984be2979b6d5a50cc5f038ae7.pdf

Nelissen, S., & Van den Bulck, J. (2018). When digital natives instruct digital immigrants: Active guidance of parental media use by children and conflict in the family. *Information, Communication & Society, 21*(3), 375–387.

Pew Research Center. (2018, February 5). *Mobile fact sheet*. Internet and Technology. Retrieved from http://www.pewinternet.org/fact-sheet/mobile/

Putnam, R. D. (2000). *Bowling alone: The collapse and revival of American community*. New York: Simon & Schuster.

Razorfish & CafeMom. (2009). Digital mom: A two-part report published by Razorfish and CafeMom. In *Retrieved from* http://www.etnografiadigitale.it/wp-content/uploads/2012/03/Digital-mom.pdf

Rogers, E. M. (1983). *Diffusion of innovations* (3rd ed.). New York: Free Press.

Rogers, E. M., & Shoemaker, F. F. (1971). *Communication of innovation: A cross-cultural approach* (2nd ed.). New York: The Free Press.

Rudi, J., & Dworkin, J. (2014). Youth online media use: Associations with youth demographics, parental monitoring, and parent-child relationships. *Journal of Youth Development, 9*(1), 59–70.

Rudi, J. H., Dworkin, J., Walker, S. K., & Doty, J. L. (2015a). Parents' use of information and communications technologies for family communication: Differences by age of children. *Information, Communication and Society, 8*(1), 78–93.

Rudi, J., Walkner, A., & Dworkin, J. (2015b). Adolescent-parent communication in a digital world: Differences by family communication patterns. *Youth & Society, 47*(6), 811–828.

Sarkadi, A., & Bremberg, S. (2004). Socially unbiased parenting support on the internet: A cross-sectional study of users of a large Swedish parenting website. *Child: Care, Health & Development, 31*(1), 43–52.

Smith, A. (2010). Technology trends among people of color. Pew Research Center Internet and Technology. Retrieved from http://pewinternet.org/Commentary/2010/September/Technology-Trends-Among-People-of-Color.aspx

Steinberg, L., & Silk, J. S. (2002). Parenting adolescents. In M. H. Borenstein (Ed.), *Handbook of parenting: Vol. I. Children and parenting* (2nd ed., pp. 103–133). Mahwah, NJ: Erlbaum.

Subrahmanyam, K., & Greenfield, P. (2008). Online communication and adolescent relationships. *The Future of Children, 18*(1), 119–146.

Valkenburg, P. M., & Peter, J. (2013). Five challenges for the future of media-effects research. *International Journal of Communication, 7*, 197–215.

Van den Bulck, J., Custers, K., & Nelissen, S. (2016). The child-effect in the new media environment: Challenges and opportunities for communication research. *Journal of Children and Media, 10*(1), 30–38.

Van den Bulck, J., & Van den Bergh, B. (2016). The child effect in media and communication research: A call to arms and an agenda for research. *Annals of the International Communication Association, 29*(1), 35–48.

Walker, S., Dworkin, J., & Connell, J. (2011). Does quantity matter? Variation in parent use of information technology and social media. *Family and Consumer Sciences Research Journal, 40*(2), 106–119.

Zickhur, K., & Smith, A. (2012). *Digital differences*. Washington, DC: Pew Internet and American Life Retrieved from http://pewinternet.org/Reports/2012/Digital-differences.aspx

# Chapter 3
# Families and Technologies in an Era of Migration

**Lynn Schofield Clark**

Three years ago, my niece Sally moved from Argentina to South Korea to teach English. She introduced her immediate family to the popular South Korean app Kakao Talk, a messenger service similar to Facebook Messenger and WhatsApp. When Sally's parents moved from the USA to Germany, they started a new Kakao Talk chat that included Sally's aunts and uncles, cousins, and grandparents. Soon, there were five separate chats on Kakao Talk, with some including only Sally's immediate family, another including only the cousins, and other chats including different groupings of family members. Around the same time, one of Sally's second cousins started a family Facebook page, and family members who had not seen one another in years began getting in touch and sharing news of their lives. Now, my 80-something-year-old mother-in-law checks in with extended family members almost every day via several social media platforms.

This story shares some similarities with the experiences of many families around the world. Economic, political, and social changes have influenced patterns of migration that in turn have led families to become geographically dispersed. Thus, families increasingly find themselves seeking ways to maintain connections across distance, and communication technologies seem to provide solutions to these challenges. Interestingly, researchers who have explored how communication technologies are integrated into everyday life have noted a contradiction in the ways that families think about technologies. On one hand, many families come to treat certain domestic technologies, such as the landline telephone, as if they are invisible, or handy in the solving of everyday problems (Haddon, 2007; Lim, 2008). On the other hand, family members—particularly parents—worry about the incursion of technology into new spaces, wondering if this change might foster negative results for their children, relationships, or for society as a whole (Livingstone, Masceroni, &

L. S. Clark (✉)
Department of Media, Film & Journalism Studies, University of Denver, Denver, CO, USA
e-mail: Lynn.Clark@du.edu

 
J. Van Hook et al. (eds.), *Families and Technology*, National Symposium on Family Issues 9, https://doi.org/10.1007/978-3-319-95540-7_3

Staksrud, 2015). Often, technologies hold a contradictory role in family life as a result of these contrasting views of and experiences with communication technologies. In my book, *The Parent App* (Clark, 2013), for instance, I argued that parents' time-poor lifestyles have led us to create media-rich homes so that our children can be safe at home while parents are working. Even as parents use technologies to keep in touch and make arrangements for and with their children, they worry that too much reliance on technology may compromise their abilities as good parents.

Much of the research on families and technologies has responded to the perception that digital and mobile media are *disruptive technologies*, in that digital and mobile media are understood to be reordering both how we organize ourselves in social relations and how we keep track of these relations over time (Conole, de Laat, Dillon, & Darby, 2008). Many of us experience these disruptions in our family lives, as we call upon younger family members to set up a ringtone, download an app, or transfer photos for us. We tend to adopt the theory of "digital natives," assuming that younger people are somehow naturally inclined to understand technology better than those who are older (Palfrey & Gasser, 2008). In fact, abundant scholarship has pointed out that the vast majority of young people are not more knowledgeable than adults about information and communication technologies (Hargittai, 2010; Kennedy, Judd, Churchward, Gray, & Krause, 2008). In response to the digital natives theory, numerous scholars have pointed out that whereas some technologies are disruptive, the practices that drive their use—making and maintaining connections, finding and sharing information—are in many ways continuous with technologies of the past (Latzer, 2009).

What does seem to be new, however, are the heightened effects of what sociologist Ulrich Beck (1992) has termed the *risk economy*. A risk economy is one in which good-paying professional jobs are being eliminated by computerization, and labor has become less tied to geographic location. The rise of a global and interrelated economic system defined by contingency has deepened long-standing struggles for resources throughout the world, in turn heightening political, economic, and cultural conflicts and forcing thousands of people into displacement each year. Today, more than 65 million people in the world are displaced from their homes. That is an average of 1 in 100 of the world's residents. Technologies both contribute to the automation that is driving displacement and a reordering of the labor force. Technologies are also being used by individuals, groups, and organizations to mitigate the dehumanizing effects that have come about as a result of this reordering and displacement.

The empirical data presented in this chapter are drawn from national and international studies that look at migration, families, and technology, as well as from more than a decade of ethnographic interviewing and observations in urban schools that serve young people and their families, many of whom are from new immigrant, asylum-seeking, and refugee backgrounds. Integrated into this chapter are examples from studies that explore similarities and differences across geographic and national contexts. The chapter begins with a review of the contemporary migration situation in the USA. I then detail technology experiences of immigrant families in order to identify some of the gaps in the research. The chapter concludes with a review of current research on families, technologies, and migration, followed by suggestions for future research.

## Migration to the USA

Movement and migration have long been a part of the human experience. The USA has more immigrants and more persons with connections to a legacy of immigration than any other country in the world. Only 2% of the current US population can trace their heritage to American Indian and Alaskan Native roots, meaning that the vast majority of those residing in the USA today count themselves or their ancestors among those who have migrated to the USA from another location in the world (U.S. Census Bureau, 2017).

According to 2010 Census categories, the largest ethnic groups in the USA are white, not Hispanic or Latino (64%); Hispanic or Latino (16%); black or African American (12%); and Asian (5%; Pew Research Center, 2015). Of the US's total population of 323 million people, more than 40 million, or 13.4% of the current population, were born outside of the USA. This is triple the proportion of the total 1970 population born outside the USA, but still lower than the 14.8% of immigrants that made up the total population at the nation's high immigration point in 1890 (López & Bialik, 2017). When we speak of research on families and technologies, therefore, it is important to recognize that new immigrant communities are expected to provide most of the US population gains in the near future, with immigrant children now making up 25.5% of the total population of US children, most of whom (88%) were born in the USA (Pew Research Center, 2015). The term "immigrant" is used here to signify a broad range of statuses, including asylum-seeking and refugee, that reference the varied reasons for migration to the USA. In spite of this specific and contemporary use of the term, it is important to underscore that in the USA, most of us are descendants of immigrants, and many of us have migrated within or across a variety of geographic borders over the course of our lives.

Migration to the USA is a part of worldwide migration trends. As is the case elsewhere in the world, the largest immigrant groups in the USA have shifted over time. Whereas in 1960, the countries from which most US immigrants originated included Italy, Germany, UK, Canada, Poland, and the Soviet Union, today's largest immigrant groups originate from Mexico, India, China, and the Philippines. Although the rate of immigration from Latin America and Mexico has dropped since 2000, the proportion of immigrants from Mexico remains at 27.6% (Zong & Batalova, 2016). The fastest-growing racial group in the USA, however, is Asian, as the number of Asian immigrants surpassed Hispanic immigrants in 2010, according to the US census (Pew Research Center, 2012). Asians are projected to become the largest immigrant group in the USA by 2055, with India being the country of origin for the largest group of Asian immigrants to the USA in 2015 (López & Bialik, 2017). Black African and Caribbean are also among the fastest-growing immigrant groups in the USA (López & Bialik, 2017).

As is true in other countries around the world, contemporary shifts in migration are largely playing out in urban areas rather than in rural areas and in small towns (USDA Economic Research Service, 2016). In the past few decades, a shift from large urban to smaller urban areas is also noteworthy. Members of US immigrant communities are moving out of Los Angeles, New York City, Detroit, Chicago, and New Orleans into smaller cities, some of which are in the southeast (such as Raleigh and several cities in Florida), but many of which are in the southwest and west US, including Austin, Las Vegas, Phoenix, Sacramento, Portland, and Denver. In fact, some of the fastest immigration growth is occurring in metro areas that previously had small immigrant populations, such as Dallas, Phoenix, and Denver (Balbuena & Batalova, 2011; Singer, Hardwick, & Brettell, 2008).

Denver, where I am located, is in the top 20 US metro areas for immigrants arriving from Vietnam, Korea, Russia, Ukraine, and Ethiopia (Singer et al., 2008). With more than 30% of its population claiming Hispanic or Latino heritage, Denver is also home to one of the largest concentrations of Latinos in the USA. Much of the Denver metro area was once owned by members of the Arapaho and Cheyenne tribes. Because it remains one of the fastest-growing cities in the country (Murray, 2017), Denver is seen as a city with a strong future in technology, not as a slick new Silicon Valley but as a place that is attracting "Main Street businesses that code" (Vara, 2017). Denver also passed a city ordinance limiting how city officials would work in cooperation with the controversial practices of Immigration and Customs Enforcement (ICE; Hancock, 2017). All of this makes Denver an interesting place to study new immigrant families as they negotiate technological practices and a new cultural setting.

A significant number of Hispanic/Latino, African American, and multiracial households are part of the middle- or upper-middle-class in the USA (Banks, 2009; Chavez, 2001; Clark, 2003; Lacy, 2007; Rodriguez, 1996). However, wealth and privilege remain concentrated among white European American families in the USA, and in certain geographic areas of the country, as well. The wealth gap between white households and their black and Hispanic counterparts widened after the 2008 recession due to declines in the housing values of black and Hispanic families (Rooney, 2011). Given the affordability of older urban neighborhoods compared with wealthy suburban neighborhoods and the desire to live near communities of shared heritage, new immigrant families often choose to live in urban areas that have large black, Latino, and Asian populations. This is important to note because the selection of a neighborhood influences the family's options for schooling, as US schools are funded by local property taxes.

In recent years, mid-sized and smaller urban areas have seen the influx of wealthier white families into gentrifying urban neighborhoods, a trend that began several decades earlier in large coastal US cities such as New York and Boston. Even with this influx of wealthy neighbors into urban areas, public urban schools have remained underfunded, and wealthier families have opted out of neighborhood schools and into private schools or schools located in wealthier areas (Gordon, 2016). The reality is that when students and families are afforded a choice to opt out of their neighborhood school and into a wealthier area's school, only the families with access to alternate transportation are able to take advantage of this choice, since public and school subsidized transportation is often unavailable between lower income and wealthier neighborhoods. It is clear that given the preceding information about schools and neighborhoods, young people growing up in new immigrant families in the USA are more likely than their wealthier (and white) peers to attend schools that are underfunded, to have access only to outdated technological equipment, and to have teachers who are burdened with more responsibilities and fewer opportunities for training in technology and education innovations. Thus, in an era of migration, research should examine how parents of immigrant children negotiate limited access to technology in schools and their communities.

## *How Communication Technologies Facilitate Migration*

Social and digital media facilitate migration in many ways. With the strengthening of mobile communication infrastructures across the world, job-seekers can conduct information searches and respond to employment opportunities in their aspirant communities more quickly than ever before, and even while they are still far away (Paragas, 2010). Those considering migration can also leave their current locations with the knowledge that, once relocated, these same technologies can be employed to maintain connections with loved ones back home. Social and digital media lower the threshold of decisions to migrate as through social, mobile, and digital connections, family members are able to leverage weak social ties (such as distant relatives or longtime friends) that make migration possible (Dekker & Engbersen, 2014). Those seeking to migrate are able to establish a new infrastructure of latent ties prior to departure from their homeland and may plug into a network that offers unofficial insider information, further easing their transition. Such connections are important as many immigrants experience continued downward mobility after migration (Horst & Miller, 2006).

Several scholars have explored the ways in which social and digital media have come to play important roles in transnational families. The phrase, transnational families, refers to family groups in which one or more family member lives in a different geographic context for a significant period of each year. Parents in transnational families employ new media in a variety of ways to maintain co-presence, embracing a "polymedia" approach that includes texting and video conferencing in order to connect with one another in real time (Madianou & Miller, 2013). Such practices have led to an empowered experience of distant mothering, according to Madianou (2012). Others have affirmed that mobile technologies, in particular, create ways for family members to stay connected across distances and cultures (Benítez, 2012; Clark & Sywyj, 2012; Fortunati, Periterra, & Vincent, 2012; Madianou & Miller, 2013; Panagakos & Horst, 2006; Parreñas, 2005).

Immigrant parents in the USA share many frustrations in relation to what they often view as the overly sexualized, commercial, and disrespectful youth culture of their new home society (Landale, Thomas, & Van Hook, 2011). At the same time, young people in many of these families share a struggle to uphold their family's values while adapting to the values of the peer culture that is a part of their everyday environment (Berry & Sam, 1997). In many immigrant families, both parents and children are English language learners. Young people have greater access to language education than their parents do, however, and usually come to possess greater English language fluency than their parents (Zong & Batalova, 2016). In a manner similar to many US-born parents, immigrant parents generally assume a fairly traditional gender division of household labor. Thus, while parents, and especially fathers, believe that it is their responsibility to establish and maintain family policies regarding digital and mobile media use, it is often the mothers who oversee the day-to-day realities of the household. What is different in immigrant households is that due to their language proficiency and sometimes their access to technology in schools, young people in these families serve as conduits and interpreters of the new home culture, and they are often the experts in the house when it comes to digital and mobile media (Clark, 2013). Thus, children themselves come to play a key role as "technological brokers" in immigrant households (Katz, 2010). This is sometimes viewed through the lens of risk on the part of immigrant parents who fear that their children's lives will be very different from theirs, and from the lives the children may have had growing up in the parents' home context.

Due to migration and related generational differences in immigrant families, the enhanced influence of the children in the family may echo Dworkin's (Chap. 2) discussion of how children come to have more power in familial decision-making. It is important to observe, however, that in families from immigrant cultures, children are expected to be respectful, compliant, and family focused (Brown et al., 2007). Thus, rather than experiencing authority as upended, technological proficiency is bracketed off from or subsumed within other ways in which parents are presumed to maintain, and children are presumed to respect, parental authority in the family (Clark, 2013; Clark & Sywyj, 2012). Children and parents seek out communication technologies in a way that is consistent with their values of what I've called *respectful connectedness*, where the emphasis is on family media uses that are respectful, compliant, and family focused (Clark, 2013). Some young people do not resent parental restrictions on the use of technology. My research team found this to be true among our subject migrant families who had come to the USA from north and east Africa and southeast Asia. Young people saw their family's restrictions on digital and mobile media as a sign of how the family cares for them. Seventeen-year-old Josna explained that her parents demanded that she share a Facebook page with her sister. Once, someone Photoshopped pictures of her face and her sister's face onto naked bodies. She explained that she came to see her parents' decision to have her share a Facebook page with her sister as a way of protecting them both. She and her sister did not feel alone when this happened, but their shared page served as a reminder that they are part of a community that can respond together to these kinds of offenses. Josna's parents' restrictions made sense to her in the context of the protection that her joint page offered to her sister and her together.

Furthermore, rather than harboring the US presumed expectations of developing from adolescence into independent adults, among immigrant born families there is an expectation of continued social and economic interdependence and a prioritizing of familial bonds over personal autonomy (Gullotta & Adams, 2008). Thus, similar to the parents Nathanson (Chap. 1) has discussed, parents in migrating families desire influence. They want to mediate in their children's media and technology uses, but as immigrant families, they often do so within contexts that are quite different.

One common concern of immigrant families involves surveillance. Several young people I interviewed noted that their family members had asked them not to have a Facebook page out of fear that Homeland Security or ICE might be able to locate undocumented family members through social media networks. This ability to locate people was also mentioned as a concern among families that were escaping abusive situations.

## *Digital and Social Media Risks Related to Access*

While more than 92% of US teens reported going online daily, and more than 75% said that they had, or had access to, a mobile phone in 2015 (Lenhart, 2015), discrepancies in access and use remain, particularly in immigrant families. One study found that one in ten immigrant Hispanic families have no internet access at all, compared with 7% of US born Hispanics and 5% of US born whites (Rideout & Katz, 2016). In the same study, 44% of immigrant Hispanic parents said that they do not use computers at home, work, or even occasionally (Rideout & Katz, 2016).

Note that 75% of young people say they have or *have access to* a mobile phone (Lenhart, 2015). My own research has found that in many cases, young people from new immigrant families were still sharing a mobile phone with other members of their family as recently as 2017. Often, this occurs due to limited finances and children who age into mobile phone use before the family decides to (or can) make a personal phone purchase for a child. The practice of sharing a phone was also explained in relation to the parents' desire to maintain some control over the technology. For instance, Laticia, a sixteen-year-old from Mexico, noted that she was expected to turn over the mobile phone to her mother as soon as her mother returned from work. There are many reasons that immigrant families might adopt unique strategies for integrating technologies into their lives, and further research is needed to identify and explore these issues.

Another interesting area of research relates to the widespread use of mobile phones and Internet access. Although research organizations such as Pew once measured the adoption of mobile devices separately from the ability to access the Internet, researchers have found that with the increasing ubiquity of mobile phones and then smart phones, members of some communities first began receiving Internet access via mobile phones rather than through a laptop or tablet (Rideout & Katz, 2016). Most researchers believe that while smart phones afford certain advantages over older models, the adoption of a mobile device as the primary means for accessing the Internet is a negative development for young people, as it is much easier to access online materials and to participate in the production of original content with a laptop or tablet than it is on a phone (Watkins, 2009). This pattern of adoption has been especially prevalent among young African Americans and Latinos (Watkins, 2009). Because mobile phones are less expensive and easier to attain than laptops or tablets, this pattern of adoption is likely to be found among young people in new immigrant communities, as well, although research is needed to provide empirical support for this. Currently, research is under way that is examining the hidden costs and workarounds that are developing among young members of marginalized communities who are utilizing mobile phones as a primary or only gateway to internet access (Watkins et al., 2018).

There are also marked differences in who pays for mobile phones and for phone plans. Lower-income young people are more likely than their middle-class counterparts to have a prepaid cell phone plan and to pay for it themselves. When teens in lower-income families paid for their own mobile phone plans, this further accentuated gaps between parents and teens, and between first-generation, Spanish-dominant adult Latinos and their Latino children in particular (Straubhaar, Spence, Tufekci, & Lentz, 2012). This is the case because parents tend to grant autonomy to the person who pays for the phone.

In addition to what researchers have termed "gradations in digital inclusion," what has also come to be of interest among those studying young people and access to digital and mobile media is the "participation gap." Some young people have less access not only to technologies but also to the opportunities for participation that they enable (Hargittai, 2010; Jenkins, 2006; Livingstone & Helsper, 2007). Cost remains a key factor for why lower-income families do not have high speed internet access at home (Rideout & Katz, 2016). Further research is needed to learn how immigrant young people and their families are coping with the lack of ready access to high speed internet access, and how they are responding to the deepening inequities that are related to and exacerbated by differential access.

## Digital and Social Media Risks Related to Online Harassment

Limited access to technology remains a primary concern of immigrant parents, but another concern is the perceived prevalence of online harassment that their children encounter. Research has demonstrated that online patterns of harassment correlate with offline patterns, and that young people are harassed on the basis of their race/ethnicity, national or tribal affiliation, sexual orientation, and religious practices (Low & Espelage, 2013; Maynard, Vaughn, Salas-Wright, & Vaughn, 2016; Scherr & Larson, 2009). Research on cyberbullying demonstrates that online harassment is part of a broader landscape of peer victimization that can also include sexual harassment, dating violence, and fights (Levy et al., 2012). For many young people, such encounters in social and digital media spaces are quite difficult. As one example, Santosh, a seventeen-year-old, noted that he has experienced various levels of harassment both online and off. When one of his online friends referred to him on his Facebook wall using a racially loaded term, Santosh decided to ignore it, even though he found it "painful" and "horrible." He said he was hoping this friend would stop using that word, because otherwise, "there would be some problems" (Clark, 2013). Some young immigrant students felt hurt when experiencing both racism and misrecognition of their ethnic heritage. One fourteen-year-old high schooler originally from Kenya, for instance, recounted harassment he had experienced online, saying of one text he received, "They used the n-word but I don't understand because that is not my nationality. But it really hurt me." He then blocked the perpetrator's contact information so that he would receive no further contact from him (Clark, 2013). Race, religion, and country of origin also presented intersecting experiences of discrimination for some young people. Several young women from Somalia who were between 12 and 18 years of age noted that they had been harassed both online and off for wearing hijab and had simultaneously experienced racial and cultural insults in both online and offline spaces.

In contrast to middle- and upper-middle-class young people who might find in Facebook a place where one can explore the possibilities of developing an acquaintance into a friendship or a romantic relationship, young people from marginalized backgrounds—due to economics, race, or ethnicity—have reason to be more cautious. Young people living in low-income and non-dominant communities understand themselves to be under increasing surveillance, and thus opt out of social and digital media use or adopt self-censoring practices to cope with evolving online privacy norms (Boyd, 2014; Marwick & Boyd, 2014; Vickery, 2015). This has implications for the presence–or absence–of immigrant young people in social and digital media spaces, as will be discussed further in a later section.

Because of the sorting that occurs in public schools, it is important to note that young people who grow up in new immigrant families are much more likely than white European young people to attend schools that include a wide diversity of people their own age (Orfield & Frankenberg, 2013). On the plus side, this means that young people of differing racial/ethnic lineages and geographic roots find themselves grouped into classes with others who are similarly grappling with varying degrees of racism, religious discrimination, racial/ethnic misrecognition, linguistic challenges, and other forms of exclusion as they may similarly work to forge bi- or multicultural identities for themselves. Thus, some find friends among those with similar backgrounds who provide solidarity and support. However, even as classes, sports, and extracurricular activities introduce young people to those of differing cultural heritages, religions, family compositions, and socioeconomic backgrounds, young people in highly diverse urban schools often settle into social groups of racial/ethnic homophily, just as do those from less culturally diverse schools (Currarini, Jackson, & Pin, 2010). Sometimes, encounters across difference are welcomed as opportunities for new friendships, informal intercultural learning, and personal development. At other times, such encounters can be tense and conflict-ridden, and social media become spaces of heightened emotions. How social and digital media practices enable or hinder relations of solidarity and tension in both in-group and cross-cultural settings, and how such in-school encounters differ when supplemented or challenged through online means, is an important area for future research.

## *Social and Digital Media Competency Programs for Immigrant Children*

Several large and comparative studies have focused on digital media and learning or "connected learning". These studies consider the ways that young immigrants live and learn in digital and social media spaces as they traverse between school and informal settings. Ethnographic studies of immigrant children's experiences with social and digital media literacy and competency development have demonstrated that digital technologies can serve as catalysts for collaborative learning across home, school, and community settings (Barron et al., 2014; Barron, Walter, Martin, & Schatz, 2010). A year-long study of a class in a London suburb began with aims to uncover how schools, homes, and peers were densely networked in a manner to create connections that could be leveraged for more meaningful learning. However, results led the researchers to be more circumspect of the potential for digital technologies to catalyze learning across home, school, and community settings (Livingstone & Sefton-Green, 2016). The authors observed "a general tendency toward the social reproduction of advantage or disadvantage… [that made them] cautious in the face of the undoubtedly exciting calls to reimagine education in ways that rely on families to support and extend learning," noting that such reordering of educational priorities might risk exacerbating socioeconomic inequalities (p. 189).

As a means of addressing socioeconomic inequalities, in many US urban communities where immigrant young people live, after-school and summer community programs provide mentoring and pedagogical resources for the development of social and digital media competency. Proportionally, few young people take advantage of these programs, but studies show that those who do are more likely to do well in higher education and to pursue leadership opportunities in their workplaces and communities (Jenson et al., 2013). One comprehensive study of US youth digital media programs conducted in 2008 found that 58% of after- school community media programs serve a high percentage of newcomers to the USA, even though these programs are woefully underfunded; half of the programs surveyed operated on annual budgets of $100 K per year or less, and 69% had been serving their constituents for 10 or fewer years (Turner, 2011). The study's authors concluded that "what is clear is that these programs offer a lifeline for individual youth in underserved communities" (p. 40). More longitudinal research is therefore warranted regarding the role of these programs in the lives of immigrant young people and their communities.

**Digital Media Competency and Development of Citizen Identity** A number of scholars have asserted that providing young people with opportunities to develop digital media competency enhances participation in civic life among political newcomers. For instance, "When people have digital and media literacy competencies, they recognize personal, corporate and political agendas and are empowered to speak out on behalf of the missing voices and omitted perspectives in our communities. By identifying and attempting to solve problems, people use their powerful voices and their rights under the law to improve the world around them" (Hobbs, 2010, p. 17; see also Clark & Marchi, 2017). A study of youth media production in Israel concluded that the programs that most effectively prepare young people for civic engagement harness adults as conversation partners (Levin, 2011). Similarly, "People do not automatically acquire an effective public voice or the motivation to use it. They must be taught" (Levine, 2008, p. 125). Adults and youth can effectively work together in what Soep (2011) terms "collegial pedagogy" that leverages the video materials that youth record and embeds those materials in broader narrative frames for purposes of both pedagogy and dissemination. In a cross-national context, when students from differing countries were brought together for common educational experiences via a shared social media platform, students were able to critically consider questions of relative privilege and poverty, "shifting youth's self-understandings as a result" (Stornaiuolo, Hall, & Sahni, 2011, p. 276). More research is needed to ascertain the information technology and curricular designs that prove most effective with both homogeneous and heterogeneous groups of immigrant and domestic young people. Also important is a better understanding of how immigrant young people interpret their interactions with US born adults.

**How Apps and Social Media Sites Shape Online Engagement** Social media platforms through which people communicate with one another do not exist in a neutral space. Platforms are designed to encourage connectivity that, in turn, generates profits for platform stakeholders as valuable data is gathered about its users and their practices (Van Dijck, 2013). Amazon and Facebook have long employed such proprietary algorithms. Twitter and Instagram each instituted sorting mechanisms in the early 2017, and each saw profits increase dramatically shortly thereafter. Meanwhile, Snapchat, which has less algorithmic sorting, saw its use decline dramatically after the launch of Instagram Stories (Constine, 2017). Most digital experiences today are thus shaped by algorithms that push toward us what is presumed to be our "preferred content." These sites also make recommendations based on prior user experiences and personalize our search results, most of the time in ways of which most users are unaware (Eslami et al., 2015).

Even more important than algorithmic ranking might be individuals' choices of where to direct their attention. Individuals' choices limit exposure to content that might otherwise challenge one's views and beliefs (Bakshy, Messing, & Adamic, 2015). The problem with this argument, as Sandvig (2015) has pointed out, is that the particular study that emphasized individual choice as being more limiting than algorithmic authority was conducted by Facebook's own staff, and overlooks the fact that if Facebook is accelerating the tendency toward confirmation bias and polarization, that is surely a problem for democracy. Evaluating any claims about the influences of social media on thought and decision-making is difficult when Facebook refuses to provide either access to the data they collect, or information about the algorithms that sort (Pooley, 2016). Thus, there is much that is unknown, and cannot be known, about how online experiences with platforms are shaped for differing groups of people, including, of course, immigrant families.

We do know that the emergent "hybrid media system" is comprised of various actors (both human and technological) that shepherd information flows according to their own logics in ways that can modify or even undermine the agency of others (Chadwick, 2017). The "dark frontier" of this hybrid media system was revealed in the 2016 US election and its aftermath, as fake news, social media bot activity, and the orchestrated hacks and leaks that undermined Clinton's campaign coalesced at least in part because of the incentive structures of social media platforms (Chadwick, 2017).

Are some voices, and perhaps even some languages, more likely to be favored algorithmically than others in social media spaces? Do the algorithms of social media spaces render the lived experiences of immigrant groups less visible, and therefore less likely to engender empathy among those already predisposed to ignore such groups? What is possible in terms of regulating the circulation of the fake news that reinforces stereotypes, reinforces the anti-immigrant movement, and amplifies the voices of a hateful minority at the expense of the growing majority? Such questions are important, and this is why many interested in the role of immigrant families in the future of democracy feel compelled to both study efforts to educate people on the ways that digital media shape and potentially limit our experiences and to advocate for greater transparency from the media organizations that increasingly structure those experiences.

## The Internet of Things: Data Collection and Surveillance

The Internet of Things (IoT) is a phrase that is employed to suggest that revolutionary implications are to come with the incorporation of wireless and data technologies into home appliances. The use of the term obscures the fact that the automation of consumer durable goods is part of a century-long trend (Streeter, 2014). Although the phrase implies revolution, in a more banal description IoT is about accessing remote data in a manner that allows for the more efficient exchange of goods and services. Of course, any gathering of data is far from banal, particularly among communities that already feel at risk. During the aftermath of Hurricane Harvey, for example, many immigrants put themselves at greater physical risk as a result of fear that agencies providing aid might, as a compelling rumor suggested, harvest and share data about immigration status, thus jeopardizing their futures as well as their immediate chances of receiving aid. Any efforts to embed supposedly harmless processes of data collection into one's home and personal life are therefore suspect for many, particularly in a political environment that has already demonstrated a proclivity for prioritizing punishment over humanitarian concerns. There is little wonder that many, including members of immigrant families, eschew the seemingly mundane health and fitness and personal data tracking apps that are widely adopted among other populations, as well as even federally funded programs designed to provide internet access (Byron, 2017; Rideout & Katz, 2016). Research in this area is likely to reveal sustained reluctance on the part of immigrant families, and may serve as a caution for those who wish that technological solutions might emerge to solve endemic social problems.

## Conclusion

Studies of the digital and social media experiences of immigrant families in the USA. Young people and their families embrace restrictive approaches to parenting in a digital age even as young people develop proficiency as bicultural intermediaries. Studies provide optimism for the aspirations that immigrant families and children bring to their US experiences, but also highlight the enduring skepticism that accompanies new technological developments in a politically fraught context.

Suggestions for future directions in research, as noted in this chapter, highlight a need to develop an understanding of the younger immigrant, asylum-seeking, and refugee child's experiences with social and digital media competency development. Furthermore, there is a need to understand the risks they and their families face in social and digital media spaces, including issues of limited access, risk of harassment, and tendencies to self-censor. Future research should continue to analyze opportunities for enriching social and digital media competencies among these groups. Finally, researchers need to understand how the platforms, algorithms, and data-gathering mechanisms of social media shape online engagement for immigrant, asylum-seeking, and refugee family members. We need to be conscious of technological discourses that have glossed over the dark frontiers of our hybrid media environment, tempering our enthusiasm for technological solutions with a foregrounded concern to protect the human rights of immigrant families.

Above all, this chapter highlights the need for scholars, educators, and advocates to leave behind any deficit-based approaches to the study of immigrant families, children, adolescents, and media that tend to see middle class forms of parenting as the ideal norm. We need to provide a check on the tendency to criticize parents as culpable for what are more accurately described as social structural failures that do not support the unique needs of a growing number of US families. My colleagues and I have argued elsewhere that future studies should seek to better understand the contextual factors that influence media engagement in diverse family settings and structures (Alper, Katz, & Clark, 2016). We must also seek to better understand the creative ways that children and families are working to address the challenges they face, as such innovations provide directions for policies that govern the digital and social media in which we are increasingly immersed.

## References

Alper, M., Katz, V., & Clark, L. S. (2016). Researching children, intersectionality, and diversity in the digital age. *Journal of Children and Media, 10*(1), 107–114.

Bakshy, E., Messing, S., & Adamic, L. (2015). Exposure to ideologically diverse news and opinion on Facebook. *Science, 348*(6239), 1130-1132. doi: 10.1126/science.aaa1160

Balbuena, C., & Batalova, J. (2011, December 8). *Green card holders and legal immigration to the United States*. Migration and Policy Institute. Retrieved from http://www.migrationpolicy.org/article/green-card-holders-and-legal-immigration-united-states-1

Banks, P. A. (2009). *Represent: Art and identity among the black upper middle class*. New York: Routledge.

Barron, B., Gomez, K., Pinkard, N., Martin, C. K., Austin, K., Gray, T., … Zywica, J. (2014). *The digital youth network: Cultivating digital media citizenship in urban communities*. Boston, MA: MIT Press.

Barron, B., Walter, S., Martin, C. K., & Schatz, C. (2010). Predictors of creative computing participation and profiles of experience in two Silicon Valley middle schools. *Computers & Education, 54*(1), 178–189.

Beck, U. (1992). *Risk society: Towards a new modernity*. Thousand Oaks, CA: SAGE.

Benítez, J. L. (2012). Salvadoran transnational families: ICT and communication practices in the network society. *Journal of Ethnic and Migration Studies, 38*(9), 1439–1449. https://doi.org/10.1080/1369183X.2012.698214

Berry, J. W., & Sam, D. L. (1997). Accculturation and adaptation. In J. W. Berry, H. Segal, & C. Kagitcibaci (Eds.), *Handbook of cross-cultural psychology, volume 3: Social behavior and applications* (2nd ed., pp. 291–326). Boston: Allyn and Bacon.

Boyd, D. (2014). *It's complicated: The social lives of networked teens*. New Haven, CT: Yale University Press.

Brown, B. B., Bakken, J. P., Nguyen, J., Von Bank, & H. G. (2007). Sharing information about peer relations: Parent and adolescent opinions and behaviors in Hmong and African American families. *New Directions for Child and Adolescent Development, 2007*(116), 67–82. https://doi.org/10.1002/cd.189

Byron, P. (2017). Friendship, sexual intimacy & young people's negotiations of sexual health. *Culture, Health & Sexuality, 19*(4), 486–500.

Chadwick, A. (2017). *The hybrid media system: Politics and power*. Oxford, NY: Oxford University Press.

Chavez, M. (2001). *Everyday injustice: Latino professionals and racism*. Lanham, MD: Rowman & Littlefield.

Clark, L. S. (2013). *The parent app: Understanding families in the digital age*. Oxford, NY: Oxford University Press.

Clark, L. S., & Marchi, R. (2017). *Young people and the future of news*. Cambridge: Cambridge University Press.

Clark, L. S., & Sywyj, L. (2012). Mobile intimacies in the USA among refugee and recent immigrant teens and their parents. *Feminist Media Studies, 12*(4), 485–495. https://doi.org/10.1080/14680777.2012.741861

Clark, W. (2003). *Immigrants and the American dream: Remaking the middle class*. New York, NY: Guilford Press.

Conole, G., de Laat, M., Dillon, T., & Darby, J. (2008). 'Disruptive technologies', 'pedagogical innovation': What's new? Findings from an in-depth study of students' use and perception of technology. *Computers & Education, 50*(2), 511–524. https://doi.org/10.1016/j.compedu.2007.09.009

Constine, J. (2017). Snapchat is stifled by its un-algorithmic feed. Tech crunch. Retrieved August 30, 2017, from http://social.techcrunch.com/2017/04/29/sortchat/

Currarini, S., Jackson, M. O., & Pin, P. (2010). Identifying the roles of race-based choice and chance in high school friendship network formation. *Proceedings of the National Academy of Sciences, 107*(11), 4857–4861. https://doi.org/10.1073/pnas.0911793107

Dekker, R., & Engbersen, G. (2014). How social media transform migrant networks and facilitate migration. *Global Networks, 14*(4), 401–418. https://doi.org/10.1111/glob.12040

Eslami, M., Rickman, A., Vaccaro, K., Aleyasen, A., Vuong, A., Karahalios, K., … Sandvig, C. (2015). "I always assumed that I wasn't really that close to [her]": Reasoning about invisible algorithms in the news feed. In *CHI '15 Proceedings of the 33rd Annual ACM Conference on Human Factors in Computing Systems* (pp. 153–162). New York, NY: ACM.

Fortunati, L., Periterra, R., & Vincent, J. (2012). *Migration, diaspora and information technology in global societies*. London: Routledge.

Gordon, H. R. (2016). We can't let them fail for one more day': School reform urgency and the politics of reformer-community alliances. *Race Ethnicity and Education, 19*(1), 1–22.

Gullotta, T., & Adams, G. (2008). *Handbook of adolescent behavioral problems*. New York: Springer.

Haddon, L. (2007). Roger Silverstone's legacies: Domestication. *New Media & Society, 9*(1), 25–32. https://doi.org/10.1177/1461444807075201

Hancock, M. B. (2017). *Mayor Hancock statement on passage of public safety enforcement priorities act*. Retrieved August 29, 2017, from https://www.denvergov.org/content/denvergov/en/mayors-office/newsroom/2017/mayor-hancock-statement-on-passage-of-public-safety-enforcement-.html

Hargittai, E. (2010). Digital na(t)ives? Variation in internet skills and uses among members of the "net generation". *Sociological Inquiry, 80*(1), 92–113. https://doi.org/10.1111/j.1475-682X.2009.00317.x

Hobbs, R. (2010). *Digital and media literacy: A plan of action* (a white paper). The Aspen Institute, Communications and Society Program. Retrieved from https://assets.aspeninstitute.org/content/uploads/2010/11/Digital_and_Media_Literacy.pdf

Horst, H., & Miller, D. (2006). *The cell phone: An anthropology of communication*. New York, NY: Berg.

Jenkins, H. (2006). *Convergence culture where old and new media collide*. New York: NYU Press.

Jenson, J. M., Alter, C. F., Nicotera, N., Anthony, E. K., & Forrest-Bank, S. S. (2013). *Risk, resilience, and positive youth development: Developing effective community programs for at-risk youth: Lessons from the Denver Bridge Project*. Oxford University Press. Retrieved from http://books.google.com/books?hl=en&lr=&id=Ith3VhC_AdkC&oi=fnd&pg=PP2&dq=info:J49gl1rpIpAJ:scholar.google.com&ots=pIA4ERR6ym&sig=wNhzEqnIQQvDhXvXteGhkVl1EJI

Katz, V. S. (2010). How children of immigrants use media to connect their families to the community. *Journal of Children and Media, 4*(3), 298–315. https://doi.org/10.1080/17482798.2010.486136

Kennedy, G. E., Judd, T. S., Churchward, A., Gray, K., & Krause, K.-L. (2008). First year students' experiences with technology: Are they really digital natives? *Australasian Journal of Educational Technology, 24*(1). https://doi.org/10.14742/ajet.1233

Lacy, K. (2007). *Blue-chip black: Race, class, and status in the new black middle class*. Berkeley: University of California Press.

Landale, N., Thomas, K., & Van Hook, J. (2011). The living arrangements of children of immigrants. *Future of Children, 21*(1), 43–70.

Latzer, M. (2009). Information and communication technology innovations: Radical and disruptive? *New Media & Society, 11*(4), 599–619. https://doi.org/10.1177/1461444809102964

Lenhart, A. (2015,). *Teens, social media & technology overview 2015*. Pew Research Center, Internet and Technology. Retrieved from http://www.pewinternet.org/2015/04/09/teens-social-media-technology-2015/

Levin, D. (2011). 'Because it's not really me:' Students' films and their potential as alternative media. In J. Fisherkeller (Ed.), *International perspectives on youth media: Cultures of production and education* (pp. 138–154). New York: Peter Lang.

Levine, P. (2008). A public voice for youth: The audience problem in digital media and civic education. In L. Bennett (Ed.), *Civic life online: Learning how digital media can engage youth* (pp. 119–138). Cambridge, MA: MIT Press.

Levy, N., Cortesi, S., Gasser, U., Crowley, E., Beaton, M., Casey, J., & Nolan, C. (2012). *Bullying in a networked era: A literature review* (SSRN Scholarly Paper No. ID 2146877). Rochester, NY: Social Science Research Network. Retrieved from https://papers.ssrn.com/abstract=2146877

Lim, S. S. (2008). Technology domestication in the Asian homestead: Comparing the experiences of middle class families in China and South Korea. *East Asian Science, Technology and Society: An International Journal, 2*(2), 189–209. https://doi.org/10.1007/s12280-008-9045-6

Livingstone, S., & Helsper, E. (2007). Gradations in digital inclusion: Children, young people and the digital divide. *New Media & Society, 9*(4), 671–696. https://doi.org/10.1177/1461444807080335

Livingstone, S., Masceroni, G., & Staksrud, E. (2015). *Developing a framework for researching children's online risks and opportunities in Europe*. London: EU Kids Online https://www.researchgate.net/publication/285593314_Developing_a_framework_for_researching_children%27s_online_risks_and_opportunities_in_Europe

Livingstone, S., & Sefton-Green, J. (2016). *The class: Living and learning in the digital age*. NYU Press.

López, G., & Bialik, K. (2017). *May 3*. Pew Research Center, Fact Tank: Key findings about U.S. immigrants Retrieved from http://www.pewresearch.org/fact-tank/2017/05/03/key-findings-about-u-s-immigrants/

Low, S., & Espelage, D. L. (2013). Differentiating cyberbullying perpetration from non-physical bullying: Commonalities across race, individual, and family predictors. *Psychology of Violence, 3*(1), 39–52.

Madianou, M. (2012). Migration and the accentuated ambivalence of motherhood: The role of ICTs in Filipino transnational families. *Global Networks, 12*(3), 277–295. https://doi.org/10.1111/j.1471-0374.2012.00352.x

Madianou, M., & Miller, D. (2013). *Migration and new media: Transnational families and polymedia*. New York, NY: Routledge.

Marwick, A. E., & Boyd, D. (2014). Networked privacy: How teenagers negotiate context in social media. *New Media & Society, 16*(7), 1051–1067. https://doi.org/10.1177/1461444814543995

Maynard, B. R., Vaughn, M. G., Salas-Wright, C. P., & Vaughn, S. (2016). Bullying victimization among school-aged immigrant youth in the United States. *Journal of Adolescent Health, 58*(3), 337–344. https://doi.org/10.1016/j.jadohealth.2015.11.013

Murray, J. (2017, March 28). Denver's growth spurt slows down—A little—As the city's population nears 700,000. The Denver Post. Retrieved from http://www.denverpost.com/2017/03/28/denvers-growth-spurt-slows-down/

Orfield, G., & Frankenberg, E. (2013). *Educational delusions?: Why choice can deepen inequality and how to make schools fair*. Berkeley: University of California Press.

Palfrey, J. G., & Gasser, U. (2008). *Born digital: Understanding the first generation of digital natives*. New York, NY: Basic Books.

Panagakos, A. N., & Horst, H. A. (2006). Return to cyberia: Technology and the social worlds of transnational migrants. *Global Networks, 6*(2), 109–124. https://doi.org/10.1111/j.1471-0374.2006.00136.x

Paragas, F. (2010). Migrant workers and mobile phones: Technological, temporal and spatial simultaneity. In R. Ling & S. W. Campbell (Eds.), *The reconstruction of space and time: Mobile communication practices* (pp. 39–65). New Brunswick, NJ: Transaction Publishers.

Parreñas, R. (2005). Long distance intimacy: Class, gender and intergenerational relations between mothers and children in Filipino transnational families. *Global Networks, 5*(4), 317–336. https://doi.org/10.1111/j.1471-0374.2005.00122.x

Pew Research Center. (2012, June 19). *The rise of Asian Americans*. Retrieved from http://www.pewsocialtrends.org/2012/06/19/the-rise-of-asian-americans/

Pew Research Center. (2015, September 28). *Chapter 5: U.S. Foreign-Born Population Trends*. Retrieved from http://www.pewhispanic.org/2015/09/28/chapter-5-u-s-foreign-born-population-trends/

Pooley, J. (2016, November 11). *We can't know whether Facebook is to blame for Trump's win*. Slate. Retrieved from http://www.slate.com/blogs/future_tense/2016/11/11/we_can_t_know_whether_facebook_is_to_blame_for_trump_s_win.html

Rideout, V., & Katz, V. S. (2016). Opportunity for all? Technology and learning in lower-income families. In *A report of the Families and Media Project*. New York: Joan Ganz Cooney Center at Sesame Workshop Retrieved from http://www.joanganzcooneycenter.org/wp-content/uploads/2016/01/jgcc_opportunityforall.pdf

Rodriguez, G. (1996). *The emerging Latino middle class*. Pepperdine University Institute for Public Policy. https://publicpolicy.pepperdine.edu/davenport-institute/content/reports/latino.pdf

Rooney, B. (2011, July 26). *Recession worsens racial wealth gap*. CNN Money. Retrieved from http://money.cnn.com/2011/07/26/news/economy/wealth_gap_white_black_hispanic/index.htm

Sandvig, C. (2015). *What Facebook's "It's not our fault" study really means*. WIRED. Retrieved from https://www.wired.com/2015/05/facebook-not-fault-study/

Scherr, T., & Larson, J. (2009). Bullying dynamics associated with race, ethnicity, and immigration status. In S. R. Jimerson, S. M. Swearer, & D. L. Espelage (Eds.), *International handbook of school bullying: An international perspective* (pp. 223–234). New York, NY: Routledge.

Singer, A., Hardwick, S., & Brettell, C. (2008, April 30). Twenty-first century gateways: Immigrants in suburban America. Migration Policy Institute. Retrieved from http://www.migrationpolicy.org/article/twenty-first-century-gateways-immigrants-suburban-america

Soep, E. (2011). All the world's an album: Youth media as strategic embedding. In J. Fisherkeller (Ed.), *International perspectives on youth media: Cultures of production and education* (pp. 246–261). New York: Peter Lang.

Straubhaar, J., Spence, J., Tufekci, Z., & Lentz, R. G. (2012). *Inequity in the technopolis: Race, class, gender, and the digital divide in Austin*. Austin, TX: University of Texas Press.

Streeter, T. (2014, September 29). Internet [draft] [#digitalkeywords] [Blog post]. Retrieved from http://culturedigitally.org/2014/09/internet-draft-digitalkeywords/

Stornaiuolo, A., Hall, G., & Sahni, U. (2011). Cosmopolitan imaginings of self and other: Youth and social networking in a global world. In J. Fisherkeller (Ed.), *International perspectives on youth media: Cultures of production and education* (pp. 263–280). New York: Peter Lang.

Turner, K. (2011). Mapping the field of youth media organizations in the United States. In J. Fisherkeller (Ed.), *International perspectives on youth media* (pp. 25–49). New York: Peter Lang.

USDA Economic Research Service. (2016). *Rural economy & population*. Retrieved from https://www.ers.usda.gov/topics/rural-economy-population/

U.S. Census Bureau (2017). 2017 National population projections tables, Table 11: Race and Hispanic origin of the native and foreign born. Retrieved from https://www.census.gov/data/tables/2017/demo/popproj/2017-summary-tables.html

Van Dijck, J. (2013). *The culture of connectivity: A critical history of social media*. Oxford University Press.

Vara, V. (2017). *Can the American heartland remake itself in the image of Silicon Valley? One startup finds out*. Wired. Retrieved from https://www.wired.com/2017/05/can-denver-become-like-silicon-valley/

Vickery, J. R. (2015). `I don't have anything to hide, but…': The challenges and negotiations of social and mobile media privacy for non-dominant youth. *Information, Communication and Society, 18*(3), 281–294.

Watkins, S. C. (2009). *The young and the digital: What the migration to social network sites, games, and anytime, anywhere media means for our future*. New York: Beacon Press Retrieved from https://www.amazon.com/dp/B004Z1TBY6/ref=dp-kindle-redirect?_encoding=UTF8&btkr=1

Watkins, S. C., Cho, A., Bermudez, A. L., Vickery, J. R., Shaw, V., & Weinzimmer, L. (2018). *The digital edge: How black and Hispanic youth are reimagining the digital divide*. New York University Press.

Zong, J., & Batalova, J. (2016, March 17). Mexican immigrants in the United States. Migration Policy Institute. Retrieved from http://www.migrationpolicy.org/article/mexican-immigrants-united-states

# Part II
# Dating and Mating in the Internet Age

# Chapter 4
# Online Dating: Changing Intimacy One Swipe at a Time?

**Pepper Schwartz and Nicholas Velotta**

Few aspects of romantic coupling have shifted as radically in the past fifty years as how we find our mates. Looking back a mere century ago, couples were finding their partners primarily through familial ties and proximity (Coontz, 2006). While arranged marriage was never a custom in the USA, channeled marriages were. Parents took great care to introduce their adult child to events that would offer cultural, religious, and/or economic homogeneity, or even better, advantage. Churches had dances, the wealthy had coming-out parties, and fraternities and sororities created alliances based on feelings of equivalent superiority. This practice of community-sourced matchmaking—which was once considered the superior means for singles to find an acceptable spouse—has been all but retired in metro areas, which means that it is no longer a marriage conduit for the vast majority of love-seeking Americans.

It should not come as any surprise that this cultural and behavioral shift in mate finding converges with the rise of technology—first cars, then phones, later, the Internet, and online dating. More individuals are seeking "love at first byte" in lieu of more conventional routes to love such as the workplace or at local bars. Even still, locations like singles bars remain a staple of social life, though they are no longer a main locus of looking for a date; these days, it would not be uncommon to come across couples in a singles bar on the date they scheduled using a dating site or app.

The World Wide Web along with various reappraisals of how to find *The One* have ushered in a complex romantic reality that takes place both online and in vivo simultaneously. In this chapter, we give the often-chaotic landscape of internet dating a history and modern-day context. We discuss how different populations use online dating sites and apps. Further, we postulate how their usage may be changing the way couples form and maintain relationships and how dating technologies impact the individuals who use them. Also, we evaluate the hypothesis put forth by pundits that both the plentitude of people available online and the style of some

P. Schwartz (✉) · N. Velotta
Department of Sociology, University of Washington, Seattle, WA, USA



J. Van Hook et al. (eds.), *Families and Technology*, National Symposium on Family Issues 9, https://doi.org/10.1007/978-3-319-95540-7_4

dating sites (à la Tinder's streamlined "just swipe" interface) has changed not only American dating but American mating, and perhaps worldwide patterns as well (see Jayson, 2013; Slater, 2013a).

## Precursors to Modern Online Dating

Prior to electronic messages, "winks," and "pokes," the first attempts at broadcasting romantic interest to the masses were via classified ads. Personal advertisements appeared in newspapers and were, loosely speaking, amalgamations of the author's bio, physical stats, interests, and what they were looking for in a partner. Opportunities were somewhat stratified by the locus of the ads. For example, early advertisements were found in The Village Voice and the New York Review of Books, which would certainly select for a specific kind of person: urban, urbane, relatively high income level, educated, and—in this early format—heterosexual. Readers who found these faceless profiles interesting were given numbers to dial and could leave messages in the hopes that the author would be similarly inclined to meet for an in-person date.

The similarities between classified ads and modern day online dating are apparent, minus all the technological features that site developers offer their clientele. Classifieds etched out a basic framework of the dating economy from which future dating services could draw upon. Some clear themes found in the ads include: (1) a greater return on investment (e.g., more dates for less effort); classifieds written by women garnered an average of 15 replies and for men, an average of 11 replies (Ahuvia & Adelman, 1992); (2) male use outnumbered female use, with men placing twice as many ads as women (Williams, Sawyer, & Wahlstrom, 2016); and (3) the ability to list both physical and personality traits was extremely important to users and readers (Cicerello & Sheehan, 1995; Davis, 1990; Dunbar, 1995).

Given that the hype around classifieds was at its peak in the 1990s (Williams et al., 2016), it may be surprising that the first computer-based dating service arrived thirty years prior. A Harvard project aptly named *Operation Match* was launched in 1965 and had singles "submit several pieces of information about themselves and what they wanted, have these cross-referenced in a database, and receive a handful of recommended partners" (Weigel, 2016, p. 170). A similar service, *Project TACT* (1964), catered to Upper Eastside New Yorkers. These trailblazers were ahead of their time and technological ability. Author Moira Weigel (*Labor of Love: The Invention of Dating*) describes the rudimentary services as "basically like outsourcing the role of a meddlesome aunt who sets you up on blind dates to a stranger who had a bigger Rolodex" (Weigel, 2016, p. 171). Both databases eventually closed shop due to a lack of processing power (Leonhardt, 2006). However, they contributed a new model of matchmaking for aspiring capitalists to expand on decades later: computerized, data-driven dating services.

Heterosexual singles, who sought technologically enhanced dating and were suspicious of the low-investment and anonymity of classified ads, may have gotten their first route to love in the 1980s with video dating. For a monthly service fee, video dating companies would distribute a taped autobiography of clients who listed what they were looking for in a partner (Finkel, Eastwick, Karney, Reis, & Sprecher, 2012; Weigel, 2016; Woll & Cozby, 1991). The major characteristics that endured from these video services included the ability to see the person prior to meeting them and, perhaps even more influential, the notion that singles had an endless pool to pick from (Woll & Cozby, 1991). A common theme among video dating services was the organization's aggressive marketing of how many singles their clients would be exposed to and could potentially meet (Woll & Young, 1989). The appearance of infinite eligibles also fostered greater choosiness in users (Woll & Cozby, 1991). Participants were exercising harsher judgements towards who they would and would not date both in their own profile video and individually off-tape. This may sound familiar to people who currently use online dating services: today, dating sites almost universally tout the millions of active users they have—giving the message that choosiness is not only O.K. but necessary to narrow down options to Mister or Miss Right. Unfortunately for the early video entrepreneurs, video dating never reached mainstream markets (Finkel et al., 2012). Nonetheless, their appearance left an indelible sense of how right and easy it was to be *choosey* in the new dating economy.

## Rewriting the Online Dating Narrative

Prior to what Malcolm Gladwell would later refer to as the tipping point for mass use of online dating, the services were seen as somewhat pitiable. Popular opinion characterized online dating as a place where socially awkward and unattractive singles would likely go to find a mate (Harmon, 2003). As a result, individuals who found each other through online dating were loath to admit it. This denigration of online dating was so pervasive throughout the 1990s that early in their history, dating companies had to vehemently defend their clientele. Companies asserted that their users were attractive, high quality individuals and pointed out that attractive singles might use online services because they were too busy with their careers to search for love on their own (Weigel, 2016). A second hurdle was acclimating the public to the idea that they had to pay for meeting someone they might love. Initially, many fees were steep, and there was resistance, even outrage, at the dollar amount some new online dating companies were charging. Government regulators paid close attention to the customer service and refund policies of such businesses (which were sketchy at best in some companies) but admitted that the claims of malpractice might be underreported due to clients' fears of stigma if they were to publicly file an issue (Blodgett, 1986).

So, for much of its early introduction into the marketplace, online dating was initially considered as both embarrassing and potentially dangerous. Some commenters saw the sites as incubators for grifters looking to take advantage of lonely hearts or misrepresent themselves in the virtual reality (T. L. Anderson, 2005;

Gibbs, Ellison, & Heino, 2006). The fears of online dating were not totally unfounded either. Cable news and TV shows like *To Catch A Predator* (MSNBC), and now *Catfish* on MTV, continue to promote this narrative by focusing on liars and predatory individuals trying to seduce, cheat, or ask money of naive daters via online dating and hook-up sites. True perspective on what was actually happening for most users was hard to get since, aside from safety concerns, conversation about experiences on the sites was scarce. The stigma of being an online dater was so real, that even good results were unshared. When asked how they met, couples might not feel free to admit they met online. And, although these were clear hurdles to mainstream acceptance, another narrative of online romance began to propagate in the late 1990s and early 2000s, one many articles, news reports, movies, and books referred to as "love at first byte."

Around this pivotal moment in attitude change, the first major player entered the e-dating economy in 1995: Match.com. Gary Kremen, founder and then-CEO of Match, lauded the site for its immense potential to "bring more love to the planet than anything since Jesus Christ" at a time when approximately five percent of Americans had access to the Internet (Kauflin, 2011). What may have seemed like an audacious claim by a tie-dye-shirt-wearing-matchmaking-newcomer ended up becoming true. Within 10 years of its immergence, Match.com had registered 40 million people (Ansari & Klinenberg, 2016). A key factor differentiating Match from other dating services at the time was the ability for users to select their own matches—something that other new dating sites took note of. If video dating had touted choosiness, Match.com taught us the art of quickly scrolling through seemingly endless dating profiles in search of *The One*, or at least the one for that night.

Soon Match.com was joined by other major industry players like eHarmony, PlentyOfFish, Zoosk, and OkCupid. Each competitor was keen to put its personal spin on the merits of using their site, sometimes evoking social science as its foundation for matching. eHarmony started out as the religious-based market for serious singles looking for traditional long-term relationships and offered a 150-item intake questionnaire. Later on, PhD's were employed to do studies on its clientele. PlentyOfFish also uses a behavioral science rationale and in 2017, its homepage declared that the site gives users access to "More dates, more relationships, more visits than any other dating site"—claiming we all personally know someone who has found a partner on the site (PlentyOfFish.com, 2017). Zoosk markets its "Behavioural Matchmaking technology," a type of artificial intelligence which learns from client's actions online, supposedly procuring better matches with more use (Lawler, 2014; Zoosk Inc, 2017). OkCupid has users answer many multiple-choice questions and allows users to indicate specific answers they want from potential matches. OkCupid takes these data and uses an algorithm to calculate compatibility scores or "match percentages." There are no questions about physical appearance in OkCupid's database, something that the cofounder and lead of OkCupid's analytics team, Christian Rudder, believes enables matches of the "inner-selves" (Rudder, 2014).

## Matchmaking as a "Science"

As new companies sought a competitive edge, a tactic for self-validation was to present their online matchmaking as scientific. For the major players previously discussed, terms like behavioral matchmaking technology and match percentages stand out. The era of finding *The One* by chance started to be edged out by claims of using a more systematic approach: finding *The One* with *science* or, more accurately, *quasi-science*.

In their most basic form, many of these sites (eHarmony in the lead) began hiring social scientists to construct matching algorithms. eHarmony had psychologist Steve Carter help develop their algorithm (eHarmony, 2017); Match.com and its sister site Chemistry.com brought on anthropologist and intimacy expert Helen Fisher in 2005 as their Chief Scientific Advisor (Match.com, 2017); PerfectMatch.com hired co-author and sociologist Pepper Schwartz, to create their algorithm. The list goes on, but what remains murky is what these algorithms *do*. How effective are they at pairing up human beings in a way that supersedes the individual's own life experience and real-world judgement?

Few sites or studies offer sufficient answers to this question. After all, sites posit their algorithm much like a secret recipe—if the key ingredients are made public the product loses value and competitors can use the algorithms for themselves. In addition to the secrecy, to our knowledge none of these algorithms have been independently reviewed for their claims. Luckily, one example we can draw on is PerfectMatch's algorithm detailed in *Finding your Perfect Match* (Schwartz, 2006b). Schwartz used a variation of the Myers–Briggs Type Indicator, a personality inventory intended to make C. G. Jung's theory of psychological types useful in people's lives. Far from being guaranteed as an infallible matching system, the PerfectMatch.com algorithm helps people identify their own personality traits and choose which of those they would or would not like to see in a mate. So, if someone's responses reveal them to be an introvert, their preference may be to look for another introvert. If they feel they need a partner who is more talented than they are at negotiating the social world or talking about feelings, they could search for an extrovert. The PerfectMatch.com algorithm addresses eight major personality characteristics.

Each site that applies behavioral science to the process of matching users has done so in varied ways. Helen Fisher of Chemistry.com and Match.com has begun experiments using these online data mines to determine how physical and personality characteristics linked to various hormone and neurotransmitter levels may influence which mates will be successful together (Fisher, 2016; Frazzetto, 2010). In her recently revised and updated book, *Anatomy of Love: A Natural History of Mating, Marriage, and Why We Stray*, Fisher outlines four basic personalities and mindsets that most people fit into: serotonin-expressive individuals (dubbed "Builders" for their apparent traditional beliefs and calm, cautious attitude), dopamine-expressive individuals ("Explorers" who are innately curious and energetic), testosterone-expressive individuals ("Directors" who tend to be assertive and skeptical), and estrogen/oxytocin-expressive individuals (named "Negotiators" in reference to their ability to work well with others and their empathetic mindset; Fisher, 2016). Looking at what each group searches for in a mate, Fisher observes patterns such that Builders seek similarity in other Builders. The same is true for Explorers who desire someone adventurous like themselves. Seeking difference, Directors and Negotiators tend to gravitate towards one another in a sort of complementary fashion.

Taking their approach even farther, some sites began to innovate and use matching systems whose rationales are not widely accepted by many behavioral scientists. For example, GenePartner.com (founded in 2008) gives users the ability to order $99 DNA swab kits that they can send to labs in Switzerland that will produce a "GenePartner ID" (McGrane, 2009). From this, they can be matched to others within their GenePartner ID database with the hope that such an ID could eventually be interchangeable among other dating sites. Similar promises are made by other gene-driven sites (Frazzetto, 2010), with fees climbing as high as $2000 for a lifetime membership (Finkel et al., 2012).

Whether we can utilize science to successfully match individuals online remains to be verified. However, the overall popularity of dating sites claiming to be science-driven is undeniable. The promise of scientific help feeds into a larger narrative that finding *The One* is becoming increasingly hard to do. A number of social trends and current values make online dating the mating mode of the moment. Chalk it up to later ages at marriage with reduced access to a suitable pool of eligible singles; divorces that send people back into the dating pool after their twenties; increased choosiness; increased individualization; lowered social stigmas around online dating; the appearance that there is an infinite pool of singles to choose from (prompting the thought, "How will you ever know when you find *The One* with so many to choose from?"); and many more social factors which we have yet to touch on. Outsourcing the search is becoming a perfect fit of practicality and need. When mega-sites like eHarmony, Match.com, Chemistry, OkCupid, and Zoosk offer more or less scientific forms of data-based matchmaking, hopeful daters are reassured. As marriage hopefuls age and find themselves with an unenviable track record in the dating market, businesses that claim their algorithms will augment human judgement and match people better than they have been able to do for themselves offer a compelling argument. Take eHarmony, for example. In television ads, the face and founder of the site, Neil Clark Warren, usually encounters a single woman talking about how she relies on her offline methods of finding a man. His response is along the lines of, "And how's that going?" at which time cut-away scenes of the woman on awkward and unsuccessful dates are shown to undermine her ability in finding *The One* using more traditional methods. The ads close with eHarmony's slogan, "Stop waiting. Start communicating" hammering home the notion that trying to find your soulmate without their help will be a long, unsuccessful wait.

To be fair, these sites do help many people find their mate. It is worth noting, however, that the majority of these sites offer no hard evidence to show that their algorithms can actually procure better dates, partners, marriages, sex lives, etc. than human judgement alone. eHarmony is a partial exception. They did a study that compared the marriages formed through their site to other more conventional methods and found their marriages to have higher marital adjustment scores (Carter & Buckwalter, 2009). However, the research was done by in-house researchers and the raw data is not available for scrutiny making it unverifiable. Additionally, eHarmony omitted the potential confounding effects that selection bias may play in their results. The eHarmony group may be fundamentally different from the control group in a way that prompted them to use the site to find dates rather than utilize other methods to meet a partner as the control group did (Finkel et al., 2012).

## Niche Markets

The major players in online dating target the heterosexual mass market, even though many online dating businesses enable sexual minorities to filter the gender of their matches once signed up for their site. Heterosexual lives have indeed been changed by these businesses. By 2012, it was estimated that 20-to-over-30% of marriages began online (Cacioppo, Cacioppo, Gonzaga, Ogburn, & Vanderweele, 2013; Rosenfeld & Thomas, 2012). As incredible as that statistic is, the rise of online dating has had even more dramatic impact on same-sex pairings. Over 60% of same-sex couples met using the Internet by 2012 (Rosenfeld & Thomas, 2012). Why the difference in usage? For one, being a minority in itself means being less likely to find another minority mate through day-to-day, face-to-face interactions. Additionally, for LGBTQ individuals who prefer or need to conceal their sexual orientation from family, friends, or coworkers, the Internet may serve as a supplementary source of romantic possibilities to their less fruitful social network.

Similarly, other numerically smaller markets like elderly daters, racial and religious minorities, and the polyamorous community have gained a vital resource in online dating sites. While LGBTQ users can choose from sites such as Adam4Adam, PinkCupid, and Gay Friend Finder, older men and women can now choose among sites like SeniorMatch.com, OurTime, SinglesOver60, MatureSinglesClick, and Senior FriendFinder. Polyamorous users have sites like PolyMatchMaker and PolyamorousPassions.com. Racial minorities have a surfeit of options depending on their race—BlackPeopleMeet and Black Singles (for African Americans); AsianPeopleMeet, Chnlove, Shaadi (for Asians); LatinoPeopleMeet, Amigos.com, and LatinAmericanCupid (for Hispanic daters); Shadi and Helahel.com (for Muslims). There is even GayMuslimDating.com for gay Muslim singles. There are sites dedicated to other niche markets, from JDate (for Jewish users) and Christian Mingle (for Christians) to FarmersOnly, EquestrianSingles, and dating sites available only to people from the Ivy League or who belong to Mensa. (Sites do come and go; these are sites available at the time of writing.)

We have gone from a world in which we would never expect to find certain attributes in a partner we happened to meet through real-world connections, to a reality in which we can specifically filter for important traits we want. An individual with a fetish for BDSM, for example, who would have little reason to expect a blind date or random stranger to enjoy BDSM as well, may find it difficult to satisfy this aspect of their sexuality. Rather than tip toe around the topic, hope it comes up at some point in their relationship, or simply repress their desire to engage in these actions, they can log into FindSpankingPartners.com or BDSMSingles.com to find a mate (for a night or for the long-term). Niche sites like these help users bypass the possible stigma and awkwardness that they may face trying to engage in these actions without prior knowledge of a partner's sexual desires. The growing individualization of sites has not only become useful, but for many people it is essential to have a defined, specific market. The long-tail economic model that companies like Amazon specialize in is now the norm for online dating sites. And, it is from this model that the mobile dating apps arose.

## There's an App for That

Apple Inc.'s App Store opened in 2008 enabling businesses to develop their own mobile applications, or "apps," for iPhone users to take with them on the go. Apps optimized the unique features that smartphones offer, most specifically here, their GPS operations. Consumers soon had access to one specific app that would forever change the landscape of digital dating. In 2009, Grindr, a dating app targeted at gay men, was launched and marketed heavily for its hook-up potential (see Queerty, 2009). It quickly became a staple of gay culture. The app was simple: Create an account, add a screen name, provide a profile picture (or opt for no picture), and scroll through the other profile pictures of men within a specified distance from your current location. You could then send messages and determine whether you wanted to meet up in real life (usually for a sexual tryst). The app made finding a partner rapid and almost entirely based on profile pictures and physical stats like height, weight, and body type. Grindr also offered a premium version of its app (Grindr XTRA), enabling users to skip in-app advertisements, view a larger pool of men in their area, and filter the profiles shown to them by various factors such as race, height, and age (Grindr, 2017).

Grindr was not the first mobile dating app, but its innovative approach to streamlining the mate selection process helped seal its place as a staple in gay hook-up and romance culture. Now, according to a 2017 statement by Grindr CEO Joel Simkhai, the app caters to three million daily active users and is also launching an "electronic collection of articles, videos, photography, and more that celebrate and represent the modern LGBTQ world" (Cuby, 2017). Grindr, while built for a quick review of an inventory of potential sex partners, has been used for more than hook-ups. Many gay men use the app to find romance, sex, and friends. Unlike the heterosexual world where hook-ups often disqualify the two people involved for a serious relationship, a recent online survey of 4000 gay men found that a substantial number of men seek both romance and sex simultaneously on hook-up oriented apps like Grindr. Forty-five percent of respondents reported that they would "prefer a date but will go with a hook-up if it feels right" and another 10% are using apps to find a date or relationship exclusively (GrabHim.Net, 2015). Whether or not Grindr leads to more relationships than heterosexual apps is unestablished, but the app laid down a smooth user interface model for forthcoming heterosexual and gay dating apps to follow.

Various companies tried to replicate Grindr's success with the heterosexual market, even Grindr itself, though only one took home the trophy. Tinder became available in 2012, with founders targeting college campuses that have major partying reputations as the app's first users. This was not simply for convenience, but rather a ploy aimed at capitalizing on the market of young adults looking for casual sex (hook-ups) rather than long-term relationships (Ansari & Klinenberg, 2016). Tinder caught on rapidly and was soon hailed as the straight version of Grindr, reaching valuations of $1.6 billion by 2015 (Cook, 2015). Users sign up using their Facebook credentials making the process almost simultaneous. They select their match preferences (i.e., gender, age range, and max distance), pick a few profile pictures for other users to see, and begin "swiping" through other profiles. Swiping may seem like a strange verb to describe the process of viewing profiles if you have yet to experience Tinder. However, creators designed the interface to be similar to a deck of cards with users playing Tinder's game by swiping through profiles that include a picture, name, and age. Click on the profile card and see a bit more information about the potential match, including mutual Facebook connections and a 500-word or less self-description. Users can then swipe the profile card to the left of their mobile's screen to indicate they are not interested or right to indicate interest. If both parties swipe right, they get a match and are then allowed to initiate communication between one another.

A profitable combination of a well-designed user interface and mutual interest matching have set Tinder apart from other straight dating apps. Rather than have users fill out lengthy questionnaires and running matching algorithms (like competitors Match.com, Chemistry.com, OkCupid, and others), Tinder has created a convenient way for users to log in and start getting matches right away; no waiting around. The app is truly the straight Grindr with users seeing all profiles within their desired proximity. What is more, the game-inspired structure of the interface has enabled Tinder to be seen as less serious than other apps which likely reduced the stigma of online dating by making it more of a social activity. In focus groups across the USA on the subject of Tinder, there was a common theme of people signing up for Tinder simply out of "amusement or as a joke and swiping profiles with friends in a group setting" (Ansari & Klinenberg, 2016, pp. 114). This light-hearted entry attitude seems to diminish over time and users begin using the app more seriously.

The other component of Tinder's success is its mutual interest matching scheme. An obstacle recognized by dating services from the time of classifieds has been the overwhelming male presence. Requiring mutual interest prior to enabling communication between parties provided a more secure space for female users. They would receive messages only from men they had expressed interest in—profiles they swiped left never came back to agitate them with endless annoying messages such as "Hey," "What's up?," "Hey again." This is especially important seeing as the app catered to sexual conquests. Women were not going to join if they were harassed by unwanted sexual innuendos, lewd commentary on their profile pictures, sexually explicit requests, etc. Not to say this mutual interest element does not draw in men too. In fact, the app's design helps relieve possible feelings of rejection for both parties. If you match, you know that the person would be open to talking and possibly meeting up with you. If you do not match, you will likely forget about that profile as you continue to swipe through the never-ending deck of new ones. The chances of crafting what you think to be a perfect message only to be ignored have been reduced thanks to this simple yet essential mutual interest component.

As best we can tell, this is where the dating app market is heading: Efficient, entertaining, and GPS-savvy. For example, the more recent app Bumble, which launched in 2014, focuses on GPS location, a game-like user interface, and mutual interest as well. However, it requires the woman to message her matches within 24 h of their match, otherwise the match disappears. This approach addresses the issue of female usership via a requirement of mutual interest, but unlike Tinder, Bumble's platform empowers women to be romantic initiators, which has not traditionally been the case online. The app's administrators take pride in denouncing and deleting the accounts of men who abuse the service by making sexist or derogatory comments. This female-focused approach has paid off for Bumble. The company now holds the title of second top grossing Lifestyle app (first being Tinder) and claims 800 million matches (with 10 billion swipes) per month (Bennett, 2017).

Technological innovation has spiked in ways past generations have never seen and the online dating industry has developed within this overall cultural change. We have gone from Harvard's *Operation Match* which required massive IBM computers to process a relatively small number of singles, to Match.com and others who now broadcast opportunities for digital dating with pools of millions to choose from and a rapidly expanding dating app market. The success of these technologies is proof enough of the desire multiple generations of single and divorced people have for finding sexual and/or lifetime partners, and the fact that traditional modes of meeting people no longer work well for considerable numbers of men and women. It is important to note though that the psychological consequences of using these sites have been widely unstudied, and we have yet to elaborate on whether the proclaimed efficiency of these sites to provide their clientele with suitable partners lives up to expectations. With the following section, we will be evaluating how the interfaces and in-app/in-site features of various internet dating platforms impact the user's ability to find their match.

## Efficiency of Dating Sites and Apps

The financial success and popularity of dating sites is easily established, but the sociological insight from such technological traction is a bit less easy to pin down. We believe that, in part, traction is built on a cultural shift towards increasing individualization and individualism within relationships. While Stephanie Coontz has written in her book on the evolution of marriage that our society has gone from "yoke mates to soul mates" (Coontz, 2006), it is also true that there has been more emphasis on the rights of the individual to fulfill their own personal goals, regardless of marital status. While love continues to be a central theme in the majority of people's lives, it can sometimes seem that love, as expressed in affection, sex, and loyalty, is not enough anymore. We want a partner to make us a better person, build our self-esteem, improve our self-worth, and become our other half on top of loving us in our best and worst moments. At the same time, we are working more, spending more time child rearing, and actually giving less overall time to our relationships than generations before us (Finkel, Cheung, Emery, Carswell, & Larson, 2015). The paradox is clear: Both men and women expect more deeply fulfilling relationships than in any generation before them; yet, this same generation has fewer resources—such as time—to invest into each other.

Online dating companies at least *appear* to help people out here—rather than invest multiple nights to get to know a potential mate, dating services permit users to pre-screen dates before even agreeing to meet them in person. Not only do profile pictures and profile biographies help speed up the selection process, sites and apps integrate social media for users to inspect too. On Tinder, users can check out what pictures someone posts on their Instagram, what mutual friends they have on Facebook, even what music someone listens to on Spotify. And, the list of integrated media continues to grow with further software updates.

Many users also take advantage of the in-app/site messaging services, texting each other at length before they ever schedule a date. This computer-mediated communication (CMC) makes different dating sites more attractive to their specific clientele as well. For example, dating services that allow users to send non-text file formats like gifs (short animated image files) capitalize on the millennial market who avidly use this form of CMC to communicate with each other in ways that individuals of an earlier generation may not understand or perhaps enjoy if they were to receive them. Other sites like Chemistry.com focus on getting their users to *stop* using their CMC, urging them to meet as soon as possible. "They shouldn't call them dating sites," says Chemistry's love expert Helen Fisher. "They should call them introducing sites. They [dating sites] provide the newest way to do the same old thing, which is places to meet people" (Sentementes, 2011). In effect, this approach might attract those who have little time to waste on texting and those who would rather meet up in person relatively soon to make judgements about a potential match.

Profile information, social media integration, and different CMC formats cater to the overall trend of online daters looking for someone who is their perfect match but in a manner that reduces the amount of effort required for searching. Increasing media integration presumably makes the dating site more like a one-stop-shop for potential mates. Users can now make a large number of judgements about a person before committing to a date with them. In fact, *Bustle* magazine reported that users of Tinder who connect their Spotify music account to their dating profile have 84% more matches than those who do not integrate the music platform (Emery, 2017). This is a figure that is most pertinent to millennial users who make up the bulk of each app's market: 72% of Spotify's weekly content streamers are millennials (McIntyre, 2016), and 50% of Tinder's users are within the college age range

(Romano, 2016), with an average age of 27 years old (Ansari & Klinenberg, 2016). Whether these matches are more successful than those not influenced by musical tastes remains to be known. However, the idea that simply sharing a favorite song on your dating app might make you a more desirable match is so unusual in terms of the history of dating, that it is probably worth further investigation.

## *More Integration Is Not Always Better*

One question that this app-integration surfaces is whether the mere presence of outside apps alters what users begin to look for in matches. For example, some people may post pictures on Instagram that have less to do with their actual personality and have more to do with artistic expression. However, because these images are presented on someone's dating profile, it would not be shocking if their matching potential were influenced by other users taking their Instagram pictures into account. Matches that might have otherwise panned out well may be cut-short due to irrelevant information being assessed as legitimate criteria for pursuing or dropping a given individual. Psychological studies back this hypothesis. Our first impressions of others' personality traits are made rapidly (within mere seconds) and are often flawed. Frequently, these judgements are based solely on the appearance of the target (not accounting for other relevant information needed to make correct judgements about one's personality), which has been found to decrease the accuracy of our judgement and often leads us to take actions based on erroneous assumptions (Olivola & Todorov, 2010). With increased exposure to and interaction with the person in question, we are able to form more accurate judgements about what they are really like (Carney, Colvin, & Hall, 2007). Unfortunately, dating sites and especially apps like Tinder and Grindr provide platforms that promote visually based assessments with ephemeral exposure times (i.e., a second or two and then a swipe left to oblivion). That makes it likely that users overweigh people's profile appearance (including their pictures, Instagram posts, Facebook friends, musical tastes, etc.) when drawing inferences about whether or not their personalities would have good chemistry in person.

This critique of online dating is not only made by outsiders. OkCupid's co-founder, Christian Rudder, recognizes the dilemma of presenting so much trivial information for users to see before even meeting a match. Rudder explains that people are being turned down due to deal breakers that have no realistic effects on whether the pair would work out in real life. "People make choices from the information we provide because they *can*," says Rudder, "not because they necessarily should" (Rudder, 2014, p. 100). In this way, dating companies might be over-integrating social media and other apps into their online and mobile platforms. If some users had met and developed a desirable chemistry, the small quirks of their musical tastes or Instagram photos may become endearing facets of their character rather than redlines barring them from even getting a first date. As much as this scenario does sound probable in some cases, we suspect that dating apps will continue furthering their outside-app integrations given their popularity among users.

## *Time Spent on Dating Apps*

Also up for debate is whether the simple and game-like designs of dating apps and sites actually save their client's time. It is not uncommon for many users to be on their digital dating profile for a substantial amount of time. This is especially true for dating apps: In 2014, Tinder reported that the average user logs into their profile 11 times a day, spending an average of an hour and a half on the app every day (Bilton, 2014). Grindr users may top that, spending an average of about 2 h on the mobile app daily (Miksche, 2016). Looking at the CMC component of dating sites, users of OkCupid can spend significant amounts of time on composing relatively small messages. The average user types three characters for every single character actually sent and the average message length is just over 100 characters (Rudder, 2014). In fact, this current 100-character average is 66% smaller than the average character lengths recorded by the site just before the Apple App store launched in 2008. This means that men and women are spending more time crafting and revising their messages in order to make them as small as possible. Perhaps they want the appearance of brevity in their online communications but do not mind consuming more time to craft them in this manner. It certainly means that they take this process more seriously than the product online would suggest.

Interestingly, some users have noticed this texting-time inefficiency and have taken to copy-and-paste methods of messaging, whereby they have a pre-written template that they can easily paste and send out to as many profiles as they want without consuming much time at all. Rudder, the lead of OkCupid's analytics team, says that although these messages may seem highly impersonal to their recipient, they are actually the most efficient to use when measuring the replies received per unit of effort. Up to 20% of OkCupid's clients use some variation of this copy-and-paste method of messaging. For the other 80% of clients, spending the time to create original messages remains their modus operandi (Rudder, 2014).

Perhaps one of the biggest indications that these sites are not as efficient as they claim to be is the growth of a new industry for the so-called online dating experts. Books and blogs on how to use dating sites and apps started hitting the market soon after the dating sites themselves. Take Lisa Hoehn, for example: She is a self-proclaimed serial online dater who not only founded ProfilePolish.com, a dating profile makeover service, but has also authored the book, *You Probably Shouldn't Write That: Tips and Tricks for Creating an Online Dating Profile That Doesn't Suck,* which she markets on its back cover as "...a complete, no-nonsense approach to becoming the most attractive person on any dating site or app" (Hoehn, 2016).

Is there some disillusionment with the online experience? Certainly. And, some of it shows up in odd ways. For example, reality television with dating and marriage themes have found unexpected enthusiasm from the public for shows that put people together who ordinarily would not meet. An extreme example is a popular Lifetime show called *Married at First Sight*, in which a panel of relationship experts (including co-author Schwartz) arrange legal marriages of two people who are complete strangers to one another and who meet only when they step up to the altar to marry. It would be fair upon hearing about this show to think that no American (or no American who did not come from an arranged marriage culture) would consider such a risky mating system no matter how many experts used behavioral science to put them together. But in fact, the show has been a success—not only in having a large viewership but by the fact that more than 50,000 people have volunteered to be married in this manner. What makes people volunteer? It is not cynicism or a search for fame for the great majority of them. The common themes are that dating is difficult; good men and women are hard to find; most people are not available for commitment; they are not getting any interest online or they are getting the wrong kind of interest; and overall, they have lost their faith in their own ability to find a good match. Producers and experts hear potential candidates complain about bad experiences from online dating that have exhausted them. Some attractive and financially stable candidates, who an objective observer might think would do extremely well in any dating market, feel that trying to use traditional and online methods to find a lifelong partner with little to no success has left them demoralized and more than willing to hand over the responsibility of finding a spouse to someone skilled and dedicated to the process. This extreme attempt at finding love is certainly far from the norm, but the desperation is not necessarily limited to the USA. Not only has *Married at First Sight* gained a large popularity in American television markets, but it is now being shown in more than 120 television markets over the world. (Some with the US cast and some with their own version.) It is clear that while online dating is a huge help to many, its cornucopia of available singles does not always translate into a solid match. Moreover, even people who are successful online (i.e., have lots of dates, requests, or successful initiations) seem wrung out after both short- and long-term engagement with these technological opportunities and introductions.

## The Paradox of Choice and Online Dating Fatigue

Finding a partner was once a search confined to early adulthood. Even as recently as 1990, the average age of marriage was a youthful 23 for women and 26 for men (Borresen, 2013). Now, however, an initial youthful search can extend over decades and dating can continue over the life cycle as people break-up, divorce or become widowed, etc. People's optimism and energy flag after a few years of using sites that show them hundreds of new faces day and night. Some impact on dedicated online daters is supported by science. In their much cited studies, Iyengar and Lepper (2000) demonstrate that humans are less likely to make a decision and take action when they are given an excessive number of options (as opposed to a limited number of options), and they score lower on satisfaction ratings when choosing a product from an extensive array of options rather than a limited selection. Moreover, although there is clear evidence that people will be less satisfied and more indecisive when given a greater number of choices, choice itself seems to create the appetite for more choice. When choosing between having an expansive range of options versus a smaller selection, more people gravitate towards the selection with the greatest number of options (Iyengar & Lepper, 2000; Schwartz, 2006a). These findings have been shown to apply to trivial decisions like picking a flavor of jam at the supermarket (Iyengar & Lepper, 2000) and to more important, long-term decisions like investing into different retirement savings plans (Iyengar & Kamenica, 2010). If we apply this finding to internet dating, it stands to reason that clients of dating sites are attracted to the large number of users that the sites grant them access to, but that very level of options makes it frustrating and difficult to act with confidence. A dater might wonder, "Did I just swipe away the love of my life?" Furthermore, and perhaps most worrisome to intimacy researchers, this excess of choice in the digital dating world might cause a malaise that makes it less likely for someone to feel that the choice they made is worth pursuing or maintaining.

Online daters complain, "No one is looking for commitment." This perception is likely based on the fact that so many online contacts withdraw after one or a few dates—perhaps because there are so many choices to try or perhaps because their own confidence in choosing well has become so shaky that they feel they have to keep revisiting the marketplace. If the offshoot of trying one person out of many available means that being content with that choice is less likely, then this will fuel reentry into the dating market or dating multiple people at one time. Both results may keep people in circulation rather than committing to a promising beginning. In other words, because daters know that there are vast numbers of potential partners online, they are less certain who is really *The One*. This is a state of mind we have already observed when discussing the increased choosiness brought on first by video dating and later exaggerated by online dating. Here, though we expect that the ambivalence towards picking a partner is partially due to uncertainty and choice overload, rather than simple choosiness. An excerpt from focus groups with users of online dating services illustrates this well:

> I love my girlfriend, but when we were first getting serious, I would go on Instagram and see all these hot girls. And it's like, 'Whoa should I be dating these girls? Or just settle down and be in a relationship?' It felt like the opposite of 'out of sight, out of mind.' They were in sight and IN my mind. (Ansari and Klinenberg, 2016, pp. 190-191)

These patterns of choice overload when given more choice in potential partners have also been noted in speed-dating experiments. Participants involved in speed dating are more likely to turn down 100% of their potential matches when given larger variability in their available selection (i.e., potential mates had wider variability in traits such as weight, height, occupation, etc.; Lenton & Francesconi, 2011). Although this does not directly show that the number of available mates reduces our ability to commit to one match, the same rationale applies whereby the more choices and variability we must process, the less likely we are to be content in making a decision. Nonetheless, dating sites continue to be a major player in mating and people often get over their battle fatigue and start anew.

So, are online dating sites really more efficient in pairing off single men and women than traditional methods alone? In some ways, it seems they are. Many researchers have validated the statistic that over 20% of heterosexual marriages now begin online (Cacioppo et al., 2013; Rosenfeld & Thomas, 2012), and for same-sex relationships that percentage has more than doubled (Rosenfeld & Thomas, 2012). This is a huge cultural shift, and if the number of relationships and marriages initiated online is the measure used to assess online dating's effectiveness, then it seems to be doing extraordinarily well. Additionally, online dating has allowed minorities and niche populations to meet in-group, single members in a way that would have been unimaginable prior to online dating. For busy or isolated people who seek long-term relationships but who cannot (or choose not) to frequent bars, social events, or locations where other singles might be present, online dating is almost their only hope for finding someone they consider special. While dating sites and apps may require continuous monitoring, messaging, and searching, they also provide an easy-to-use technology that can be used any time, day or night, with little or no stigma attached. Online dating is custom-made for the person who is a busy single mom, an ambitious worker staying late or carrying three jobs, or just someone in a small town with few choices.

At the same time, we should note that research measuring the overall efficiency for the online dater him- or herself, or for that matter, the relationships formed after years spent looking for a partner online, is minimal. Online dating keeps metamorphosing, and at the present, unless someone is lucky and finds a partner rather quickly, there are significant emotional costs to the online search. Among the costs are the fatigue that comes with having to make so many quick decisions; regretting some of them; auditioning and exposing oneself many times to a stranger's gaze and evaluation; and feeling rejected by lack of attention online as well as by unsuccessful dates when interest turns out to be one-sided. Many other subtle injuries happen in a dating market where people owe each other nothing and spot-market behavior is common. (Spot market, an economic term, refers to the behavior of one-time exchanges as opposed to interactions that are done within what is known to be a protracted and continuing negotiation or partnership). The paradox of having many choices is that people also feel entitled to create a number of requirements, and a high number of deal breakers, assuming that somewhere in this pile of people, there is someone who can fit most or all of what they want. Hence, another nail in the coffin of commitment.

Still, that said, there are plenty of offline relationships created on these sites. If there were not, the sites would not be so furiously flourishing. However, we are somewhat unnerved by how few scholarly studies we have found on the overall effectiveness of online dating sites compared to traditional methods. It is possible that the efficiencies noted earlier are undercut by tangential factors (such as the emotional costs that many long-term users experience or a newfound lack of confidence in traditional methods of mate selection). In the same vein, little has been done to empirically examine the subsequent pairings begun online and how their online initiation may have impacted their relationship. The next sections explore, to the extent possible, whether online daters and their relationships display any long-term psychological or relationship satisfaction differences from those formed offline.

## The Online Dater's Psychology

As much as dating sites provide an easy place to meet potential mates, they also serve as massive data mines for researchers looking to understand modern trends in dating. Mentioned previously, Helen Fisher conducted experiments using her access to Chemistry.com's data to construct four sets of personality types and assess their compatibility with one another. Data from Match.com was used to investigate why significant amounts of users who were statistically perfect for each other according to their matching algorithm never made it past a first date. The answer: What we say we want in a partner is not necessarily what we go after online (Slater, 2013b). How, then, do we select mates? The answer is perhaps less than shocking given the direction much of the literature has pointed us towards thus far. Once again, appearance is the number one factor driving us to pursue our online matches (Ansari & Klinenberg, 2016; Levine, 2015).

### *How to Be Attractive Online*

Upon reviewing his own data, OkCupid's Christian Rudder estimates that the photos that people use on their profiles motivate up to 90 percent of the action on the site (Ansari & Klinenberg, 2016). Although more attractive people receive more attention overall, those who get the most messages compared to anyone (approximately 70% more) are people who appear polarizing or have features that people seem to either love or hate (Rudder, 2014). This means that someone rated an average of 3-out-of-5 in terms of attractiveness receives more interest than a 5-out-of-5 stunner. The principal behind this, so speculates Rudder, is perceived competition. For example, a heterosexual male believes that a woman who is seen as universally attractive (scoring a 5-out-of-5) would be attracting the attention of nearly all suitors. This intense competition, he thinks, makes her much less likely to respond to his advances given her access to ample alternatives. On the other hand, a woman who is judged a 5 by some and 1 by others—scoring an average 3-out-of-5 overall—is thought to be more realistic to approach online. The male user speculates that everyone is not vying for her (the 3's) attention and perceives himself as having a higher matching potential given her uniqueness. He personally thinks she is a 5 and is extremely attracted to her but knows others do not agree due to her polarizing looks. This social psychological theory of online daters aligns well with other research findings that we tend to approach and form relationships with those who are most equally attractive to us (Feingold, 1988; Halberstadt et al., 2016). Given that there are far fewer extremely attractive individuals in the world than there are average and polarizing individuals, it stands to reason that the 5's of the world would be messaged less online than the most attractive of the 3's.

But, it is not just about facial attractiveness on these sites. *How* one's profile picture is taken can also have major effects on the number of messages they receive. For women, showing more cleavage, giving flirtatious looks directly into the camera, and taking the picture from above their head and at an angle (nicknamed the "MySpace angle") increase the number of new messages they receive. For men, looking away from the camera, posing with an animal, and showing off muscles are all factors that increase their online dating success (Rudder, 2010a). In other research, having group photos has been shown to increase desirability, specifically when the user is in the center of the group where they can benefit from "center-stage" effects (Raghubir & Valenzuela, 2006). The center-stage effects function as mental heuristics whereby the observer of a group perceives the individual (or individuals) in the center of the group as better in a host of arenas. A gendered aspect to the center-stage heuristics has been found wherein heterosexual women observing a male's group picture with women flocked to either side of him and smiling at the male actually see the male as more preferable than when the women in the group picture have neutral facial expressions towards him (Jones, DeBruine, Little, Burriss, & Feinberg, 2007).

Some data even suggests that having a profile picture where you cannot see the user's face may be a good idea in certain scenarios. The common theme for successful, non-face pictures (gauged by receiving more messages than the average user) is to show something intriguing, unique, or sexy (Rudder, 2010a). Examples given on OkCupid's official blog include a scuba diving picture and a sexually charged picture of a woman's legs tied with colorful bondage rope. Pictures such as the latter also imply specific intentions for using the dating site—in this case sexual intentions. A user's profile picture can be a window into what they want out of the dating site and what type of users they are looking to attract.

Some recent research has focused on how profile photos may portray personality traits and therefore affect desirability. For example, in one study researchers found that profile pictures where male actors had been beautified and enhanced with lighting effects and different wardrobes garnered higher trustworthiness ratings from female participants than non-doctored photos of the same actors (McGloin & Denes, 2016). Greater perceived trustworthiness correlated with higher attractiveness ratings as well—a finding observed in other online dating research (see Jin & Martin, 2015). However, this only occurred when the female participants were viewing male profiles. When male participants were shown enhanced female profile pictures, they found them more attractive but less trustworthy (McGloin & Denes, 2016). This contradicts other data on offline dating and attraction which finds trustworthiness positively correlated with attractiveness—or even a mediator of attraction (Singh et al., 2009; Singh et al., 2015). Online it seems that men are more attracted to women they perceive as less trustworthy. This could be an extension of the male dater's belief that universally attractive women have a larger pool of eligibles and therefore run a gambit, always trying to look for a better male to date. This does not seem to reduce her physical attractiveness, but it would surely make men who ascribe to this mindset more dubious when gauging an attractive woman's trustworthiness. All that said, the studies we cite here use college-based samples, and we cannot generalize the findings to online daters of older ages. Aside from age, other subject characteristics such as race, religiosity, and socioeconomic status likely influence online dating behaviors as well. One of the limitations of this chapter is space, and unfortunately, we are unable to dedicate enough of it to cover all of these individual variables adequately. We recommend that readers who are seeking more information about how demographic variables impact a range of online dating behaviors consider Rudder's (2014) book, *Dataclysm*, as a source for such information.

## Usernames and "About Me" Sections

Once a user is determined to be attractive based on their profile picture, the next logical step is to read what they have to say about themselves. One of the first indicators of personality (aside from profile pictures) is a person's username or screen name. Men are more attracted to usernames that indicate physical attractiveness, whereas women are more attracted to usernames that indicate intelligence (Whitty & Buchanan, 2010). Both men and women enjoy playful screen names like "SeeUSoon?" or "ParentsLoveMe" (Khan & Chaudhry, 2015).

Often times, the most daunting part of building an online profile is writing an About Me section. This is the part of online dating that is meant to give users a deeper look into who you are and what you are looking for. Like other aspects of online dating, there are strategies for writing these profile autobiographies (often referred to as bios) in a way that other users will find attractive. One method to achieve an attractive bio is a 70:30 ratio. Devoting the bulk of the profile bio (about 70%) to your positive traits ensures that users will get a better understanding of who you are (Khan & Chaudhry, 2015). On the other hand, it is important to avoid seeming too self-absorbed in your About Me statement. To prevent this, the advice is to dedicate 30% of your About Me space to detail what it is you are looking for in a partner.

When users list their positive traits, they may want to keep in mind their audience. Findings show that heterosexual men respond most to women who advertise their physicality (e.g., their fitness routines) but avoid more rough activities like rugby and weight lifting (Khan & Chaudhry, 2015). Heterosexual women are most attracted to men who are risk takers and display some sense of bravery. Regarding trustworthiness—which can be a primary mediator for interpersonal attraction, both men and women find profiles more trustworthy and authentic when users are deemed traditional or "uptight" (i.e., advertising more intellectual, solitary tasks such as reading), compared to more free-spirited users who emphasize social and party-oriented traits (Jin & Martin, 2015).

## *Pressure to Be Perfect*

Users are interpreting a great deal about prospective partners from the relatively small amount of information that profiles provide. The pressure to make one's profile stand out above all the other online users is a strife for many online daters. As mentioned, some abdicate the responsibility of creating their online profile to alleged experts who promise to make their clients more attractive than they could ever make themselves. More often than not, users who want a little help zhooshing up their profile ask friends and relatives; one-in-five online daters admit to explicitly asking for someone else's help building their dating profile (Lenhart & Duggan, 2014). Women are especially likely to seek outside collaboration for their profile with 30% reporting that they had enlisted someone to create or review their dating profile (compared to only 16% of men). The need to present our best-selves might be higher than ever given the ability for online daters to spend as much time as they desire tweaking, revising, or overhauling their profiles. It certainly makes sense that we want our friends to help us since they can provide outside validation that others will find our profile attractive and hopefully speed up the process of designing the perfect profile.

Is this constant pressure to appear better than others online impacting our mating psychology? It seems likely as the rapid, evaluative nature of online dating promotes what are called "assessment mindsets" (Finkel et al., 2012). Much like the spot-market behavior described earlier, assessment mindsets encourage people to approach potential matches as in-the-moment, snap decisions. Rather than viewing potential matches as investments of psychological resources over time where both parties are working towards a shared goal, assessment mindsets focus on evaluative techniques where people consider their access to alternatives and try to determine compatibility as efficiently as possible. Although offline dating requires a degree of assessing too, the exaggerated online version of assessment mindsets may degrade early-on social interactions with potential partners: "First encounters are often awkward, and an assessment mindset may channel the assessor's attention in ways that inhibit fluid, spontaneous interaction" (Finkel et al., 2012, p. 29). Our eagerness to judge, so hypothesizes Finkel et al., may encourage the online dater's penchant for commoditizing and objectifying people, subsequently infringing on his or her ability to invest and build relationships through meaningful social interactions.

**Lying Online** When our personality and overall date ability is being assessed so harshly, it is almost understandable that many users exaggerate or even flat-out lie on their dating profile. A study of 1000 online daters from the USA and UK, commissioned by the dating site BeautifulPeople.com, found that 53% of Americans admit to lying on their profile, while 44% of Britons reported lying on their accounts (R. Anderson, 2016; Hodge, 2012). These figures make clear that there is a propensity to fib online, but even more telling, it seems as though there is an expectation for users to lie on their dating profiles. In a survey of Match.com users, over 80% of the online daters believe that others misrepresent their appearance online; 49% feel that others lie about their relationship goals; and 40% believe that others lie about their marital status (Gibbs et al., 2006). A culmination of studies and analyses finds that the most popular things for online daters to lie about on their profile include: male's height (on average men exaggerate height by 2 in.); income (inflated by 20 percent); recent profile pictures (data on OkCupid shows that the more attractive a profile picture is, the more likely it is to be out-of-date); and age (the second most popular lie for women, followed by weight). Even claiming to know celebrities and working in the film/entertainment industry are among the top 10 lies told by both male and female users (Hodge, 2012; Rudder, 2010b; Toma, Hancock, & Ellison, 2008). It appears that along with pressuring users to present their best selves, online dating more often than not inspires users to take it one step farther and add a little pizzazz to their account by stretching or fully fabricating the truth in some way that would put them ahead.

## After the First Date: Success with Online Dating

Are relationships initiated online better than those initiated offline? This question is center stage in both the popular press and in academic journals, but the reality is that data remains scant and inconclusive. Most studies focus on relationship initiation via online sites rather than the longevity of relationships formed online. Others are in-house studies, a number of which we have already touched on, that rarely provide transparent raw data. This data does allow some interesting perspectives though on long-term trends we may see in online daters. To begin with, many online users do not even meet anyone online. One-third of online daters have never gone on a date with someone they found on a dating site (Lenhart & Duggan, 2014). Whether these users have different goals online (such as having a romantic encounter confined to cyberspace or simply seeing what is out there) might factor into their decision to never meet other users. Still, 33% is a sizeable minority of online daters who do not make it to a first date.

For the other 66% of users who wish to transfer their online connection into a real-world meeting, research indicates that they should do so sooner rather than later. Online daters who form a meaningful connection via the CMC of a site are likely to experience even better subsequent in-person impressions of each other when the time between online conversation and in-person meeting are short (McKenna, Green, & Gleason, 2002; Note: The interval time was especially short with participants meeting each other within the same day). Other research finds that when people continue using CMC to interact over a longer period of time before meeting face-to-face, they experience the opposite of an enhanced first impression. Instead, these couples find that they are less attracted to their partner in real life than they had been online (Ramirez & Zhang, 2007). One may expect that this is an effect of creating a mental impression of someone online and being disappointed when, after weeks of fantasizing about how perfect they are for you and investing psychological resources in communicating and visualizing the potential match, the person fails to meet expectations. A similar conclusion is that, "...additional time spent on CMC without a reality check may allow strategic self-presentation [by the message sender] …and idealization or particularization [by the message receiver] … to continue unabated" (Finkel et al., 2012, p. 35). This in turn will make their first meeting a hard reality check, disconfirming the fantasy identity one or both parties had made for the other.

Determining the success of online dating requires understanding what success means to the individual user. Those looking for a hook-up or casual meet-up would measure their success very differently than users seeking a long-term relationship or marriage. Data from the longitudinal and nationally representative survey, *How Couples Meet and Stay Together*, has shown that heterosexual relationships initiated online actually tend to transition faster into marriage than relationships started in offline venues (Rosenfeld, 2017). A self-selection effect, whereby marriage-ready individuals are more likely to be seeking a mate online, and therefore transition faster into marriage, may mediate this effect. In this way, for those users seeking long-term commitment, online dating may be an especially successful route to marriage. Another finding that bodes well for commitment-seeking online daters is that there is little difference in the break-up rates reported by couples who found each other online and those who met in-person (Rosenfeld, 2017). Additional research is needed to understand whether the faster transition to marriage and similar break-up rates are due to self-selection processes and whether those looking for something besides matrimony experience online dating in a different light.

Other online daters define their success by their ability to hook-up or find casual-sex online. Tinder and Grindr are by far the most well-known dating mediums that target users looking for casual dates and hook-ups, though this perception may be more stereotype than fact (Gatter, Hodkinson, & Kolle, 2016). The sex-only stigma that surrounds Grindr has some gay men looking for new, long-term relationship oriented apps—one of which just opened this year called Chappy (Chappy App, 2017). Chappy markets itself on Grindr's failure to focus on gay men seeking long-term partnerships (QX Team, 2017). The app allows users to decide whether they are searching for "Mr. Right" or "Mr. Right Now" and company data analysts are already reporting some of their findings. Chappy claims that the best time to find a long-term oriented partner (a Mr. Right) is between Sunday and Thursday, while those looking for a one-night stand tend to use the app most on Fridays and Saturdays (QX Team, 2017).

One of the most controversial internet dating sites, Ashley Madison, seeks to connect users looking for extra-dyadic relationships. Other sites are used for such purposes, but Ashley Madison has made a name for itself marketing specifically to users seeking affairs with the upmost discretion. Here, success in online dating is defined by finding someone to have an extramarital affair with rather than someone to marry. In a quite embarrassing fiasco, the security of the site (its major selling point aside from finding sexual liaisons) was breached by hackers, and the identities, addresses, and sexual preferences of many users were revealed to the public. In the same breach, it was revealed that many of the women that male users had been chatting with on the site were actually robots (or in some cases, prostitutes), making many skeptical of the site's enthusiastic claims about high female usership (Morgan,

2017). Now, almost two years after the data breach, the site's Vice President of Communication reports that the site is taking in 400,000 new users per month and that usership has grown 50% since the cyberattack in 2015 (Morgan, 2017). An independent analysis of such claims has yet to be seen.

It has become evident that success in online dating is measured on a subjective scale, with online daters subscribing to sites that best align with their relationship goal at that moment. Whether the relationships, casual encounters, or sex lives of the users of various sites are more fulfilling than those initiated offline is not well-established. However, from the data we are able to review regarding the rapid adoption of online dating, high user activity, and ability to initiate real-world relationships online, we expect that for better or worse, online dating is sticking around. What is more, people seem happy to use these sites. In one study, of those participants who had personally used online dating ($N = 759$), only 24% rated their experience as negative as opposed to the 76% who had rated their experience as either positive or neutral (Rosen, Cheever, Cummings, & Felt, 2008). As President Lincoln famously said, "public sentiment is everything," and even without conclusive data on what internet dating holds for the long-run success of couples, marriages, and sexual flings initiated online, the American dating market and now many global markets gravitate towards online dating as the place to find a relationship, in whatever capacity that entails.

## Global Use of Online Dating

Thus far, we have focused on the cyber-dating trends here in the USA. However, the use of online dating is widespread across the globe. India, a place where arranged marriage is still the common route to a wedding, has become more interested in modern dating apps. In India, dating apps are likely to be used by parents looking for a mate for their son or daughter because many specific requirements (such as caste, class, and astrological signs) necessitate a wider choice in eligible candidates. There is also much competition for eligible spouses since the median age in India is now a youthful 27.6 (Central Intelligence Agency, 2013).

While arranged marriages remain culturally desirable and prevalent, semi-arranged marriages, where the prospective groom or bride has some form of veto power and input into who he or she will marry, have begun growing in popularity and now account for an estimated quarter of all marriages in India (Jejeebhoy, Santhya, Acharya, & Prakash, 2013). These semi-arranged marriages are often formed using online matchmaking sites (such as the massively popular Shaadi.com), usually with the father of the bride seeking out a suitable male partner online and then presenting him to the bride for a final judgement (Harris, 2015). Some young singles have even more say in who they pair up with, enabled in part by recent rise in availability of dating apps. India is now Tinder's top Asian market. Its success has inspired a large number of new Indian dating apps, most of which cater to serious long-term relationships and a more conservative clientele, in contrast to Tinder's casual dating focus (Walia & Punit, 2015).

The Indian apps make a concerted effort to express how secure and safe dating apps are for their users (see Behal, 2015; Mehta, 2016) because young adults often do not want their parents to know they are dating. Casual dating and love pairings with parental consent (as opposed to family-arranged pairings) remain uncommon in India, so for users of these dating apps, security and discretion are quite important if they want to escape parental repercussions. Love marriages and pairings are still the minority, but many people will date (especially while in other countries for college, internships, or residencies) until the time comes for their parents to find them a spouse. Most young people will then accept their parent's authority. We believe though that internet dating will increase many young men and women's desire to pick their own mate, since they will have developed personal preferences and gained knowledge through dating about who they would find compatible. This is especially likely in urban areas where technology is already becoming more integrated into the dating market (Harris, 2015; Walia & Punit, 2015).

China is in the vanguard of Asian countries adopting online dating. Chinese singles are much more likely than Indian singles to adopt casual dating and hooking up. Mainland Chinese have their own Tinder-esc app called Momo which has a reported 91.3 million users and has successfully integrated live videostreaming into its platform to make it more of a dating app and social media hybrid (Li & Lipscomb, 2017; Ng, 2017). However, familial and communal approval of relationships still has strong influence on how Chinese singles use dating sites. Traits that were considered significant when parents negotiated arranged marriages remain important in the cyber-dating realm with many sites asking users to report their annual incomes, housing situations, and education level (Li & Lipscomb, 2017; Zheng, 2017).

In contrast to the trends we see in China and India, online dating use remains underwhelming in Japan. After looking into why young Japanese people seem less than enthusiastic about online dating, it was surmised that the trend is a symptom of radical economic and cultural shifts for the country's younger generations. As women have become more financially independent and the workforce has become increasingly competitive, many Japanese men feel a loss of dominance and fear rejection should they approach a single woman about potentially dating. Japanese men reported that being on dating sites puts them at risk of being perceived as a "charai" (a derogatory term used to describe Japanese playboys; Ansari & Klinenberg, 2016). Yet at the same time, women frequently reported that they desired men to be more assertive when it comes to dating. Men who display passive dating etiquette are now referred to as "herbivore men." Likewise, women who initiate romantic connections are referred to as "carnivorous women." One survey estimates that about 60% of the young male population self-identifies as herbivores, while other polls estimate the prevalence may be even higher (Harney, 2009). The fear of being portrayed as too self-assured or "douchey" is so pervasive (for women and especially men) that it is considered strange to use pictures of yourself as your profile photo (Ansari & Klinenberg, 2016). Others have noted that a stigma still surrounds online dating, and many Japanese people worry about potential online scams (Fowler, 2015).

There is a paradox here: The number of arranged marriages has been declining for years in Japan (Retherford & Ogawa, 2006), but romantic marriages have not filled in to maintain the number of committed relationships in this country. Individual choice, enabled by online dating and less restrictive cultural mores about dating, has not created more marriages or even more committed relationships. Indeed, Japanese men and women have opted out of coupledom entirely. One survey found that around one-third of young Japanese men and women have no dating experience (Ansari & Klinenberg, 2016). Another recent survey found 70% of unmarried men and 60% of unmarried women aged 18 to 34 are not currently in a relationship, and over 40% of men and women in the same age bracket report still being virgins (Aoki, 2016). The absence of a thriving online dating economy, geared towards either serious relationships or hook-ups, is evidence of this widespread lifestyle shift among Japanese singles.

This lack of interest in online dating and more general fears about initiating romantic connections have the Japanese government concerned. Japan is currently facing a declining population crisis; the population is estimated to drop from 127 million to 87 million by 2060 (Fowler, 2015). In an effort to stem the population drop-off, the Japanese government has allocated funds into dating services, including a dating site that will send cash and wedding presents to couples who go on to get married after meeting on the site (Ansari & Klinenberg, 2016). If this sounds extreme, much of the same government inducements to date also exist in Singapore and in Indonesia since educated young Chinese women in these countries have low marriage rates and low fertility rates, a fact that does not bode well for these countries eventual need for population replacement and the fullest utilization of a highly valued gene pool. Singapore, for example, truly worried about the marital futures of its citizens, has started up government-run dating sites and works towards creating an environment cohesive for dating agencies to grow in, even organizing conferences to introduce young men and women in the hopes that some go on to date.

Most western, and many eastern, countries now have and encourage online dating. We explored the trends found in only a handful of countries. However, it is worth noting that the countries we chose to highlight in this brief section are considered collectivistic societies where long-term partnerships have traditionally been a domain controlled by the family. That seems to be changing somewhat, but it is not clear if gender roles are changing to empower women as well as men and parents in the dating space. If, as it has been documented, relationship initiation and relationship building is increasingly being handed over to the young people themselves, then this may disadvantage women unless they feel more comfortable initiating and managing dating opportunities.

One goal of this section is to illustrate that awareness of world trends in online dating can enrich the study of relationship formation, mores, and goals as they continue to evolve at a rapid pace. The data from these technologies enables researchers to understand where a dating and mating economy currently is and where it may be heading based on the characteristics of the popular dating sites and apps that people are using in a particular region. This is particularly evident when looking at the contrasts between Japan and other Asian nations like India and China. Today's dating economy, both on the individual level (e.g., what people choose to display on their dating profile) and on the societal level (e.g., what patterns exist in different populations using online dating), is much different than it was even ten years ago. We believe the proliferation of dating apps and sites serves as a platform for more individualistic attitudes towards mate selection—even in collectivist cultures. Increasingly, young adults have the freedom to have a choice—at least where partner selection is concerned. This is particularly novel for women; while cultural restrictions on marriage and partner selection have existed for both men and women in almost all societies in human history, relatively few societies have given women freedom to get to know men on their own. Even more liberal interpretations of choice are often little more than limited amounts of veto power. The acceptance of increasingly sophisticated online dating technology into traditional societies certainly encourages a reconceptualization of spousal formation. It may even change social perceptions of what marriage is.

## Discussion

It is more than apparent that online dating has reorganized the dating, mating, and sexual world. Online dating has segmented the dating pool much in the same way that major online companies such as Google have segmented users into marketing targets, advertising targets, and philanthropic target populations. The silos can be general or specific, but the fact is that we now have organized groups according to age, sexual preference, hobbies, education, desires, and just about every other kind of specific standing we can imagine. It also seems apparent that derivatives of original ideas are now populating the web. For example, hook-up sites proliferate, but also *anti*-hook-up sites get created. We now have Bumble that is run by women countering the male orientation of Tinder. Just recently, Chappy launched for long-term gay relationships in contrast to the hook-ups promoted by the gay dating app Grindr.

The online dating space has become a hotbed of innovation and elaboration. An uncertain economic period with little job security and the concomitant possibility of getting super rich very quickly has spurred all kinds of entrepreneurship. And, the dating space is a relatively low-cost entry into trying to make it big fast without having to own (at least initially) anything that is anchored in bricks and mortar.

The business of dating is not the only thing we believe has been altered by the proliferation of online matchmaking. The abundance of online possibilities, geared for every age group, has made singlehood less threatening and less time bound. We think that this has a paradoxical effect. It makes people less desperate about being paired because there are *Plenty of Fish* in the sea (to use the name of a now popular site). On the other hand, the necessity of working hard at creating a profile and putting yourself into the marketplace consumes much more time than going out to the bars on Friday or Saturday night. The online market is both efficient (lots of choices accessed from at-home perusal) and inefficient (taking longer to form relationships because people online are complete strangers, or because of our tendency to be less certain when given an abundance of alternatives).

Furthermore, and most paradoxical of all, we hypothesize that there is a new kind of burnout for those who do a lot of online dating without a satisfying result. Unsuccessful time online, due to little interest from others or lackluster dates, may indeed have long-term effects but it most certainly has short-term ones. People drop-out of dating but perhaps worse, they have the same kind of self-image destruction over a lifetime that was historically limited to the selection processes of the teen or young adult years. Both men and women can be rated and rejected in these anonymous circumstances at any time, in any age group, or interest group.

On the other hand—and in online dating, there is always another hand—the dating space is always open; always has new people to introduce; and always offers another chance. Older people who thought that there was no passion or romance after widowhood or a late in life divorce can have renewed and reasonable optimism that they could find a new love or romantic companion. Gay men and lesbians in small towns with limited ability to seek out partners can now have the big city populations to choose from. Yes, people can feel fungible on the web, but they are also findable.

Certainly, there is some hand-wringing over all of the dashed hopes, imperfect pairings, and occasional chicanery, that is justified. Still, we believe that ultimately the positive impact of online dating outweighs the negative. One reason for our optimism is because of the continuing invention of new sites and more permissive romantic guidelines for the people using them. There really is a site for anyone ready to try their luck at finding love (or a one-night stand) online, and most societies encourage their people to do so. Furthermore, while online dating can be punishing, its profitability shows that men and women of all descriptions ultimately want its services.

As for future directions for behavioral scientists, sociologists should watch the evolution of dating online carefully since its various transitions certainly reflect social change and impact family structure, marriage, fertility, sexual patterns, and lifestyles. Psychologists and social psychologists are likely to continue finding online dating interesting because of how it affects the individual's capacity to love, connect, and commit. All behavioral scientists might well consider how persisting intense user engagement with online dating may affect both the long-term personality of and stability of intimate relationships. Whatever our personal take may be on the positives or negatives of online dating, we think it is realistic to believe that online dating is going to be a significant part of the romantic and sexual landscape for the foreseeable future.

## References

Ahuvia, A., & Adelman, M. (1992). Formal intermediaries in the marriage market: A typology and review. *Journal of Marriage and Family, 54*(2), 452–463. https://doi.org/10.2307/353076

Anderson, R. (2016). The ugly truth about online dating: Are we sacrificing love for convenience? *Psychology Today*. Retrieved from https://www.psychologytoday.com/blog/the-mating-game/201609/the-ugly-truth-about-online-dating

Anderson, T. L. (2005). Relationships among internet attitudes, internet use, romantic beliefs, and perceptions of online romantic relationships. *Cyberpsychology & Behavior, 8*(6), 521–531. https://doi.org/10.1089/cpb.2005.8.521

Ansari, A., & Klinenberg, E. (2016). *Modern romance*. New York: Penguin Books.

Aoki, M. (2016). In sexless Japan, almost half of single young men and women are virgins. *The Japan Times*. Retrieved from https://www.japantimes.co.jp/news/2016/09/16/national/social-issues/sexless-japan-almost-half-young-men-women-virgins-survey/-.WaHeEK2ZOsy

Behal, A. (2015, April). Could this dating app be India's take on Tinder? *Forbes* Retrieved from https://www.forbes.com/sites/abehal/2015/04/27/could-this-dating-app-be-indias-take-on-tinder/

Bennett, J. (2017, March 18). With her dating app, women are in control. *The New York Times*. Retrieved from https://www.nytimes.com/2017/03/18/fashion/bumble-feminist-dating-app-whitney-wolfe.html

Bilton, N. (2014, October 29). Tinder, the fast-growing dating app, taps an age-old truth. *The New York Times*. Retrieved from https://www.nytimes.com/2014/10/30/fashion/tinder-the-fast-growing-dating-app-taps-an-age-old-truth.html

Blodgett, N. (1986). The dating game: Regulating the video matchmakers. *ABA Journal, 72*(9), 25.

Borresen, K. (2013, November 14). 5 good reasons to get married while you're young, according to research. *The Huffington Post*. Retrieved from http://www.huffingtonpost.com/2013/11/14/married-young_n_4227924.html

Cacioppo, J. T., Cacioppo, S., Gonzaga, G. C., Ogburn, E. L., & Vanderweele, T. J. (2013). Marital satisfaction and break-ups differ across on-line and off-line meeting venues. *Proceedings of the National Academy of Sciences of the United States of America, 110*(25), 10135–10140. https://doi.org/10.1073/pnas.1222447110

Carney, D. R., Colvin, C. R., & Hall, J. A. (2007). A thin slice perspective on the accuracy of first impressions. *Journal of Research in Personality, 41*(5), 1054–1072.

Carter, S. R., & Buckwalter, J. G. (2009). Enhancing mate selection through the internet: A comparison of relationship quality between marriages arising from an online matchmaking system and marriages arising from unfettered selection. *Interpersona: An International Journal on Personal Relationships, 3*(Supp 2), 105–125 Retrieved from https://interpersona.psychopen.eu/article/view/78

Central Intelligence Agency. (2013). *The World Factbook 2013–2014*. Retrieved from https://www.cia.gov/library/publications/the-world-factbook/geos/in.html

Chappy App. (2017). .A new chapter in gay dating. Retrieved from https://blog.chappyapp.com/home/2016/12/2/introducing-chappy

Cicerello, A., & Sheehan, E. P. (1995). Personal advertisements: A content analysis. *Journal of Social Behavior & Personality, 10*(4), 751–756.

Cook, J. (2015, April 1). Tinder would be worth $1.6 billion as a standalone business. *Business Insider*. Retrieved from http://www.businessinsider.com/jmp-securities-analyst-note-on-tinder-2015-4

Coontz, S. (2006). *Marriage, a history: How love conquered marriage*. New York: Penguin Books.

Cuby, M. (2017, March 27). Grindr is giving users everything they need with new content hub 'into'. *Paper*. Retrieved from http://www.papermag.com/grindr-is-giving-users-everything-they-need-with-new-content-hub-into-2332290891.html

Davis, S. (1990). Men as success objects and women as sex objects: A study of personal advertisements. *Sex Roles, 23*(1/2), 43–50. https://doi.org/10.1007/BF00289878

Dunbar, R. (1995). Are you lonesome tonight? (mate selection by humans). *New Scientist, 145*, 26–31.

eHarmony. (2017). eHarmony management team: Meet Steve Carter. https://www.eharmony.com.au/about/profile/steve/

Emery, L. R. (2017, March 2). Tinder users who have spotify integrated get more matches, & here are the top anthems on the dating app. *Bustle*. Retrieved from https://www.bustle.com/p/tinder-users-who-have-spotify-integrated-get-more-matches-here-are-the-top-anthems-on-the-dating-app-41903

Feingold, A. (1988). Matching for attractiveness in romantic partners and same-sex friends: A meta-analysis and theoretical critique. *Psychological Bulletin, 104*(2), 226–235. https://doi.org/10.1037/0033-2909.104.2.226

Finkel, E. J., Cheung, E. O., Emery, L. F., Carswell, K. L., & Larson, G. M. (2015). The suffocation model: Why marriage in America is becoming an all-or-nothing institution. *Current Directions in Psychological Science, 24*(3), 238–244. https://doi.org/10.1177/0963721415569274

Finkel, E. J., Eastwick, P. W., Karney, B. R., Reis, H. T., & Sprecher, S. (2012). Online dating: A critical analysis from the perspective of psychological science. *Psychological Science in the Public Interest, 13*(1), 3–66.

Fisher, H. (2016). *Anatomy of love: A natural history of mating, marriage, and why we stray*. New York: W. W. Norton & Company Inc.

Fowler, B. (2015, April 4). Japanese singles are posting strange photos on their online dating profiles. *Business Insider*. Retrieved from http://www.businessinsider.com/the-japanese-are-clueless-about-online-dating-2015-7

Frazzetto, G. (2010). The science of online dating. *Science and Society, 11*(1), 25–27. https://doi.org/10.1038/embor.2009.264

Gatter, K., Hodkinson, K., & Kolle, M. (2016). On the differences between Tinder™ versus online dating agencies: Questioning a myth. An exploratory study. *Cogent Psychology, 3*(1). https://doi.org/10.1080/23311908.2016.1162414

Gibbs, J., Ellison, N., & Heino, R. (2006). Self-presentation in online personals: The role of anticipated future interaction, self-disclosure, and perceived success in internet dating. *Communication Research, 33*(2), 152–177 doi:10.1177_0093650205285368.

GrabHim.Net. (2015). Stop the presses! Our gay dating app survey results are in! *GrabHim.Net*. Retrieved from https://grabhim.net/2015/03/17/stop-the-presses-our-gay-dating-app-survey-results-are-in/

Grindr LLC. (2017). Grindr: Gay and same sex guys chat, meet and date on the app store. Retrieved from https://itunes.apple.com/us/app/grindr-x-tra/id319881193?mt=8

Halberstadt, J., Jackson, J. C., Bilkey, D., Jong, J., Whitehouse, H., McNaughton, C., & Zollmann, S. (2016). Incipient social groups: An analysis via in-vivo behavioral tracking. *PLoS One, 11*(3), e0149880. https://doi.org/10.1371/journal.pone.0149880

Harmon, A. (2003). Online dating sheds its stigma as losers.com. *New York Times*. Retrieved from https://www.nytimes.com/2003/06/29/us/online-dating-sheds-its-stigma-as-loserscom.html

Harney, A. (2009, June 15). The herbivore's dilemma: Japan panics about the rise of "grass-eating men" who shun sex, don't spend money, and like taking walks. *The Slate*. Retrieved from http://www.slate.com/articles/news_and_politics/foreigners/2009/06/the_herbivores_dilemma.html

Harris, G. (2015, April 24). Websites in India put a bit of choice into arranged marriages. *The New York Times*. Retrieved from https://www.nytimes.com/2015/04/26/world/asia/india-arranged-marriages-matrimonial-websites.html

Hodge, G. (2012, December 10). The ugly truth of online dating: Top 10 lies told by Internet daters. *HuffPost*. Retrieved from http://www.huffingtonpost.com/greg-hodge/online-dating-lies_b_1930053.html

Hoehn, L. (2016). *You probably shouldn't write that: Tips and tricks for creating an online dating profile that doesn't suck*. Philadelphia: Running Press.

Iyengar, S., & Kamenica, E. (2010). Choice proliferation, simplicity seeking, and asset allocation. *Journal of Public Economics, 94*(7), 530–539. https://doi.org/10.1016/j.jpubeco.2010.03.006

Iyengar, S., & Lepper, M. R. (2000). When choice is demotivating: Can one desire too much of a good thing? *Journal of Personality and Social Psychology, 79*(6), 995–1006. https://doi.org/10.1037/0022-3514.79.6.995

Jayson, S. (2013). Online dating has changed everything, author says. *USA Today*. Retrieved from https://www.usatoday.com/story/news/nation/2013/01/23/love-algorithms-online-dating/1856853/

Jejeebhoy, S. J., Santhya, K. G., Acharya, R., & Prakash, R. (2013). Marriage-related decision-making and young women's marital relations and agency. *Asian Population Studies, 9*(1), 28–49.

Jin, S. V., & Martin, C. (2015). "A match made…online?" The effects of user-generated online dater profile types (free-spirited versus uptight) on other users' perception of trustworthiness, interpersonal attraction, and personality. *Cyberpsychology, Behavior, and Social Networking, 18*(6), 320–327. https://doi.org/10.1089/cyber.2014.0564

Jones, B. C., DeBruine, L. M., Little, A. C., Burriss, R. P., & Feinberg, D. R. (2007). Social transmission of face preferences among humans. *Proceedings of the Royal Society B, 274*(1611), 899. https://doi.org/10.1098/rspb.2006.0205

Kauflin, J. (2011, December 16). How Match.com's founder created the world's biggest dating website—and walked away with just $50,000. *Business Insider*. Retrieved from http://www.businessinsider.com/match-gary-kremen-2011-12

Khan, K. S., & Chaudhry, S. (2015). An evidence-based approach to an ancient pursuit: Systematic review on converting online contact into a first date. *Evidence-Based Medicine, 20*(2), 48–52. https://doi.org/10.1136/ebmed-2014-110101

Lawler, R. (2014, April 16). Online dating site Zoosk files for $100M IPO, with $178M in revenues and a $2.6M net loss in 2013. *TechCrunch*. Retrieved from https://techcrunch.com/2014/04/16/zoosk-s1-ipo/

Lenhart, A., & Duggan, M. (2014). *Couples, the Internet, and social media: How American couples use digital technology to manage life, logistics, and emotional intimacy within their relationships*. Pew Research Center, Internet & Technology. Retrieved from http://www.pewinternet.org/2014/02/11/couples-the-internet-and-social-media/

Lenton, A. P., & Francesconi, M. (2011). Too much of a good thing? Variety is confusing in mate choice. *Biology Letters, 7*(4), 528–531. https://doi.org/10.1098/rsbl.2011.0098

Leonhardt, D. (2006, March 29). Computing the mysteries of attraction. The New York Times. Retrieved from https://www.nytimes.com/2006/03/29/business/computing-the-mysteries-of-attraction.html

Levine, D. (2015, February 12). Online dating–The psychology (and reality): A science writer explores dating sites like Match.com, Tinder, eHarmony, Chemistry, interviewing experts along the way. Elsevier. Retrieved from https://www.elsevier.com/connect/online-dating-the-psychology-and-reality

Li, J., & Lipscomb, A. (2017, July 17). Love on the cloud: The rise of online dating in China. *USC US-China Today*. Retrieved from http://www.uschina.usc.edu/article@usct?love_on_the_cloud_the_rise_of_online_dating_in_china_20518.aspx

Match.com. (2017, June). About the contributors. *Up to date: The official Match.com blog*. Retrieved from http://blog.match.com/about-the-contributors/

McGloin, R., & Denes, A. (2016). Too hot to trust: Examining the relationship between attractiveness, trustworthiness, and desire to date in online dating. *New Media & Society, 20*(3), 919. https://doi.org/10.1177/1461444816675440

McGrane, S. (2009, June 29). Can genetics help you find love? *Time Magazine*. Retrieved from http://content.time.com/time/magazine/article/0,9171,1905505,00.html

McIntyre, H. (2016, April 20). Millennials are leading the Spotify revolution. *Forbes*. Retrieved from http://www.forbes.com/sites/hughmcintyre/2016/04/20/millennials-are-leading-the-spotify-revolution/

McKenna, K. Y. A., Green, A. S., & Gleason, M. E. J. (2002). Relationship formation on the internet: What's the big attraction? *Journal of Social Issues, 58*(1), 9–31. https://doi.org/10.1111/1540-4560.00246

Mehta, I. (2016, July 15). 4 dating apps that are changing how Indians look for love. *Huffington Post*. Retrieved from http://www.huffingtonpost.in/2016/02/14/india-dating_n_9231056.html
Miksche, M. (2016, May 5). Grindr, Tinder, Scruff: A recipe for loneliness. *The Advocate*. Retrieved from http://www.advocate.com/current-issue/2016/5/05/grindr-tinder-scruff-recipe-loneliness
Morgan, R. (2017, May 21). Ashley Madison is back and claims surprising user numbers. *The New York Post*. Retrieved from http://nypost.com/2017/05/21/ashley-madison-is-back-and-claims-surprising-user-numbers/
Ng, B. (2017, August 25). Momo rakes in millions with live streaming. *EJ Insight*. Retrieved from http://www.ejinsight.com/20170825-momo-rakes-in-millions-with-live-streaming/
Olivola, C. Y., & Todorov, A. (2010). Fooled by first impressions? Reexamining the diagnostic value of appearance-based inferences. *Journal of Experimental Social Psychology, 46*(2), 315–324.
PlentyOfFish.com. (2017). Retrieved from https://www.pof.com/
Queerty. (2009). Cruise local guys on your iPhone. *Queerty*. Retrieved from https://www.queerty.com/cruise-local-guys-via-gps-20090326
QX Team. (2017, August 3). Chappy: The app that's changing the game in gay dating! *QX Magazine*. Retrieved from http://www.qxmagazine.com/2017/08/chappy/
Raghubir, P., & Valenzuela, A. (2006). Center-of-inattention: Position biases in decision-making. *Organizational Behavior and Human Decision Processes, 99*(1), 66–80.
Ramirez, A., & Zhang, S. (2007). When online meets offline: The effect of modality switching on relational communication. *Communication Monographs, 74*(3), 287–310.
Retherford, R. D., & Ogawa, N. (2006). In F. R. Harris (Ed.)., *The baby bust: Who will do the work? Who will pay the taxes? Japan's baby bust: Causes, implications, and policy responses* (pp. 5–47). Lanham, MD: Rowman & Littlefield.
Romano, E. (2016, April 9). Survey says college students mostly use Tinder to find friends. Dating Sites Reviews.com. Retrieved from https://www.datingsitesreviews.com/article.php?story=survey-says-college-students-mostly-use-tinder-to-find-friends
Rosen, L. D., Cheever, N. A., Cummings, C., & Felt, J. (2008). The impact of emotionality and self-disclosure on online dating versus traditional dating. *Computers in Human Behavior, 24*(5), 2124–2157. https://doi.org/10.1016/j.chb.2007.10.003
Rosenfeld, M. J. (2017). Marriage, choice, and couplehood in the age of the internet. *Sociological Science, 4*(20), 490–510. https://doi.org/10.15195/v4.a20
Rosenfeld, M. J., & Thomas, R. J. (2012). Searching for a mate: The rise of the internet as a social intermediary. *American Sociological Review, 77*(4), 523–547 doi:10.1177_0003122412448050.
Rudder, C. (2010a, January 20). The 4 big myths of profile pictures. The OkCupid Blog. Retrieved from https://theblog.okcupid.com/the-4-big-myths-of-profile-pictures-41bedf26e4d
Rudder, C. (2010b, July 7). The big lies people tell in online dating. *The OkCupid Blog*. Retrieved from https://theblog.okcupid.com/the-big-lies-people-tell-in-online-dating-a9e3990d6ae2
Rudder, C. (2014). *Dataclysm: Love, sex, race, and identity–What our online lives tell us about our offline selves*. New York: Broadway Books.
Schwartz, B. (2006a, June). More isn't always better. *Harvard Business Review*. Retrieved from https://hbr.org/2006/06/more-isnt-always-better
Schwartz, P. (2006b). *Finding your perfect match: 8 keys to finding lasting love through true compatibility*. New York: Penguin Group.
Sentementes, G. G. (2011, February 11). Love in the time of dot-coms. *The Baltimore Sun*. Retrieved from http://articles.baltimoresun.com/2011-02-11/business/bs-bz-interview-helen-fisher-20110210_1_chemistry-com-match-com-online-dating
Singh, R., Simons, J. J. P., Young, D. P. C. Y., Sim, B. S. X., Chai, X. T., Singh, S., & Chiou, S. Y. (2009). Trust and respect as mediators of the other- and self-profitable trait effects on interpersonal attraction. *European Journal of Social Psychology, 39*(6), 1021–1038. https://doi.org/10.1002/ejsp.605

Singh, R., Wegener, D. T., Sankaran, K., Singh, S., Lin, P. K. F., Seow, M. X., … Shuli, S. (2015). On the importance of trust in interpersonal attraction from attitude similarity. *Journal of Social and Personal Relationships, 32*(6), 829–850. https://doi.org/10.1177/0265407515576993

Slater, D. (2013a, January/February). A million first dates: How online romance is threatening monogamy. *The Atlantic*. Retrieved from http://www.theatlantic.com/magazine/archive/2013/01/a-million-first-dates/309195/

Slater, D. (2013b). *Love in the time of algorithms: What technology does to meeting and mating*. London: Penguin Books.

Toma, C. L., Hancock, J. T., & Ellison, N. B. (2008). Separating fact from fiction: An examination of deceptive self-presentation in online dating profiles. *Personality and Social Psychology Bulletin, 34*(8), 1023–1036. https://doi.org/10.1177/0146167208318067

Walia, S., & Punit, I. S. (2015, September 15). The business of dating apps is disrupting Indian culture. *Quartz India*. Retrieved from https://qz.com/506596/the-business-of-dating-apps-is-disrupting-indian-culture/

Weigel, M. (2016). *Labor of love: The invention of dating*. New York: Farrar, Straus and Giroux.

Whitty, M. T., & Buchanan, T. (2010). What's in a 'screen name'? Attractiveness of different types of screen names used by online daters. *International Journal of Internet Science, 5*(1), 5–19.

Williams, D., Sawyer, S., & Wahlstrom, C. (2016). Involvement: Dating, pairing, & courtship. In D. Williams, S. Sawyer, & C. Wahlstrom (Eds.), *Marriage, families, & intimate relationships: A practical introduction* (4th ed., pp. 94–118). London: Pearson.

Woll, S., & Cozby, C. P. (1991). Videodating and other alternatives to traditional methods of relationship initiation. *Advances in Personal Relationships, 1*, 69–108.

Woll, S., & Young, P. (1989). Looking for Mr. or Ms. Right: Self-presentation in videodating. *Journal of Marriage and the Family, 51*(2), 483.

Zheng, S. (2017, February 11). Popularity of dating apps in Hong Kong shows technology and love make a good match. *South China Morning Post*. Retrieved from http://www.scmp.com/news/hong-kong/education-community/article/2069897/popularity-dating-apps-hong-kong-shows-technology

Zoosk Inc. (2017). *What is Zoosk*. Retrieved from https://about.zoosk.com/en/about/

# Chapter 5
# Technology in Relational Systems: Roles, Rules, and Boundaries

**Katherine M. Hertlein**

With over 4.1 billion people using the Internet across the globe (Internet World Stats, 2018), couples and families discover new ways of communicating and using the Internet to increase intimacy, solve problems, and forge new connections. At the same time, couples and families are plagued with serious problems related to technology and new media including boundary issues, privacy, online gaming addiction, online sex addiction, infidelity, cyberbullying, cyberstalking, sexting, and sexually charged information easily accessible to youth (Blinka, Škařupová, & Mitterova, 2016; Hertlein & Blumer, 2013). The purpose of this chapter is to present a framework to understand how technology can create challenges for family structure and how we can use these same technologies to positively support our relationship structure.

## The Couple and Family Technology Framework

Historically, the way the Internet and new media are discussed in the scholarly literature is through the lenses of individualism, isolation, and dysfunction. For example, many of the models that exist to explain technology use are geared toward explaining why individuals (without consideration of their context) select to engage in certain online activities over others. Isolated topics attended to in research include topics such as internet addiction; Facebook and social media use among teens; screen time; videogame use among young adults; texting in romantic relationships; and cyberbullying and sexting (or other risky behavior) among teens. Each of these topics tends to be evaluated and discussed in isolation from the others rather than discussed as they occur within an individuals' larger context. Second, the lens is less

K. M. Hertlein (✉)
Marriage and Family Therapy Program, University of Nevada, Las Vegas, NV, USA
e-mail: katherine.hertlein@unlv.edu



J. Van Hook et al. (eds.), *Families and Technology*, National Symposium on Family Issues 9, https://doi.org/10.1007/978-3-319-95540-7_5

about the advantages of technology, and more about how technology contributes to depression, anxiety, infidelity, suicidal ideation, stress, etc.

The Couple and Family Technology (CFT) framework (Hertlein, 2012; Hertlein & Blumer, 2013) is the first attempt to provide a comprehensive and systemic view of how we are impacted by technology. In this view, it addresses the areas missed (or dodged) by previous scholars. First, the CFT framework presents seven characteristics of technology and new media (predominantly the Internet) that affect couples and families. The seven characteristics of technology identified in the CFT framework are accessibility, affordability, anonymity, acceptability, approximation, accommodation, and ambiguity. Each of these characteristics or factors affects the structure of relationships (defined as the roles, rules, and boundaries of relationships), and the process of relationships (defined as relationship initiation, relationship maintenance, and relationship termination). Thus, the CFT framework explores how these seven factors shape the ways couple and family relationships are organized and function around technology and the Internet. Development of the framework was influenced by the work of Haddon (2006) and Lanigan (2009). Importantly, the framework considers the context in which the individual is embedded as well as future decisions to use technology and the manner in which technology is integrated into the family.

## Impact of Technology on Relationship Structure

Structure, as conceptualized by the Couple and Family Technology Framework, is defined by three primary elements: roles, rules, and boundaries. As people assume certain functions in a relationship (either in couples or in families), they take on roles to which certain rules are assigned. The rules enable the system to carry out its functions. When roles change, rules change; when rules change, boundaries change, leaving an indelible mark on the system in both positive and negative ways.

There are several ways that technology use impacts the basic structure of relationships (See Fig. 5.1). In couples, the roles may shift to include surveillance and monitoring, both critical tasks in parenting (Fox & Tokunaga, 2015; Fox & Warber, 2014; Hertlein, Dulley, Cloud, Leon, & Chang, 2017; Tokunaga, 2015; Wang, Zhou, & Zhang, 2017). Just as there are often unspoken rules about what information can be shared outside of a romantic relationship, use of the Internet may result in couples establishing rules about what is permissible to post on social media. Couples may also make decisions about when to disengage from technology such as phones and Internet and attend to their lives and relationships offline.

Technology also impacts the structure of family relationships and may necessitate changes in rules. Parents, who are in the hierarchical position to monitor youth, may find it difficult to do so when a youth is more knowledgeable about technology than they are. Parents need to have rules limiting what their child may access through technology and who has access to their child. Similar to couples, the entire family must navigate acceptable use of technology in the home or whenever family members are together.

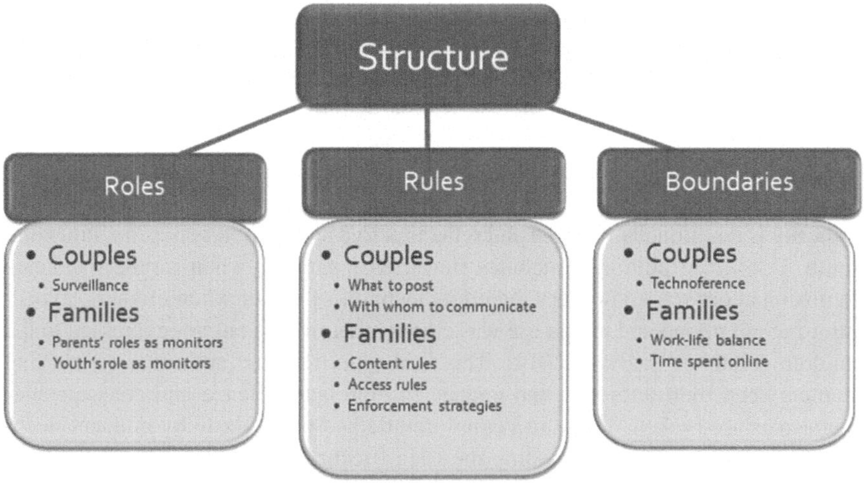


**Fig. 5.1** Roles, rules, and boundary shifts with technology

Technology shifts roles and consequently imposes new rules in couples and families in helpful ways. For example, technology can assist family members in carrying out their already-established roles with tasks such as locating educational information or resources and providing an opportunity to engage in games or activities together (Lanigan, Bold, & Chenoweth, 2009). There are other times, however, when changes in roles and rules can be confusing and create challenging situations for couples and families. Adolescents are often early adopters of technology, and as such they may take on a different role in the family (Fletcher & Blair, 2014). As a result, the role of authority in the parental system is transferred in part to one's children rather than being retained by parents. Children and adolescents became known as "digital natives" (Prensky, 2001). Not surprisingly, "Almost twice as many adolescents perceived themselves to be more proficient [at using technology] than both of their parents, as opposed to having at least one parent who was perceived as more proficient than they themselves were" (Fletcher & Blair, 2016, p. 245). In this study, distinctions were made between the type of technology for who was the expert, as being an expert in one type of technology did not predict being the family expert in another.

## *Parent's Role as Monitors*

As children develop a high level of confidence in their *technoliteracy* (Fitton, Ahmendahi, Harold, & Schifflet, 2013), they may move to a higher place of authority in the family (Fletcher & Blair, 2014; Livingstone, 2003). The role that parents once had as the exclusive monitors in families is changing. Three strategies have been employed by mothers in the case of monitoring youth's use of the Internet: abdication/loss of authority, conflicted authority, and retained authority (Fletcher & Blair, 2014). In abdication/loss of authority, mothers give up authority to others who they believe can better monitor their children. In some cases, mothers abdicate the authority to the child's father if he is deemed as having more expertise than she. Mothers may abdicate to software that advertises a protective or control function or may even abdicate to children themselves, particularly when children demonstrate more technoliteracy.

A second strategy, conflicted authority, is characterized by shared authority between mothers and school systems or between mothers and their children. Shared authority is emotionally charged and reflects active negotiation between mother and youth. Conflicted authority includes times, for example, when mothers indicate confusion about school policies regarding technology use or when mothers' expectations about phone and media use was clear in their minds but not expressed to the children (Fletcher & Blair, 2014). The final type, retained authority, means that mothers keep their authority and engage in more surveillance and consequences when rules are broken. These strategies are affected particularly by mothers' technology literacy, concerns regarding the use of technology (i.e., particularly in the case of chat rooms), and how much they value technology (Fletcher & Blair, 2014).

## *Youth's Elevated Role in Family Hierarchy*

How youth respond to their parents is a key factor that impacts role organization (and hierarchy) in families. The hierarchical gains a youth makes in a family are a direct result of (1) how accessible the Internet is, (2) parent's lack of understanding technology, (3) the affordability of many of the technologies, and (4) the level of anonymity when one engages in online interactions, which also corresponds well with the youth's identity development process. Youth who have a great sense of pride in having a high degree of technology literacy may not be willing to give up their position as the technology expert in the family. Youth development commonly includes making bids for greater degrees of autonomy, and demonstrating literacy or expertise in an area is a key strategy to argue one's case. There are several domains of autonomy-granting that occur across a youth's development, moving from the personal domain (decisions about clothes, hair, leisure time activities), to what are known as conventional domains (chores, tasks), and eventually to prudential domains (decisions about risky behavior such as drug or alcohol use; Bell, Baron, Corson, Kostina-Ritchey, & Frederick, 2014). Youth move through this process to gain independence (Wray-Lake, Crouter, & McHale, 2010). In the case of autonomy related to technology use and expertise, the domains affected simultaneously are the personal (e.g., how to spend time online, etc.) as well as the prudential domains (e.g., risk factors of online conversations such as cyberbullying, stalking, and sexting). For youth who are not granted this independence, the impact of long-term monitoring and surveillance in families may contribute to youth feeling mistrusted, interference with youths' desires for autonomy, and ongoing conflict between parents and children.

## Impact of Technology on Relationship Rules

Technology has allowed us to redefine, in beneficial ways, the rules of when and how it is permissible to communicate with others outside of the home. Historically, to make contact with someone in the middle of the night either for work or personal purposes would be considered inappropriate. In the age of technology, however, one can send an email at a time convenient for the sender (rather than considering the convenience of the recipient) and recipients can respond when the timing is right for them (Bacigalupe & Lambe, 2011; Neustaedter, Harrison, & Sellen, 2013; Rea, Behnke, Huff, & Allen, 2015). This concept has been found to be true for maintaining relationships among sibling groups as one transitions to college (Lindell, Campione-Barr, & Killoren, 2015) and in long-distance relationships (Teng & Wang, 2015). In these instances, the accessibility and affordability of communication technology gives us the flexibility to contact someone whenever and wherever we would like and promotes connection and the continued development of closeness.

### *Rules in Couple Relationships*

Technology and media, however, also introduce challenges to rules in couple and family relationships. Some couples indicate that though they do not have rules in their relationships regarding phone usage, they believe that they should (Miller-Ott, Kelly, & Duran, 2012). This is because the determination as to whether particular online behavior is acceptable in one's relationship often creates conflict between couples. It is also often the case that couples do not overtly discuss the rules they have for one another in the relationship. Instead, they assume their partner is aware of what behavior is inappropriate (Helsper & Whitty, 2010). For example, couples often have unspoken rules about internet postings and communication with individuals who could be a romantic interest. For men, texting with others outside their romantic relationship has negative implications for their partner's attachment, relationship satisfaction, and perceived relationship stability (Rueda, Lindsay, & Williams, 2015; Schade, Sandberg, Bean, Busby, & Coyne, 2013).

Couples may have rules about when the relationship is publicly announced. When one member of a developing relationship edits their Facebook status to indicate relationship ties, it is generally viewed positively by the partner. This pattern of expression, however, does not necessarily mean a more solid relationship. In fact, those who spend more time on Facebook lauding the relationship actually perceived lower levels of expression of love than those who did not post as much about one another on Facebook (Northrup & Smith, 2016). Further, if one member of the couple indicates they are in a relationship and the other indicates their status as single, this can create conflict and is associated with lower levels of relationship satisfaction for women (Papp, Danielewicz, & Cayemberg, 2012).

Accountability, while not one of the seven characteristics of technology or the Internet according to the CFT framework described earlier, affects structure and process in relationships (Hertlein & Stevenson, 2010) and may be a key factor in how adherence to expressed rules and boundaries is interpreted. First, each member of the couple is accountable for their own use of communication technology to interact with others outside of their relationship. Second, accountability applies to people's online interactions with their own partner. The less accountable people feel they are, the more likely they will engage in behavior that crosses the line (behavior they would not participate in offline). The lack of accountability combined with the ambiguity of their actions can create conflict in couples and families.

### *Rules in Families*

There are two types of rules related to technology use in families: content rules and access rules. Content rules refer to the types of information that can be posted on social media sites; the types of information that can be shared with others via cell phones or text messaging; and how to avoid strangers and unsafe individuals online (Fletcher & Blair, 2014; Vaterlaus, Beckert, Tulane, & Bird, 2014).

Rules exist to discourage inappropriate behavior and parents use enforcement strategies to encourage compliance and prevent violations (Fletcher & Blair, 2014). Enforcement strategies are employed to minimize the negative impact of technology on youth (Fletcher & Blair, 2016). The strategies employed depend on who holds the role of expert in the family. For example, in families where parents set rules about technology, enforcement strategies include checking the youth's cell phone and setting up blocks that would limit misuse. Parents who are experts and set the rules also tend to require youth to friend them on Facebook in order to monitor youth's activity (Fletcher & Blair, 2016). In this case, accessibility of the Internet favors the parent.

## Impact of Technology on Relationship Boundaries

Those who turn to online dating often hold the misconception that they have more control in the selection process and that online dating sites provide sufficient gatekeeping mechanisms and boundaries to prevent harm (Hitsch, Hortacsu, & Ariely, 2010; McKenna & Bargh, 2000). For example, adolescent females who experienced dating violence via online technologies spent much time talking to the person in whom they were interested prior to an in-person meeting (Draucker & Martsolf, 2010). The adolescent girls assumed that these men were adequately screened and deemed them as appropriate relationship material. It may be the case that the extent to which the Internet allows online daters to be anonymous and alter their self-presentation interferes with a potential partner's ability to assess how safe they are.

Individuals attempting to screen online dating partners may rely too heavily on the approximation quality of the Internet and believe they have more assurances to safety than they actually do when an offline encounter occurs.

## General Impact of Technoference

Interference of technology, or *technoference*, in a relationship can be detrimental to long-term outcomes (McDaniel & Coyne, 2016; Morgan et al., 2016). The accessibility of being contacted at any time and the partner's response to the interference, in particular, are associated with several negative outcomes. Seventy percent of women note that technology interferes in their relationships, and 62% of women report that it interrupts with couple life at least once per day. Technoference is correlated with lowered relationship satisfaction and increased conflict in relationships (McDaniel & Coyne, 2016; Morgan et al., 2016).

To operationalize the impact of technology use on romantic relationship intimacy, Campbell and Murray (2015) developed the Technology and Intimate Relationship Assessment. The items on this scale examine behaviors associated with cell phone engagement (including turning away from a partner to answer a call), other electronic distractions during time together, surveillance behaviors, experience of anxiety with one's partner's cell phone usage, and other similar items. Younger participants noted more disruption in their relationship intimacy via technology than older participants. At the same time, younger participants were more likely to report that technology overall had a positive impact on the quality of their relationships. A possible explanation is that older participants had been coupled longer, felt more secure than younger couples, and were less reliant on using technology in their relationships. There was also a significant difference between those who classified their relationship as dating versus those who classified their relationship as post-dating (Campbell & Murray, 2015).

## Time Spent Online

Technology has a significant impact on the role of work in one's home life. Laptops, smartphones, and even smartwatches have altered the landscape and rhythms of relationships (Derks & Bakker, 2014; Dimmick, Feaster, & Ramirez, 2011). Couples have a certain rhythm that becomes established in their relationships and many couples come into marital therapy citing some relational problem whose etiology is rooted in temporal patterns (Fraenkel, 1994). One member of a couple may not appreciate or deem appropriate the time that their partner spends on particular tasks. This is certainly true in today's digital world. Couples indicate amount of time spent online as problematic in their relationship (Morgan et al., 2016). For example, men who played online were more likely to experience conflict in their relationship over time spent online (Coyne et al., 2012).

Another key example regarding the dispersion of time in relationships is the issue of work and homelife balance. The electronic accessibility we have to our work outside of the workplace has compromised our ability to maintain a good balance between work and homelife, especially when one considers the significant pressure to respond to work interferences while at home due to technology (Duxbury, Higgins, Smart, & Stevenson, 2014). The decision to engage in work activities while at home could be viewed as one making their priorities known (that is, valuing work more than home). Because the technology is always on, responding to job-related issues may be tempting to do, despite the negative impact to the relationship as well as the individual's overall well-being (Derks & Bakker, 2014).

The issues that affect couples, with relation to technology use, also affect families. Youth now have a tendency to spend more time in their rooms communicating with their peers rather than engaging in physical interactions (Carvalho, Francisco, & Relvas, 2015). When parents used the internet more often from home, they reported decreased family time and cite technology as the reason (Williams & Merten, 2011). Family time is often conceptualized as how the family organizes their time as well as the activities in which the family members collectively participate. This is an important distinction to consider the activities in which the family participates. A study of Korean families examined whether children's internet use influenced declines in family time and family communication. According to the findings, total time using the *Internet* was related to perceived declines in *family* time but not related to *family* communication (Lee & Chae, 2007).

The assessment as to whether more time spent together is a key to increased levels of intimacy is a complicated question. For couples, less time together may decrease feelings of connection, which subsequently interferes with successful relationship factors including understanding, meeting one another's needs, and space to share personal disclosures essential to intimacy (Bodenmann et al., 2007). For example, time spent on video gaming has more effect on relationships than content (Coyne et al., 2012; Northrup & Smith, 2016). Yet in cases where couples cannot spend time together in person, online interactions offer a feasible alternative because of the opportunity to gain social or emotional support (Hertlein & Ancheta, 2014; Murray & Campbell, 2015).

## Online Victimization

Another boundary issue associated with the accessibility and affordability of technology is cyberbullying. Cyberbullying, for both the victim and perpetrator, is associated with impulsiveness (Floros, Simos, Fisoun, Dafouli, & Geroukalis, 2013) and tied to the affordability and accessibility of technology. For teens, the daily visibility one has to their peers fuels their jealousy and can result in harassment via text and other apps that will be delivered instantly (Rueda et al., 2015). Parents who make use of security measures on children's devices can offer more protection to reduce cyberbullying, though it is not guaranteed to prevent victimization (Floros et al., 2013).

## Using Technology to Establish more Productive Roles, Rules, and Boundaries

### *Effective Roles, Rules, and Boundaries in Couples*

The same elements of technology and new media which contribute to disrupted roles, rules, and boundaries also provide opportunities to assist couples and families in developing new and adaptive roles, rules, and boundaries. In couples, there are new rules for developing relationships, namely where and how couples can meet (e.g., online dating sites and apps). These rules may allow individuals to meet more people because they believe that technology will protect them from making an ill-advised connection. The accessibility of technology and its affordability assist in meeting new partners (Couch & Liamputtong, 2008; Hertlein, 2012; Hertlein & Ancheta, 2014; Murray & Campbell, 2015). Technology changes the standard social rules that males are most likely to initiate a social or romantic connection, and technology increases the number of potential people with whom to form a relationship in cost-effective ways. Further, meeting online is now one of the most acceptable ways to meet people and may become the rule as opposed to the deviation from the norm (Hertlein & Blumer, 2013; Paul, 2014; Rosenfeld & Thomas, 2012).

Couples may establish rules about how to resolve conflict in their relationship, which, when followed, advance relationship satisfaction (Perry & Werner-Wilson, 2011). In regard to recurring arguments between partners, many couples (85%) reported using both online and offline communication methods to resolve the issues, and 81.3% reported using two different types of online modalities to resolve the issue (Perry & Werner-Wilson, 2011). One study found couples are more successful at resolving a conflict when multiple modes of technology are engaged (Caughlin & Sharabi, 2013). In another study though, integration of multiple technologically mediated communication channels during serial arguments was negatively associated with relational closeness and satisfaction for dating partners (Pusateri, Roache, & Wang, 2015).

In terms of boundaries, the Internet allows more access to relationships with permeable boundaries between the individual and the external world. It also means, however, that there can be more permeable boundaries between each partner in the relationship, this resulting in more commitment (Hertlein & Blumer, 2013), spicing up the couple's sex life (Hertlein, 2016), and providing a communication channel that would not otherwise exist in long-distance relationships (Hertlein & Ancheta, 2014; Rea et al., 2015). The Internet may enable couples to develop idiosyncratic patterns, which can promote couple identity and a sense of connection specific to one another.

### *Effective Roles, Rules, and Boundaries in Families*

The fact that the communication on the Internet is ambiguous can highlight the importance of setting rules for how people communicate with each other and with members outside the family. When youth begin using a cell phone it is time to establish ground rules for how they communicate with peers and parents, how they alert parents of important news and events, etc. Parents can monitor cell phone use, dictate when and where a child is using the phone simply by taking the device or suspending service, limit the phone numbers that can be called on the phone, and manage access to certain sites via blocking programs. Much of the literature related to technology use by youth suggests that using technology is an effective way to build relationships while having some appropriate boundaries in place (Fitton et al., 2013). Positive outcomes have been demonstrated in cases where schools show youth how to use technology and introduce rules for technology use (Katz, Felix, & Gubernick, 2014).

How online behavior approximates offline behavior, gives youth an opportunity to develop their identity, gain social skills, experiment with limit setting, social mores, and appropriate means for emotional regulation in positive ways. Adolescents perceive technology as an integral part of their daily lives which assists them in problem solving, increases their feelings of self-efficacy both socially and intellectually, and aids in the development of coping skills (Fitton et al., 2013). Parents who allow adolescents the use of technology for these functions tend to be seen more positively by their children and thereby improve communication with them.

Finally, the accessibility, affordability, and acceptability of technology as a daily communication tool can inspire relationships beyond the traditional parent child roles. How adult children navigate relationships with their parents in a digital age can positively establish adaptable and appropriate roles in the family system. For example, gaming and other activities shared online can be an accessible and affordable way to bridge geographical as well as emotional differences between generations (Kooiman & Sheehan, 2014).

## Conclusion

The Couple and Family Technology framework delineates the complex interaction of ways the Internet affects family roles, rules, and relationships, both positively and negatively. Whether a new modality will positively or negatively affect one's life may depend on the nature of the relationship (whether it is couple or family), the type of relationship dynamic already established, the goals and motivation involved in the Internet activity chosen, and many other factors. Scholars should continue to investigate the circumstances which promote advantages of technology use in couple and family life as well as the nuances of how roles, rules, and boundaries continue to evolve in conjunction with new media.

## References

Bacigalupe, G., & Lambe, S. (2011). Virtualizing intimacy: Information communication technologies and transnational families in therapy. *Family Process, 50*(1), 12–26. https://doi.org/10.1111/j.1545-5300.2010.01343.x

Bell, N. J., Baron, E., Corson, K., Kostina-Ritchey, E., & Frederick, H. (2014). Parent–adolescent decision making: Embracing dialogical complexity. *Journal of Family Issues, 35*(13), 1780–1799. https://doi.org/10.1177/0192513X13480339

Blinka, L., Škařupová, K., & Mitterova, K. (2016). Dysfunctional impulsivity in online gaming addiction and engagement. *Cyberpsychology, 10*(3). https://doi.org/10.5817/CP2016-3-5

Bodenmann, G., Charvoz, L., Bradbury, T. N., Bertoni, A., Iafrate, R., Giuliani, C., ... Behling, J. (2007). The role of stress in divorce: A three-nation retrospective study. *Journal of Social and Personal Relationships, 24*(5), 707–728 https://doi.org/10.1177/0265407507081456

Campbell, E. C., & Murray, C. E. (2015). Measuring the impact of technology on couple relationships: The development of the Technology and Intimate Relationship Assessment. *Journal of Couple & Relationship Therapy, 14*(3), 254–276. https://doi.org/10.1080/15332691.2014.953657

Carvalho, J., Francisco, R., & Relvas, A. (2015). Family functioning and information and communication technologies: How do they relate? A literature review. *Computers in Human Behavior, 45*, 99–108. https://doi.org/10.1016/j.chb.2014.11.037

Caughlin, J. P., & Sharabi, L. L. (2013). A communicative interdependence perspective of close relationships: The connections between mediated and unmediated interactions matter. *Journal of Communication, 63*(5), 873–893. https://doi.org/10.1111/jcom.12046

Couch, D., & Liamputtong, P. (2008). Online dating and mating: The use of the internet to meet sexual partners. *Qualitative Health Research, 18*(2), 268–279. https://doi.org/10.1177/1049732307312832

Coyne, S. M., Busby, D., Bushman, B. J., Gentile, D. A., Ridge, R., & Stockdale, L. (2012). Gaming in the game of love: Effects of video games on conflict in couples. *Family Relations, 61*(3), 388–396. https://doi.org/10.1111/j.1741-3729.2012.00712.x

Derks, D., & Bakker, A. B. (2014). Smartphone use, work–home interference, and burnout: A diary study on the role of recovery. *Applied Psychology: An International Review, 63*(3), 411–440. https://doi.org/10.1111/j.1464-0597.2012.00530.x

Dimmick, J., Feaster, J. C., & Ramirez, A. (2011). The niches of interpersonal media: Relationships in time and space. *New Media & Society, 13*(8), 1265–1282. https://doi.org/10.1177/1461444811403445

Draucker, C. B., & Martsolf, D. S. (2010). The role of electronic communication technology in adolescent dating violence. *Journal of Child and Adolescent Psychiatric Nursing, 23*(3), 133–142. https://doi.org/10.1111/j.1744-6171.2010.00235.x

Duxbury, L., Higgins, C., Smart, R., & Stevenson, M. (2014). Mobile technology and boundary permeability. *British Journal of Management, 25*(3), 570–588. https://doi.org/10.1111/1467-8551.12027

Fitton, V. A., Ahmendahi, B. K., Harold, R. D., & Schifflet, E. D. (2013). The role of technology on young adolescent development: Implications for policy, research and practice. *Child and Adolescent Social Work Journal, 30*(5), 399–413. https://doi.org/10.1007/s10560-013-0296-2

Fletcher, A. C., & Blair, B. L. (2014). Maternal authority regarding early adolescents' social technology use. Journal of Family Issues, 35(1), 54–74. doi:https://doi.org/10.1177/0192513X12467753.

Fletcher, A. C., & Blair, B. L. (2016). Implications of the family expert role for parental rules regarding adolescent use of social technologies. *New Media & Society, 18*(2), 239–256. https://doi.org/10.1177/1461444814538922

Floros, G. D., Simos, K. E., Fisoun, V., Dafouli, E., & Geroukalis, D. (2013). Adolescent online cyberbullying in Greece: The impact of parental online security practices, bonding, and online impulsiveness. *Journal of School Health, 83*(6), 445–453. https://doi.org/10.1111/josh.12049

Fox, J., & Tokunaga, R. S. (2015). Romantic partner monitoring after breakups: Attachment, dependence, distress, and post-dissolution online surveillance via social networking sites. *Cyberpsychology, Behavior, and Social Networking, 18*(9), 491–498. https://doi.org/10.1089/cyber.2015.0123

Fox, J., & Warber, K. M. (2014). Social networking sites in romantic relationships: Attachment, uncertainty, and partner surveillance on Facebook. *Cyberpsychology, Behavior, and Social Networking, 17*(1), 3–7. https://doi.org/10.1089/cyber.2012.0667

Fraenkel, P. (1994). Time and rhythm in couples. *Family Process, 33*(1), 37–51.

Haddon, L. (2006). The contribution of domestication research to in-home computing and media consumption. *The Information Society, 22*(4), 195–203. https://doi.org/10.1080/01972240600791325

Helsper, E. J., & Whitty, M. T. (2010). Netiquette within married couples: Agreement about acceptable online behavior and surveillance between partners. *Computers in Human Behavior, 26*(5), 916–926. https://doi.org/10.1016/j.chb.2010.02.006

Hertlein, K. M. (2012). Digital dwelling: Technology in couple and family relationships. *Family Relations, 61*(3), 374–387. https://doi.org/10.1111/j.1741-3729.2012.00702.x

Hertlein, K. M. (2016). "Your cyberplace or mine?": Electronic fantasy dates. In G. R. Weeks, S. T. Fife, & C. M. Peterson (Eds.), *Techniques for the couple therapist: Essential interventions from the experts* (pp. 182–185). New York: Routledge.

Hertlein, K. M., & Ancheta, K. (2014). Advantages and disadvantages of technology in relationships: Findings from an open-ended survey. *The Qualitative Report, 19*(11), 1–11.

Hertlein, K. M., & Blumer, M. L. C. (2013). *The couple and family technology framework: Intimate relationships in a digital age*. New York: Routledge.

Hertlein, K. M., Dulley, C., Cloud, R., Leon, D., & Chang, J. (2017). Does absence of evidence mean evidence of absence: Managing the issue of partner surveillance in infidelity recovery. *Sexual and Relationship Therapy, 32*(3–4), 323–333.

Hertlein, K. M., & Stevenson, A. (2010). The seven "as" contributing to internet-related intimacy problems: A literature review. *Cyberpsychology: Journal of Psychosocial Research on Cyberspace, 4*(1), 1–8.

Hitsch, G. J., Hortacsu, A., & Ariely, D. (2010). Matching and sorting in online dating. *The American Economic Review, 100*(1), 130–163. https://doi.org/10.1257/aer.100.1.130

Internet World Stats (2018). Internet usage statistics: The Internet big picture. Retrieved from: www.internetworldstats.com/stats.htm. Accessed May 2018.

Katz, R. L., Felix, M., & Gubernick, M. (2014). Technology and adolescents: Perspectives on the things to come. *Education and Information Technologies, 19*(4), 863–886. https://doi.org/10.1007/s10639-013-9258-8

Kooiman, B. J., & Sheehan, D. P. (2014). Intergenerational remote exergaming with family and friends for health and leisure. *Journal of Intergenerational Relationships, 12*(4), 413–424. https://doi.org/10.1080/15350770.2014.962442

Lanigan, J. D. (2009). A sociotechnological model for family research and intervention: How information and communication technologies affect family life. *Marriage & Family Review, 45*(6–8), 587–609. https://doi.org/10.1080/01494920903224194

Lanigan, J. D., Bold, M., & Chenoweth, L. (2009). Computers in the family context: Perceived impact on family time and relationships. *Family Science Review, 14*(1), 16–32 Retrieved from: http://www.familyscienceassociation.org/sites/default/files/2Jane_Lanigan.pdf

Lee, S., & Chae, Y. (2007). Children's internet use in a family context: Influence on family relationships and parental mediation. *Cyberpsychology & Behavior, 10*(5), 640–644.

Lindell, A. K., Campione-Barr, N., & Killoren, S. E. (2015). Technology-mediated communication with siblings during the transition to college: Associations with relationship positivity and self-disclosure. *Family Relations, 64*(4), 563–578. https://doi.org/10.1111/fare.12133

Livingstone, S. (2003). Children's use of the internet: Reflections on the emerging research agenda. *New Media and Society, 5*(2), 147–166.

McDaniel, B. T., & Coyne, S. M. (2016). "Technoference": The interference of technology in couple relationships and implications for women's personal and relational well-being. *Psychology of Popular Media Culture, 5*(1), 85–98. https://doi.org/10.1037/ppm0000065

McKenna, K. Y. A., & Bargh, J. A. (2000). Plan 9 from cyberspace: The implications of the internet for personality and social psychology. *Personality and Social Psychology Review, 4*(1), 57–75. https://doi.org/10.1207/S15327957PSPR0401_6

Miller-Ott, A. E., Kelly, L., & Duran, R. L. (2012). The effects of cell phone usage rules on satisfaction in romantic relationships. *Communication Quarterly, 60*(1), 17–34. https://doi.org/10.1080/01463373.2012.642263

Morgan, P., Hubler, D. S., Payne, P. B., Pomeroy, C., Gregg, D., & Homer, M. (2016). My partner's media use: A qualitative study exploring perceptions of problems with a partner's media use. *Marriage & Family Review, 53*(7), 683–695. https://doi.org/10.1080/01494929.2016.1263589

Murray, C. E., & Campbell, E. C. (2015). The pleasures and perils of technology in intimate relationships. *Journal of Couple & Relationship Therapy, 14*(2), 116–140. https://doi.org/10.1080/15332691.2014.953651

Neustaedter, C., Harrison, S., & Sellen, A. J. (2013). *Connecting families: The impact of new communication technologies on domestic life*. New York: Springer.

Northrup, J., & Smith, J. (2016). Effects of Facebook maintenance behaviors on partners' experience of love. *Contemporary Family Therapy, 38*(2), 245–253. https://doi.org/10.1007/s10591-016-9379-5

Papp, L. M., Danielewicz, J., & Cayemberg, C. (2012). "Are we Facebook official?" Implications of dating partners' Facebook use and profiles for intimate relationship satisfaction. *Cyberpsychology, Behavior and Social Networking, 15*(2), 85–90. https://doi.org/10.1089/cyber.2011.0291

Paul, A. (2014). Is online better than offline for meeting partners? Depends: Are you looking to marry or to date? *Cyberpsychology, Behavior, and Social Networking, 17*(10), 664–667. https://doi.org/10.1089/cyber.2014.0302

Perry, M. S., & Werner-Wilson, R. J. (2011). Couples and computer-mediated communication: A closer look at the affordances and use of the channel. *Family and Consumer Sciences Research Journal, 40*(2), 120–134. https://doi.org/10.1111/j.1552-3934.2011.02099.x

Prensky, M. (2001). Digital natives, digital immigrants part 2: Do they really think differently? *On the Horizon, 9*(6), 1–6. https://doi.org/10.1108/10748120110424843

Pusateri, K. B., Roache, D. J., & Wang, N. (2015). The role of communication technologies in serial arguments: A communicative interdependence perspective. *Argumentation and Advocacy, 52*(1), 44–60. https://doi.org/10.1177/0265407509106719

Rea, J., Behnke, A., Huff, N., & Allen, K. (2015). The role of online communication in the lives of military spouses. *Contemporary Family Therapy, 37*(3), 329–339. https://doi.org/10.1007/s10591-015-9346-6

Rosenfeld, M. J., & Thomas, R. J. (2012). Searching for a mate: The rise of the internet as a social intermediary. *American Sociological Review, 77*(4), 523–547. https://doi.org/10.1177/0003122412448050

Rueda, H. A., Lindsay, M., & Williams, L. R. (2015). She posted it on Facebook: Mexican American adolescents' experiences with technology and romantic relationship conflict. *Journal of Adolescent Research, 30*(4), 419–445. https://doi.org/10.1177/0743558414565236

Schade, L. C., Sandberg, J., Bean, R., Busby, D., & Coyne, S. (2013). Using technology to connect in romantic relationships: Effects on attachment, relationship satisfaction, and stability in emerging adults. *Journal of Couple & Relationship Therapy, 12*(4), 314–338. https://doi.org/10.1080/15332691.2013.836051

Teng, Y., & Wang, S. (2015). The use of communication technologies by dating couples to maintain romantic relationship. *Mass Communication Research, 122*(1), 121–168.

Tokunaga, R. S. (2015). Interpersonal surveillance over social network sites: Applying a theory of negative relational maintenance and the investment model. *Journal of Social and Personal Relationships, 33*(2), 171–190. https://doi.org/10.1177/0265407514568749

Vaterlaus, J. M., Beckert, T. E., Tulane, S., & Bird, C. V. (2014). "They always ask what I'm doing and who I'm talking to": Parental mediation of adolescent interactive technology use. *Marriage & Family Review, 50*(8), 691–713. https://doi.org/10.1080/01494929.2014.938795

Wang, K., Zhou, M., & Zhang, Z. (2017). Can insecurely attached dating couples get compensated on social network sites? – The effect of surveillance. *Computers in Human Behavior, 73*, 303–310. https://doi.org/10.1016/j.chb.2017.03.046

Williams, A. L., & Merten, M. J. (2011). iFamily: Internet and social media technology in the family context. *Family and Consumer Sciences Research Journal, 40*(2), 150–170. https://doi.org/10.1111/j.1552-3934.2011.02101.x

Wray-Lake, L., Crouter, A. C., & McHale, S. M. (2010). Developmental patterns in decision-making autonomy across middle childhood and adolescence: European American parents perspectives. *Child Development, 81*(2), 636–651. https://doi.org/10.1111/j.1467-8624.2009.01420.x

# Chapter 6
# Are Tinder and Dating Apps Changing Dating and Mating in the USA?

**Michael Rosenfeld**

The popular media coverage of Tinder and phone dating apps in general tends to favor a kind of social doomsday scenario. Tinder and phone apps are supposedly undermining relationship commitment and making everyone superficial and prone to empty hookups. In Sales' (2015) Vanity Fair story, "Tinder and the Dawn of the 'Dating Apocalypse'," all the stereotypes of online dating were presented. According to Sale's dystopian vision, people do not even look at each other anymore; they look only at their phones. Young heterosexual male Tinder users claimed to be using Tinder and other phone apps to hook up with 100 new women per year. Men, however, have been known to exaggerate their sexual exploits (Lewontin, 1995).

Hookup culture does exist (Bogle, 2008), and phone apps such as Tinder and Grindr do facilitate hookups, some of which are intentional one-night stands, and others of which start out as one-night stands and then blossom into long-term relationships. Either the hookup or the long-term relationship can be positive outcomes, depending on what the individuals want. Some individuals want neither long-term relationships nor hookups but may prefer nothing more than an occasional flirtation; phone dating apps can provide simple flirtations as well.

One of life course theory's central themes is that an individual's roles change over the life course, and behavior necessarily changes across the life course as roles change (Elder, 1975). Adults are perfectly capable of going through a phase of hookups without any commitment and then transitioning to committed relationships in a later life stage (Bogle, 2008). One of the misleading ingredients in Sales' (2015) article is the implication that the reliance on hookups among young single subjects portends the end of committed relationships for everyone (i.e., the "dating apocalypse").

In scholarly writing about the Internet's effect on social interaction, negative views of the Internet's supposed impact predominate (Rosenfeld, 2017), much as

M. Rosenfeld (✉)
Department of Sociology, Stanford University, Stanford, CA, USA
e-mail: mrosenfe@stanford.edu



J. Van Hook et al. (eds.), *Families and Technology*, National Symposium on Family Issues 9, https://doi.org/10.1007/978-3-319-95540-7_6

negative views of Internet dating predominate in the popular press. Turkle (2011, 2015), one of the most prominent scholarly Internet skeptics, has argued that the new technologies have robbed us of the skills to be effective listeners in face-to-face interactions, because the cell phone in one's pocket is potentially always distracting one's attention away from the people who are physically present. Depression and anxiety are associated with overuse of online social networking (Primack et al., Chap. 9). If the Internet undermines our relationships, then the social effects of the Internet are to be feared.

Some couples have trouble managing the boundaries between their relationship and the outside world, because the Internet and the cell phone erode those boundaries (Hertlein, Chap. 5). Couples who disagree about how to manage the technology in their lives often find themselves in couples' therapy, leaving therapeutic professionals to see mainly the downsides and dysfunctions of technology's incorporation into personal life. However, there is potential for new technologies to be adaptive and assistive in relationships (Hertlein, Chap. 5). The positive impacts of technology on relationships are less visible to therapeutic professionals though, because people who have healthy relationships and who have found appropriate norms and positive ways to use new technologies do not generally seek relationship therapy. Positive views of the Internet's effect on social relationships at the population level have been offered (Glassner, 2010; McKenna & Bargh, 2000; Wellman, 2001). It is reasonable to assume that new technologies may have negative effects on some individuals and positive effects on others. A composite of negative effects of technology on some individuals and positive effects on others could yield neutral effects of technology in the aggregate.

Some scholars and journalists have claimed that romantic relationships formed online are necessarily shallow and less committed (Manning, 2006; Slater, 2013; Turkle, 2011, 2015; Weigel, 2016; Young, 1998) compared to relationships formed offline. Research with nationally representative data, however, has shown that couples who meet online are no more likely to break up (Cacioppo, Cacioppo, Gonzaga, Ogburn, & VanderWeele, 2013; Rosenfeld, 2017; Rosenfeld & Thomas, 2012). In contrast to the predictions about how online dating might undermine the stability of romantic relationships, heterosexual couples who met through online dating transitioned to marriage more quickly (Rosenfeld, 2017).

One potential reason for the faster transition to marriage for couples who met through Internet dating may be that wider availability of partners online leads to better matches. To the extent that mate selection is an information gathering process (Oppenheimer, 1988), the greater amount of information available on Internet dating websites may allow couples to gather information about each other more quickly. Selection bias is a third potential reason for faster transitions to marriage for couples who met through Internet dating: marriage-ready individuals may select themselves into Internet dating.

In this chapter, I endeavor to measure the impact of Tinder and other phone dating apps on dating and on existing romantic relationships in the USA. I find that, except for gay men who are avid users of the phone apps (Grindr especially), phone dating apps are having only a very modest impact on Americans' romantic lives.

Despite the claims that Tinder, Grindr, and phone dating apps in general have created an environment of non-stop hookups, I show that the majority of unpartnered heterosexual men and women in the USA, more than 80% in fact, have not gone on any dates in the past 12 months. Far from being oversexed, heterosexual Americans who are unmarried and unpartnered appear to be in something of a relationship drought, or perhaps they are satisfied with their single status and not working too energetically to acquire a partner. The viability of singlehood as a permanent or semi-permanent adult status has increased over time (Klinenberg, 2012) as the age at first marriage has increased (Rosenfeld, 2007), and as interest in remarriage (especially among older women) has declined (Rosenfeld, 2018). In this chapter I employ in-depth interview data and new nationally representative survey data to explore how, how often, and why American adults use phone dating apps such as Tinder and Grindr.

According to 2017 survey data from the project, How Couples Meet and Stay Together, only 18.7% of unpartnered heterosexual men and only 11.4% of unpartnered heterosexual women in the USA went on any dates in the past 12 months (see Table 6.2 below). That means more than 80% of unpartnered heterosexual American adults report meeting exactly zero people for dates or hookups in the past 12 months. Heterosexuals who used Tinder and other phone apps to meet people for sex or romance in the past 12 months met an average of 5 people for sex or romance in the last 12 months, far less than the scores or hundreds of hookups claimed by the people interviewed by Sales (2015). Perhaps Sales was talking to an unusually sexually active and popular subset of American men. Our in-depth interviews about Tinder and dating reflect the same order of magnitude of dates and hookups per year as do the nationally representative data: between zero and five dates or hookups with new people per year. It may be that the sexuality and attractiveness of Sales' subjects (with their 100 partners per year) was exaggerated for the audience's titillation. It would not be the first time that sex and hyperbolic descriptions of technology's impact were combined to drive some other goal, such as readership or viewership, or conservative political action.

Recent moral panics have occurred over behaviors that purportedly document the sexual profligacy among American youth (e.g., sex bracelets, rainbow parties; Best & Bogle, 2014). Sex bracelets were said to be colored bracelets that adolescent girls wear to symbolize which sexual acts they had experienced. Rainbow parties were those at which adolescent girls wearing different colored lipsticks are reported to have given oral sex to adolescent boys, resulting in rainbow striped penises. Both the sex bracelet and the rainbow party stories were widely covered in the popular media, but the stories were unsubstantiated (Best & Bogle, 2014). Moral panic can occur when fear and uncertainty override and drown out data and information. Sexuality and technology are subjects that stimulate fear and anxiety, and therefore, sexuality and technology are natural terrain for moral panic.

Social media use and phone dating have risks, some of which are new and specific to the cell phone. Sending nude pictures of oneself to a partner or a potential partner is sexting. When the recipient of the intimate pictures shares them indiscriminately that translates to revenge porn, a problem that has potential elements of harassment and extortion (Jeong, 2013; Lohmann, 2013). The new technologies are certainly not without potential dangers and pitfalls, but Internet dating and phone apps do have some unique advantages as well. For instance, it is much easier to block unwanted advances on Tinder compared to blocking the unwanted advances of someone who is standing next to you at a bar or party. The ability of phone dating apps to quickly and permanently block anyone who makes unwanted advances is one reason some of our female interviewees felt that phone dating apps have improved the safety of dating and hooking up (see Massey (2015) for descriptions of the feminist utility of using Tinder to reduce men's control over dating.) The interesting question is whether and for whom the benefits of the new technologies outweigh the risks and pitfalls.

## The Data

I rely on two distinct data sources. The first data source is in-depth interviews (lasting 2–4 h) with ten adult subjects about Tinder and dating. These ten Tinder-related interviews, conducted in 2015 and 2016 by myself and students, Taylor Orth, Fiona Kelliher, and Sandy Lee, are part of a larger body of more than 50 in-depth interviews with individuals and couples in the San Francisco Bay Area about relationships and breakups. The interviews were recorded and transcribed. All names and identifying details have been changed.

The second data source is the 2017 cohort of the How Couples Meet and Stay Together study (hereafter HCMST 2017; for prior waves 1–5 of public data from the HCMST 2009 cohort, see Rosenfeld, Thomas, & Falcon, 2015), a nationally representative study of 3510 American adults in the summer of 2017 (Rosenfeld, Thomas, & Hausen, 2018). Of the 3510 adults surveyed, 2856 had a current spouse or partner; 538 subjects were unpartnered; and an additional 107 subjects (mostly young adults) reported never having had a boyfriend, girlfriend, romantic partner, or sexual partner. The HCMST 2017 definition of current partner is a broader definition than most surveys use, including not only spouses, boyfriends, girlfriends, romantic partners, and sexual partners, but also including a "romantic partner who is not yet a sexual partner." Therefore, unpartnered subjects in HCMST 2017 are, as far as can be determined, *truly* unpartnered. The 107 subjects who reported never having had a romantic partner are not included in the analyses below. According to the weighted HCMST 2017 data, 61% of heterosexual American adults are married, 20% are partnered but not married, 15% are unpartnered (but had at least one partner in the past), and 4% (mostly men in their 20s) have never had a partner. HCMST 2017 oversampled self-identified gay, lesbian, and bisexual subjects who are more likely to meet partners online than are heterosexuals (Rosenfeld & Thomas, 2012). Of the 3394 HCMST 2017 subjects who had ever had a sexual or romantic partner, 551 self-identified as gay, lesbian, or bisexual.

HCMST 2017 subjects were asked about dating and hookups in the past 12 months: "In the past year, have you ever met someone for dating, for romance, or for sex?" If they answered *yes*, the next question asked how many people they had met for dating, romance, or sex in the past year, with closed ended choices of: *1 person*, *2–5 people*, *6–20 people*, *21–50 people*, and *more than 50 people*. I took the median of each category as the number of people met and used the value of 75 for the number of people met last year for the two HCMST 2017 subjects who said they met more than 50 people in the prior 12 months. Subjects with spouses or current partners were asked the same questions about meeting people for dates, romance, or sex in the previous 12 months, with the clarifying clause "besides (partner name)" where partner name is the name they reported for their current spouse or partner. HCMST 2017 allows for estimates of the dating behavior of both partnered and single adults in the USA. Subjects who had met at least one person in the past 12 months for dating, romance, or sex in the past year were asked "In the past year, have you ever used an app on your phone (such as Tinder or Grindr) to meet someone in person for dating, romance, or sex?" and the follow-up question asked, "Of the people you met in the past year, how many did you meet using phone apps (such as Tinder or Grindr)?"

HCMST 2017 includes information about fidelity and monogamy of married and currently partnered adults, and how much of the infidelity or nonmonogamy might be associated with phone apps or Internet dating. The results in Tables 6.1 and 6.2 are weighted by the variable "weight_combo," which weights the population to demographic benchmarks from the Current Population Survey, and which also accounts for the oversample of self-identified lesbian, gay, or bisexual adults in HCMST 2017.

The survey data and the interview data complement each other. The survey data provide a representative snapshot of how often US adults go on dates or meet people for hookups, and how they find their partners. The non-representative interview data provide detail and insight into why people make the dating choices they make. In order to understand the *why*, one has to talk to subjects face-to-face in an unscripted way, for long enough to make them comfortable telling their stories, and long enough for the interviewers to be able to understand their motivations. I begin with summaries of two interviews.

## *How Phone Dating Apps Are Used*

**Subject: Wilson** Wilson is an engaging Filipino-American man in his mid-30s. In his 20s, he had a series of three long-term cohabiting relationships with women, none of which ended well. His high school girlfriend was from a higher social class than Wilson and reminded him of this unequal origin from time to time. Wilson dated his high school girlfriend into college and found that she treated him badly, sometimes giving him the cold shoulder. Eventually, they broke up.

Wilson's second girlfriend was a woman he lived with for 4 years after college. Wilson describes this woman as engaging and charismatic, but also moody and difficult. On several occasions, Wilson came home and found that some of his belongings were missing from the apartment. He eventually found that his belongings had been dropped out of the apartment window onto the parking lot below. On one occasion, as he was previewing his slides at work just before a presentation, he found that a slide of pornography had been inserted into his presentation. His girlfriend later admitted to adding the slide. They broke up when the girlfriend moved away for professional school, and Wilson says that she is the only girlfriend he has ever missed.

Wilson's third girlfriend was mature, organized, successful, but was constantly berating Wilson to get a promotion at work, marry her, make a plan to settle down, and have children. Wilson felt he was not ready to get married and have children, nor was he particularly interested in a promotion at work. He liked to have time free on the weekends for video games, but this girlfriend wanted to schedule all his free time. After 3 years together, they broke up. Wilson's three long-term girlfriends each contributed evidence to his view that, "women are crazy."

Wilson is a refugee from the land of committed relationships. His three cohabiting relationships were full of struggle and drama, none of which he misses in his current state of living alone. His current dating strategy is hookups arranged via phone dating apps, mainly Tinder. He appreciates the fact that most of the women he meets through Tinder do not want a relationship any more than he does. In the past 3 years, he has used phone dating apps to meet with 12 separate women and had sex with 10 of them. Of the 10 women he had sex with, he saw only one woman more than once, and that occasional hookup relationship lasted 3 months.

The yield for Wilson, in terms of sexual frequency, or sexual encounters per year divided by time spent on the phone dating apps, is low compared to the sexual frequency of married people, for instance. (Married people report having sex about twice a week; see Laumann, Gagnon, Michael, & Michaels, 1994.) One of the basic rules of sex and relationships is that married people, and people with cohabiting partners, have more sex because they have solved the problem of sexual access (Laumann et al., 1994; Waite & Gallagher, 2000). Tinder and phone dating apps have not entirely removed the barriers that make it difficult for strangers to hook up. Lining up a date with a stranger is and always will be emotionally taxing. Even flirting with people who one never plans to go on dates with is time consuming, as is making arrangements for dates that might not actually take place.

Wilson opens Tinder on his phone Friday and Saturday afternoons, swipes right on a few pictures, and tries to find a local woman who is interested in meeting up that night. He says 60% of the women on Tinder check "yes" that they are willing to hook up. He ignores the other 40%. In his view, Tinder is not a place where anyone should expect to find long-term relationships; that would be "like shopping for filet mignon at Target." He finds Tinder women to be even more interested in a no-strings-attached encounter than he is. The women he messages on Tinder follow a clear pattern of not over-messaging and not over-sharing. They never talk about commitment or about the possibility of settling down one day. A few short texts, a meeting, a hookup, and then they part ways. He says women usually ask him a few questions to make sure he is not an ax murderer and then, according to Wilson, "they get down to business."

**Subject: Shae** Shae is an attractive white woman in her mid-20s. She grew up in a small town in the Midwest. Her mother knew the other mothers in town. Communication between the mothers meant that when Shae was in high school she was never able to spend time in a room alone with a boyfriend, because the mothers did not allow it. When Shae went away to college, she was frustrated and wanted to have a lot of experiences to catch up. She became a party girl in college, meeting young men, hooking up, and making out.

Shae had one bad experience in college in which she was drunk at a party. A male student she knew from political work offered to drive her home, but instead, he drove her to his place and groped her. She was too drunk and disoriented to do anything about it. This sour experience that Shae recognizes as a sexual assault dampened her enthusiasm for partying. She never told her friends or the college authorities about it.

Shae had two serious boyfriends after college, but neither relationship lasted. Neither boyfriend was popular with Shae's friends because both boyfriends were, in retrospect, "jerks." The problem, Shae realized, was that the kind of young men who sought her out at parties were the alphas–strong, tall, self-assured, take-charge young men. Shae was attracted to the alpha men at first but always found that their views on politics and relationships were out of step with her own; she describes herself as a "flag waving feminist." If there were more compatible men in Shae's social circle, Shae found that she did not get to know them well enough. The alpha males had gotten to her first, and Shae was too shy to push past the alphas at the party and find the nerdy politically progressive and quieter young men she might have been more compatible with.

One advantage that Shae experienced immediately with Tinder was her ability to be agentic about whom she was in communication with. Both parties in Tinder have to swipe right on each other's profile in order to start communicating. Even after swiping right, if the other person sent messages Shae did not like, the other party was easy to block. Once blocked, the other party would never be heard from again.

Shae met Danny through Tinder, and he was her first Tinder date. Shae was on the way to meet friends one Friday afternoon but decided to bail out on her friend's plan and log on to Tinder instead. She swiped on Danny's profile then messaged him and arranged to meet him for dinner. After dinner, when Shae said, "Let's go back to your place," she could tell that Danny was happy but was a bit flustered, and she liked flustering him. They had sex that night. Danny had been on two Tinder dates before, neither of which ended up with more than a kiss on the cheek, so Danny was not expecting sex on his first date with Shae. Danny was shy and soft spoken, two things Shae immediately liked about him.

Shae did not necessarily expect to immediately hear from Danny again, but the next day he did text her. She went on a few dates with other people she met on Tinder, but she found the men boring. Two months after first meeting Danny, Shae proposed that they date exclusively, and Danny was a little bit surprised that Shae had been seeing other people. The next month, they officially became boyfriend and girlfriend, and now they live together. Danny is the most important person in Shae's life; her first ever live-in boyfriend; her first partner who has treated her the way she wants to be treated; and she met him through a Tinder hookup. They have been together for 3 years.

For Shae, Tinder had immediate advantages. She was in control of who she would communicate with in a way that gave her more agency than she had had in face-to-face social situations. Compared to being at a bar, being on Tinder allows people to break off communication with others who irritate them and sift through candidates more safely before first face-to-face contact. One of the critiques of Tinder and the various new online dating technologies is that the new technologies undermine relationship commitment. The nationally representative data and stories like Shae's tend to paint the phone apps and Internet dating in general in a more commitment-neutral light.

## *What the Survey Data Show*

**Dating Habits of Married and Partnered Adults** How reflective are the interview stories of the experience of all adults in the USA? To answer that question, I turn to the survey data. Table 6.1 shows an analysis of dating and hooking up in the previous 12 months among HCMST subjects who had a current partner at the time of HCMST 2017 and had been in the relationship since at least 2015. Since all respondents represented in Table 6.1 were partnered at the time of HCMST 2017, the questions they were asked about dating in the past 12 months were prefaced with, "besides partner name" (where partner name is that of their current spouse or partner), and the dating and hookup behavior reported in Table 6.1 excludes dates with their current partner. Table 6.1 describes dating or hooking up that would fall into the categories of either nonmonogamy or infidelity.

Table 6.1 shows that for married heterosexual people, only a very small percentage (3.4% of men and 1.6% of women) admitted to meeting someone other than their spouse in the past 12 months for dating, romance, or sex. Men may be more prone to marital infidelity, or men may be more willing to admit infidelities. For heterosexual men and women, and for lesbians, being married (as compared to being partnered but not married) is associated with a sharp reduction in percentage of subjects who said they met someone other than their partner for dating, romance, or sex in the past 12 months. For heterosexual men, being married reduces the percentage of men who date outside the relationship from 18.6 to 3.4%, and for heterosexual women, being married reduces the percentage of outside dating from 14.4 to 1.6%. For lesbians, being married reduces the percentage who date outside the relationship from 30 to 3%.

For gay men, however, being partnered or married appears to be uncorrelated with monogamy. Twenty four percent of gay men who were partnered but not

**Table 6.1** Dating and meeting partners other than main partner in the last 12 months (for subjects *with* a current partner or spouse)

| Subject gender | Male | Male | Female | Female | Male | Male | Female | Female |
|---|---|---|---|---|---|---|---|---|
| Partner gender | Female | Female | Male | Male | Male | Male | Female | Female |
| Married | No | Yes | No | Yes | No | Yes | No | Yes |
| *n* | 260 | 1028 | 374 | 976 | 82 | 44 | 61 | 31 |
| Mean relationship duration at HCMST 2017 (years) | 6.3 | 26.2 | 6.7 | 26.8 | 10.6 | 15.7 | 6.6 | 18.2 |
| Percent who met at least one person for dating, romance, or sex (beside current partner) in last 12 months | 18.6 | 3.4 | 14.4 | 1.6 | 24 | 21 | 30 | 3 |
| Mean number of people met for dating, romance, or sex (beside current partner) in last 12 months | 0.9 | 0.1 | 0.4 | 0.04 | 1.4 | 2.6 | 0.7 | # |
| Mean number of people met for dating, romance, or sex (beside current partner) in last 12 months, if met at least one person | 4.9 | 3.2 | 2.9 | 2.5 | 5.9 | 12.0 | 2.4 | # |
| Mean number of people met through phone apps for dating, romance, or sex (beside current partner) in last 12 months, if met at least one person in any way | 1.0 | 0.5 | 1.0 | 0.3 | 5.0 | 8.0 | 0.4 | # |
| Percentage of all dates that were met through phone apps | 20 | 16 | 34 | 12 | 85 | 67 | 17 | # |

Source: HCMST 2017; weighted by weight_combo. Relationships formed in 2016 or 2017 were excluded so that all current relationships began in 2015 or earlier to ensure that current relationships would have been in effect for the 12 months prior to the survey; HCMST 2017 was fielded in July, 2017. There was only one woman with a female married partner who reported meeting anyone other than the spouse in the previous 12 months, so those cells have too small a sample to report averages and have the symbol # instead

married and 21% of gay men who were married said they met someone other than the spouse or partner for dating, romance, or sex in the past 12 months. Given the fact that gay male relationships are more stable than lesbian relationships in the USA (controling for marital status; see Rosenfeld, 2014), it is possible that gay male relationships have a higher tolerance for nonmonogamy (D'Emilio, 2002).

Note that among the dates and hookups that married heterosexuals report, only a small percentage (16% for men, 12% for women) were arranged through phone dating apps; phone dating apps were not a major draw. It is unlikely, therefore, that the existence of phone dating apps would have a destabilizing effect on heterosexual marriages in the USA, as most heterosexual marital nonmonogamy and infidelity seems to have been arranged in other ways.

**Table 6.2** Dating and meeting partners in the last 12 months for subjects *without* a current partner

| Subject gender | Men | Women | Men | Women |
|---|---|---|---|---|
| Subject LGB/straight | Straight | Straight | LGB | LGB |
| *n* | 177 | 236 | 81 | 44 |
| Percent who met at least one person for dating, romance, or sex in last 12 months | 18.7 | 11.4 | 44 | 16 |
| Mean number of people met for dating, romance, or sex in last 12 months | 0.42 | 0.55 | 3.6 | 0.7 |
| Mean number of people met for dating, romance, or sex in last 12 months, if met at least one person | 2.4 | 5.1 | 8.2 | 4.5 |
| Mean number of people met through phone apps for dating, romance, or sex in last 12 months, if met at least one person in any way | 0.2 | 1.1 | 2.8 | 2.7 |
| Percentage of all dates that were met through the phone apps | 8 | 22 | 34 | 60 |

Source: HCMST 2017; weighted by weight_combo

As has been previously noted (Rosenfeld & Thomas, 2012), same-sex couples are more likely to meet partners online than are heterosexual couples (see also McKenna & Bargh, 1998). Table 6.1 reports that 67% of the dating or hookup partners of married gay men (and 85% of the dating or hookup partners of unmarried gay men) in the past 12 months were found through phone dating apps. For gay men, Grindr (which caters exclusively to gay men) is the dominant phone app, followed in a distant second by Tinder (which promotes same-sex and different sex matches). Since there was only one married lesbian in HCMST who dated outside the marriage, the sample is too small to draw conclusions.

**Dating Habits of Adults Who Are Not Partnered** Among the heterosexual unpartnered (i.e., no spouse, boyfriend, girlfriend, sexual partner, or romantic partner) who were actively dating in the past 12 months, Table 6.2 shows a modest number of different partners from dating and hookups. According to Table 6.2, actively dating (meaning they met at least one new date or partner in the past 12 months) unpartnered heterosexual men in the USA met an average of 2.4 partners for dating or sex in the past 12 months. Unpartnered heterosexual women who were actively dating met an average of 5.1 partners in the past 12 months. These modest numbers of different people met for dating and hookups are consistent with what our interview subjects reported and with the distribution of sexual partner frequency found by Laumann et al. (1994). The results are entirely out of line with the most exaggerated reports about hookup activity from the popular press (e.g., Sales, 2015). The modest number of people met for dates or hookups in the past 12 months (2.4 for men, 5.1 for women) includes only the unpartnered heterosexual adults who were *actively* dating. The survey data show that a large majority of unpartnered heterosexual adults were meeting no one at all in the past 12 months.

Of heterosexual men in the USA who did not have a partner at the time of HCMST 2017, only 18.7% said they had met someone in the past 12 months for dating, romance, or sex. Interestingly, the percentage of heterosexual men who met at least one partner in the last 12 months is around 19% whether the men are unpartnered (Table 6.2) or partnered but not married (Table 6.1).

For heterosexual women without a current partner, only 11.4% said they met someone for a date or a hookup in the past 12 months, not statistically significantly different from the 14.4% of partnered but unmarried women who met someone in the past 12 months (Table 6.1).

There are several potential reasons why heterosexuals who are partnered but not married have the same probability of having dates and hookup partners as unpartnered heterosexuals have in finding any partners. It may be that partnered relationship status selects for people who are more appealing as partners, and that the unpartnered heterosexuals have characteristics that make them less appealing as dates. Alternatively, it may be that unpartnered heterosexuals are as committed to being single as partnered (but unmarried) heterosexuals are committed to their partners. Heterosexual relationships that lack the marital commitment appear to impose few constraints on dating outside the relationship.

For heterosexual men who did not have partners at the time of HCMST 2017, phone dating apps accounted for only 8% of women they had met in the previous 12 months. Note that even though the unpartnered heterosexual women had a lower rate of meeting people for dates, romance, or sex in the past 12 months compared to unpartnered heterosexual men (11.4% compared to 18.7%), the heterosexual women who did go on dates were more likely to have met their dates using phone apps (22% compared to 8% for heterosexual men). The greater likelihood of heterosexual women's partners to have been found through the phone apps (see Table 6.1) is an indication that phone dating apps may be more empowering or useful to women, as Shae's story illustrates.

As would be expected from prior research (Rosenfeld & Thomas, 2012), gay and lesbian respondents were much more likely than heterosexuals to meet their dates using phone apps. Interestingly, unpartnered gay men and unpartnered lesbians seem to have substantially more active dating lives than do heterosexuals. Whereas only 18% of unpartnered heterosexual men met someone for dating, romance, or sex in the past 12 months, 44% of unpartnered gay men did so. And whereas only 11.4% of unpartnered heterosexual women met someone in the past 12 months for dating, romance, or sex, 16% of unpartnered lesbians did so (though the numbers of unpartnered lesbians in HCMST 2017 is small). The dating activity gap between straight and gay Americans may suggest that the market for dating apps that appeal to heterosexuals has not yet matured. There may be a substantial pool of unmet interest among heterosexuals in finding appropriate partners.

**Who Uses Which Phone Dating Apps** Table 6.3 shows that among heterosexual American adults, only 1.4% of men and 1.3% of women reported using a phone dating app in the past 12 months to meet someone for dating, romance, or sex. There are several reasons the rate of phone dating app use among heterosexuals is so low. First, most adult heterosexuals are married, and married heterosexuals are rarely on the dating market. Second, when unmarried heterosexuals do date, they mostly use other ways of finding dates rather than phone dating apps. Third, most unpartnered

**Table 6.3** Most popular phone dating apps by gender and sexual preference

| | Straight men | Straight women | Gay men | Lesbian women |
|---|---|---|---|---|
| Most popular (*n*) | Tinder (5) | Tinder (3) Bumble (3) Plenty of fish (3) | Grindr (26) | OKCupid (3) Plenty of fish (3) |
| Second most popular (*n*) | MeetMe (3) OKCupid (3) | Match.com (2) | Tinder (9) | Tagged (2) Tinder (2) |
| Third most popular (*n*) | Match.com (2) Plenty of fish (2) | …. | Adam4Adam (5) | …. |
| *n* of phone app users who met someone through the phone app in the last 12 months | 19 | 18 | 49 | 12 |
| *n* of subjects in HCMST 2017 | 1405 | 1438 | 267 | 284 |
| Proportion of all subjects who were phone app users in the past 12 months (%) | 1.4 | 1.3 | 18.4 | 4.2 |

Source: Unweighted data from HCMST 2017

heterosexuals are not meeting anyone new. When heterosexuals are using phone dating apps, Tinder is the first choice, followed by MeetMe and OKCupid for men, and Bumble and Plenty of Fish for women.

Unlike heterosexual dating culture which has *not* been taken over by phone dating apps, gay male dating culture is powerfully driven by phone dating apps. Of the gay men in HCMST 2017, regardless of their partnership or marital status, 18.4% used a phone dating app to meet someone in the past 12 months. Among gay men, Grindr is the king of the apps, followed in a distant second by Tinder, and then Adam4Adam. One gay male interviewee reported that Grindr was a terrible app; it has a tendency to crash; and its user interface is clumsy. What it has going for it, however, is simple: the large number of gay men who are on it.

## Conclusions

For heterosexuals, the impact of phone dating apps on their dating lives has clearly been overstated in the popular press. Tinder is not, as Sales (2015) suggested, a sign of "the dating apocalypse." Most heterosexuals are stably married, and there is no evidence that phone dating apps or any other modern technology have undermined or will undermine relationship stability in the USA. Rather than following the phone dating apps to a frenzied series of dates, what is interesting about unpartnered heterosexuals is how few of them date at all. More than 80% of unpartnered heterosexual women and unpartnered heterosexual men reported meeting exactly zero new people for dates or hookups in the past 12 months. Given how few actual face-to-face dates seem to be obtained through Tinder and phone dating apps, it is possible that the main utility of phone dating apps for heterosexuals is for flirting or browsing pictures, rather than for dating or hooking up.

My findings of the romantic and sexual inactivity of unpartnered heterosexual adults in the USA do not entirely square with previous findings of the number of sexual partners that adults who are not married and not cohabiting have had in the prior year (Laumann et al., 1994). One potential reason for the discrepancy is that HCMST has a wider definition of romantic partners than other surveys have had. The unpartnered subjects in HCMST may be far outliers of romantic inactivity, a population not well enough isolated in other surveys. The National Survey of Family Growth, the leading survey of relationships and fertility in the USA, privileges marriages and cohabitation relationships over informal relationships in their survey instruments and questions. Informal relationships and unpartnered people need to be studied more, as being unpartnered is increasingly an identity that adults are comfortable with (DePaulo, 2006; Klinenberg, 2012).

It is possible that HCMST finds less romantic activity among single adults than previous surveys found because unpartnered Americans are truly having fewer dates and less romantic activity than unpartnered American adults used to have. Perhaps unpartnered status has become more stable in the USA. If unpartnered adulthood is less of an intermediate stage between long-term relationships, and more of a permanent or semi-permanent stage unto itself (as the low rate of unpartnered adults who have dates in the past year would indicate), then more research is required about what motivates and sustains adults to be unpartnered.

Among heterosexuals who have been dating, the rate of use of phone apps is higher among women than among men. Heterosexual women's faster adoption of phone dating apps might reflect advantages of security (online compared to offline). The requirement that both parties express an interest before they can communicate may advantage women, compared to the ordinary face-to-face social interactions when men expect to dominate and monopolize relationship initiatives (Sassler & Miller, 2011).

Gay men have made phone dating apps, especially Grindr, into a core part of their dating and hookup scenes. Internet dating in general is more useful to gays and lesbians than to heterosexuals, because gays and lesbians are always in a thin dating market where potential partners are difficult to identify in face-to-face social interactions (Rosenfeld & Thomas, 2012).

## Appendix: Description of the HCMST 2017 Data, Unweighted Sample Size with Weighted Row and Weighted Column Percentages

| | | Sexual identity | | |
|---|---|---|---|---|
| Relationship status | Heterosexual | Gay, lesbian, or bisexual | Sexual identity unknown | Total |
| Married | 1886 (96.8%) [63.8%] | 193 (2.9%) [35.6%] | 6 (0.4%) | 2085 (100%) [59.9%] |
| Partnered, but not married | 544 (90.0%) [21.0%] | 233 (10.0%) [43.7%] | 0 | 777 (100%) [21.2%] |
| Unpartnered, but has had a partner in the past | 413 (92.5%) [15.2%] | 125 (6.7%) [20.7%] | 3 (0.8%) | 541 (100%) [14.9%] |
| Never had a partner | 0 | 0 | 107 | 107 [4.0%] |
| Total | 2843 (90.9%) [100%] | 551 (4.9%) [100%] | 116 (4.3%) | 3510 (100%) [100%] |

## References


Best, J., & Bogle, K. A. (2014). *Kids gone wild: From rainbow parties to sexting, understanding the hype over teen sex*. New York, NY: New York University Press.

Bogle, K. A. (2008). *Hooking up: Sex, dating and relationships on campus*. New York, NY: New York University Press.

Cacioppo, J. T., Cacioppo, S., Gonzaga, G., Ogburn, E. L., & VanderWeele, T. J. (2013). Marital satisfaction and break-ups differ across on-line and off-line meeting venues. *Proceedings of the National Academy of Sciences, 110*(25), 10135–10140. https://doi.org/10.1073/pnas.1222447110

D'Emilio, J. (2002). *The world turned: Essays on gay history, politics, and culture*. Durham, NC: Duke University Press.

DePaulo, B. (2006). *Singled out: How singles are stereotyped, stigmatized, and ignored, and still live happily ever after*. New York, NY: St. Martin's Press.

Elder, G. H., Jr. (1975). Age differentiation in the life course. *Annual Review of Sociology, 1*, 165–190 Retrieved from https://www.annualreviews.org/doi/abs/10.1146/annurev.so.01.080175.001121

Glassner, B. (2010). *The culture of fear: Why Americans are afraid of the wrong things* (10th ed.). New York, NY: Basic Books.

Jeong, S. (2013). Revenge porn is bad. Criminalizing it is worse. *Wired.com*. Retrieved October 2017, from https://www.wired.com/2013/10/why-criminalizing-revenge-porn-is-a-bad-idea/

Klinenberg, E. (2012). *Going solo: The extraordinary rise and surprising appeal of living alone*. New York, NY: Penguin Press.

Laumann, E. O., Gagnon, J. H., Michael, R. T., & Michaels, S. (1994). *The social organization of sexuality: Sexual practices in the United States*. Chicago, IL: University of Chicago Press.

Lewontin, R. C. (1995, April 20). Sex, lies, and social science. *The New York Review of Books*. Retrieved from http://www.nybooks.com/articles/1995/04/20/sex-lies-and-social-science/

Lohmann, R. C. (2013, April 7). Teen sexting—the real issue: Common problems associated with teen sexting. *Psychology Today*. Retrieved from https://www.psychologytoday.com/blog/teen-angst/201304/teen-sexting-the-real-issue

Manning, J. C. (2006). The impact of Internet pornography on marriage and the family: A review of the research. *Sexual Addiction & Compulsivity, 13*(2/3), 131–165.

Massey, A. (2015, April 30). The dickonomics of Tinder: Yes, women are using Tinder to get laid. No, not with you. *medium.com*. Retrieved from https://medium.com/matter/the-dickonomics-of-tinder-b14956c0c2c7#.koj7c3pu7

McKenna, K. Y. A., & Bargh, J. A. (1998). Coming out in the age of the Internet: Identity "demarginalization" through virtual group participation. *Journal of Personality and Social Psychology, 75*(3), 681–694.

McKenna, K. Y. A., & Bargh, J. A. (2000). Plan 9 from cyberspace: The implications of the Internet for personality and social psychology. *Personality and Social Psychology Review, 4*(1), 57–75.

Oppenheimer, V. K. (1988). A theory of marriage timing. *American Journal of Sociology, 94*(3), 563–591.

Rosenfeld, M. J. (2007). *The age of independence: Interracial unions, same-sex unions, and the changing American family*. Cambridge, MA: Harvard University Press.

Rosenfeld, M. J. (2014). Couple longevity in the era of same-sex marriage in the United States. *Journal of Marriage and Family, 76*(5), 905–918.

Rosenfeld, M. J. (2017). Marriage, choice and couplehood in the age of the Internet. *Sociological Science, 4*, 490–510.

Rosenfeld, M. J. (2018). Who wants the breakup? Gender and breakup in heterosexual couples. In D. F. Alwin, D. Felmlee, & D. Kreager (Eds.), *Social networks and the life course: Integrating the development of human lives and social relational networks* (pp. 221–243). New York, NY: Springer.

Rosenfeld, M. J., & Thomas, R. J. (2012). Searching for a mate: The rise of the Internet as a social intermediary. *American Sociological Review, 77*(4), 523–547.

Rosenfeld, M. J., Thomas, R. J., & Falcon, M. (2015). *How couples meet and stay together (waves 1, 2, and 3 version 3.04; wave 4 supplement version 1.02; wave 5 supplement version 1.0)*. Stanford, CA: Stanford University Libraries Retrieved from http://data.stanford.edu/hcmst

Rosenfeld, M. J., Thomas, R. J., & Hausen, S. (2018). *How couples meet and stay together: 2017 fresh sample. [computer files]*. Stanford, CA: Stanford University Libraries Retrieved from http://data.stanford.edu/hcmst

Sales, N. J. (2015, September). Tinder and the dawn of the 'dating apocalypse'. *Vanity Fair*. Retrieved from http://www.vanityfair.com/culture/2015/08/tinder-hook-up-culture-end-of-dating

Sassler, S., & Miller, A. J. (2011). Waiting to be asked: Gender, power, and relationship progression among cohabiting couples. *Journal of Family Issues, 32*(4), 482–506.

Slater, D. (2013). *Love in the time of algorithms: What technology does to meeting and mating*. New York, NY: Penguin Books.

Turkle, S. (2011). *Alone together: Why we expect more from our technology and less from each other*. New York, NY: Basic Books.

Turkle, S. (2015). *Reclaiming conversation: The power of talk in a digital age*. New York, NY: Penguin Books.

Waite, L. J., & Gallagher, M. (2000). *The case for marriage: Why married people are happier, healthier, and better off financially*. New York, NY: Doubleday.

Weigel, M. (2016). *Labor of love: The invention of dating*. New York, NY: Farrar, Straus and Giroux.

Wellman, B. (2001). Physical place and cyberplace: The rise of personalized networking. *International Journal of Urban and Regional Research, 25*(2), 227–252.

Young, K. S. (1998). *Caught in the net: How to recognize the signs of Internet addiction—and a winning strategy for recovery*. New York, NY: John Wiley & Sons.

# Part III
# Technology and Changing Family Ties

# Chapter 7
# Television "Effects" on International Family Change

**Rukmalie Jayakody**

Television's near universal saturation in the USA—99% of households have television with an average of 2.4 televisions per household (U.S. Bureau of the Census, 2006)—makes its impacts on family attitudes and behavior widely assumed. Described as one of the most powerful idea disseminators, socializing agents, and public opinion molders in the contemporary world (Kottak, 1991) that television has effects is widely accepted. For example, profound shifts in American's acceptance of homosexuality and gay parenting have been attributed to network television programs. The late 1990s television show *Will and Grace* is credited with gaining acceptance of homosexuality, and the more recent show, *Modern Family*, with the acceptance of gay parents. While these connections between television and changes in family attitudes and behaviors are convenient and persuasive, the actual research is mixed.

Television's role in the recent US teen pregnancy decline provides a good illustration of these mixed and ambiguous findings. A National Bureau of Economic Research study contends that the MTV show *16 and Pregnant* accounted for 24% of the overall decline in teen births during the 18 months after its premier (Kearney & Levine, 2015). The study authors state their analyses "indicate that exposure to '*16 and Pregnant*' was high and that it had an influence on teens' thinking regarding birth control and abortion" (Wilson, 2014, p. 1). Bill Albert, chief program officer at the National Campaign to Prevent Teen Pregnancy, said, "this extraordinary study" shows that "the media can be, and often is, a force of good" (Wilson, 2014, p. 1).

However, an Indiana University study argued the opposite—that *16 and Pregnant*, and its spin-off, *Teen Moms*, actually glamorized teen motherhood and did not provide the cautionary tale intended. Instead, heavy viewers of these reality programs

R. Jayakody (✉)
Department of Human Development and Family Studies, Penn State, University Park, PA, USA
e-mail: jayakody@psu.edu



J. Van Hook et al. (eds.), *Families and Technology*, National Symposium on Family Issues 9, https://doi.org/10.1007/978-3-319-95540-7_7

believed that the teen mothers featured had an enviable quality of life, a high income, involved fathers, affordable access to health care, easily found child care, and easily completed schooling. These programs generally contributed to an unrealistic perception of what it is like to be a teen mother. Instead of leading to a decline in teen pregnancy, the study authors argue that the MTV shows might be a contributing factor to teen pregnancy (Martins & Jensen, 2014).

Video game research provides another example of media effects uncertainty. While public and policy discussions continue to link playing violent video games with violent behavior, and while some studies have established that link, most research concludes that no relationship exists. These recent examples, whether MTV shows encourage or discourage teen childbearing and whether there is any link between violent video game play and violent behavior, highlight the problems of attributing media effects to changes in family attitudes and behaviors.

Public debates center on whether the impacts of television on family attitudes and behaviors are, on balance, positive or negative, not whether substantial impacts occur—for the most part this is not disputed. However, despite a large literature on media effects, and strong assertions about television's impacts, "there is little agreement on the nature and extent of those assumed effects" (McQuail, 1994, p. 327). Existing research designs contain serious threats to validity—especially, selectivity of television exposure—that have undermined researchers' ability to establish a causal connection between television and family change. Furthermore, even if causality concerns are set aside, we know little about how observed associations arise (Hornick & McAnany, 2001). Although debate about television's effects on children, families, communities, and cultures is increasing, concerns have been raised about the theory, quality, and rigor of methodologies used in television and media effects research. One review stressed "the limited capacity of studies to understand its [television's] nature, intensity, duration, or effects" (National Research Council; Institute of Medicine, 2006, p. ix). Understanding the impact of television is central to theories of family change, particularly as prevention and intervention programs worldwide increasingly use television to influence fertility, sexual and reproductive health, gender dynamics, and parent–child relationships.

Therefore, despite nearly universal agreement on television effects, there is actually very little evidence of television impacts. This chapter assesses research on television's "effects" on family behavior and attitudes and reviews the research designs leading to these findings. Emphasis is placed on assessing the direction of causation, the impacts of third variables on the observed associations, and identifying the possible mechanisms through which television may influence family attitudes and behaviors. While briefly touching on the USA, this paper focuses mainly on low- and middle-income countries since interventions using television are widespread in these settings. Finally, qualitative data (ethnography, intensive interviews, and focus group interviews) from a unique study in Vietnam specifically designed to assess television's impacts will be used to illustrate and highlight some of the mechanisms and pathways discussed.

## Television Worldwide

Television access has grown worldwide as satellites now beam images into remote communities that until recently were relatively isolated. In low- and middle-income countries, using television to change attitudes and behaviors is explicit. When soliciting funds to expand electrification, the World Bank highlights television, the main domestic use of electricity, and its direct link to population health improvements. "Electrification results in fertility reductions" and "television is the channel through which electricity effects fertility" by "providing information on health knowledge" (World Bank, 2008, p. 45). Expressing a similar sentiment, India's Health and Welfare Minister, Mr. Azad, argued that, "Electricity in our villages can help control population growth. Electricity will lead to television in houses, which will lead to population control. When there is no light people get engaged in the process of population growth" (Hindustan Times, 2009). The World Bank and Minister Azad are far from alone in believing that television improves population health. A substantial literature explores this possibility and international and government organizations [e.g., United Nations Population Fund (UNFPA), United States Agency for International Development (USAID), and Centers for Disease Control (CDC)] spend billions annually on media campaigns promoting population and family health.

Dramatic family changes worldwide, extensive both in their geographic scope and in the dimensions impacted—age and universality of marriage, parent's role in mate selection, parental authority, male authority, extended kinship relations, sex and age hierarchies, relationships between men and women, intergenerational relationships, and family size and structure—highlight television as an important mechanism driving these changes. Some changes emphasize that television's influence operates through structural changes, alterations in the cost–benefit calculus attributed to changes in media technology, or increases in knowledge dissemination through media. Others emphasize that television alters family behavior and attitudes primarily through ideation, a new way of thinking resulting from contact with new ideas and information. Television, specifically designed to transmit new ideas and information, may be a particularly powerful source of ideational change, and television's power to change attitudes and behaviors has long been assumed (Butcher, 2003; Kottak, 1990; Westoff, 1999). Furthermore, new ideas transmitted through television often transcend traditional barriers of language and literacy. New models of marriage, family structure, and social arrangements are introduced through television, and these new models are often labeled as modern and defined as good (Hornick & McAnany, 2001).

## Television Effects

Indeed, associations between television, population health, and family are plentiful. More than 50 years ago, the UN Statistical Yearbook data for 96 countries indicated that television availability was significantly associated with lower fertility (Williams & Singh, 1976). In Brazil and Indonesia, timing variations in television's arrival were linked to within-country fertility variations (Cammack & Heaton, 2001; Potter, Cavenaghi, Caetano, & Assuncao, 1998). Using data from 144 countries, television ownership was found to correlate more highly with fertility than either indexes of female education or GNP per capita (Hornick & McAnany, 2001). Television ownership was related to condom use in South Africa (Vundule, Maforah, Jewkes, & Jordaan, 2001), Bangladesh (Islam, Padmadas, & Smith, 2006), Brazil (Gupta, 2000), Guatemala (Cornelius, 1997), and Nepal (Boulay, Storey, & Sood, 2002).

Demographic and Health Survey data from Africa (Burkina Faso, Ghana, Kenya, Madagascar, Namibia, Nigeria, Zambia, and Morocco) and South Asia (Pakistan, India, and Bangladesh) indicate strong associations between television exposure and contraceptive use, future intentions to use contraception, preferences for fewer children, later age at marriage, and the intention to stop childbearing (Westoff & Bankole, 1997, 1999). Television exposure has also been linked to sexual attitudes and behavior. Exposure to sexual content on television was associated with more permissive attitudes towards sexual activity outside of marriage, earlier sexual debut, and the increased risk of teen pregnancy (Brown et al., 2006; Brown & Newcomer, 1991; Chandra et al., 2007; Collins, 2005). Studies in Pakistan, Bangladesh, India, Guatemala, Peru, Kazakhstan, Brazil, Fiji, Thailand, and Vietnam report television as the most frequently mentioned source of information on contraceptives and HIV/AIDS (Chaterjee, 1999; Cornelius, 1997; Islam & Hasan, 2000; Kattumuri, 2003; Khawaja, Tayyeb, & Malik, 2004; Valente, Poppe, & Merritt, 1996).

Declines in breast feeding in Hong Kong are linked to infant formula advertising, changing attitudes towards corporal punishment of children in South Korea to public service announcements (Doe, 2000), and declines in son preference in India to entertainment shows highlighting girls' education (Das Gupta et al., 2003). The appearance of eating disorders among Fijian adolescents is attributed to Western television that showcases a very thin body ideal that is in sharp contrast to the traditional full-figure body ideal of Fijian culture. Emergency room visits by young boys is said to have sky rocketed when The World Wrestling Federation was broadcast in Israel, as boys tried to imitate the wrestling moves seen on television. Inuit games, which had strongly emphasized cooperation, shifted to competition once soccer broadcasts began via satellite television.

Despite the volume and geographical scope of these findings, researchers have yet to disentangle the causal direction or to eliminate the possibility that a third variable is responsible for the observed relationships. For example, are those who watch television programs depicting families using contraception more likely to use contraceptives themselves, or are contraceptive users selecting to watch these television programs? Are those who watched more sexual content on television more likely to have sex, or are those who are having sex more likely to watch content that reflects their experience? Is television availability responsible for fertility reductions, or is there a third variable, such as socioeconomic status, that is related to both lower fertility and television availability? Is frequent viewing of sexual content on television responsible for the earlier initiation of sexual activity, or is there a third variable, such as parental monitoring of young people's activities, that is related to both watching a lot of television and earlier sexual debut? As the majority of television effects research is based on statistical associations, it is impossible to resolve these issues.

## Using Television to Change Families

Despite lacking evidence of causal impacts, substantial funding and effort focuses on using television to deliver specific family planning and reproductive health messages. Many government and nongovernment organizations use Information, Education, and Communication (IEC) and Behavior Change Communication (BCC) strategies to promote family planning services. The UNFPA has provided substantial financial and technical assistance to more than 100 countries to develop IEC strategies, and USAID supports the world's largest family planning IEC effort. Mechanisms to promote these goals range from short, public service announcements (PSAs) to paid commercials and television miniseries. Uganda's Health Ministry credited an IEC campaign with achieving dramatic changes in sexual behavior, increasing knowledge of HIV/AIDS, and reducing new HIV/AIDS infections (Kiragu, Galiwango, Mulira, & Sekatawa, 1996). After airing a series of minidramas, Egypt's contraception prevalence rate was reported to have risen by 10% (Sadik, 1995). Viewing a PSA on Islam and family planning in Mali was linked with a sharp drop in the proportion of women who believed that Islam was opposed to family planning—from 57% to 17% (Kane, Gueye, Speizer, Pacque-Margolis, & Baron, 1998). In Brazil, vasectomy requests increased after a vasectomy television campaign aired (Kincaid et al., 1996). Zimbabwe credited IEC campaigns with increases in birth spacing and fertility reductions (Guilkey & Jayne, 1997). Although a few studies employ sophisticated statistical techniques to lessen the influence of third variables, problems with causality and selection problems remain.

Entertainment-education (E-E) approaches are considered particularly effective in changing attitudes and behaviors (Singhal & Rogers, 1999). E-E is defined as "a process of purposely designing and implementing a media message to both entertain and educate, to increase audience member knowledge about an educational issue, create favorable attitudes, shift social norms, and change overt behavior" (Singhal & Rogers, 1999, p. 5). Based on social learning theory principles that people first learn new attitudes and behaviors by observing others, the soap opera format has been extensively used to promote family planning and reproductive health. Soap operas without specifically designed messages are also reported to have influenced fertility. The depiction of small families and the introduction of nontraditional ideas about women and modernity have been linked to Brazil's fertility decline (Faria & Potter, 1999). Among the earliest E-E interventions was a 1977 Mexican 9-month series that extolled the benefits of reducing fertility (Singhal & Rogers, 1999). Mexican family planning clinics reported a 33% increase in new registrants and contraceptive sales increased by 23% one year after broadcast. A Kenyan soap opera that aired between 1987 and 1989 coincided with a 58% increase in contraceptive use. More than 20 other countries have also launched television mini-dramas promoting family planning and reproductive health. As part of its Global AIDS program, the CDC used E-E messages in soap operas in Botswana, Ethiopia, Ghana, and Zimbabwe (Galavotti, Pappas-DeLucca, & Lansky, 2001). Although IEC and BCC efforts are increasing, and reported effects are persuasive, a review of sexual health focused media interventions worldwide states that "most evaluations collected only cross-sectional data" (Gurman & Underwood, 2008, p. 56). Therefore, causality and selection problems plague these interventions.

## How Does Television Impact Family Change?

Existing media effects research has also paid insufficient attention to how observed associations arise, or the specific mechanisms through which television affects individuals and communities (Hornick & McAnany, 2001; Schrum, 2002). Television may affect change by introducing new ideas and information in its content, and also by altering social interaction (Hornick & McAnany, 2001).

### *Impacts through Television Content/Exposure*

Television content may promote change by informing, enabling, motivating, and guiding individuals. Television appears a particularly effective new idea transmission mechanism, transcending traditional language and literacy barriers with access to both elites and non-elites. New ideas that may influence family attitudes and behavior include information about contraception, smaller family size preferences (Caldwell, 1982), ideas about secularization and individualism (Bumpass, 1990; Lesthaeghe & Surkyn, 1988), consumption as an appropriate orientation (Easterlin, 1987; Freedman, 1979), more egalitarian gender relationships (Hornick & McAnany, 2001; Kottak, 1991), power structures defined less by heredity and more by achievement (Johnson, 2000), and youth autonomy. For example, television programs may show a young couple meeting and falling in love, encountering obstacles such as parental objections, and persevering to form a love match. This is the basic formula of South Korean and Chinese romantic films widely watched in Vietnam.

This depiction may alter views towards arranged marriages and create more favorable attitudes about free-choice matches. Similarly, portrayals of smaller families could introduce ideas that small families are normal and acceptable (Coale & Watkins, 1986; Mason, 1997), altering fertility preferences and behavior.

Social cognition theories explain why television content is so powerful in influencing attitudes (Wyer Jr & Srull, 1989). For attitude formation, information that enters into the equation is that which is most accessible and vivid (Fishbein & Ajzen, 1975). The most accessible concepts are those that are viewed frequently and recently. Repeatedly viewing concepts on television (e.g., advertising that glorifies consumption, youth autonomy, and small families) heightens their accessibility and makes them particularly influential in attitude formation (Schrum, 2002). Television images are also very vivid (Bandura, 1986; Schrum, 2002) in that they are "emotionally interesting, concrete, and imagery provoking" (Nisbett & Ross, 1980, p. 45). Television also provides opportunities for social learning. By watching television, viewers can learn from the experiences of others, and actors can be instructive by serving as transmitters of knowledge, values, cognitive skills, and new lifestyles and behaviors. Social models on television can also illustrate that individuals have the power to change their circumstances, and seeing actors succeed through their own efforts can motivate viewers. Additionally, television programs can illustrate the rewards of certain behaviors and show how to translate a desired vision of the future into a set of achievable sub-goals (Bandura, 1986).

The constructs and models shown on television that are frequent, recent, and vivid primarily come from the West, and Western television dominates programming worldwide. Even when national programming is available, the programming often reflects viewpoints and images from large urban centers and Western production norms. The spread of Western ideas and beliefs are central in international family change explanations (Caldwell, 1982; Freedman, 1979; van de Kaa, 1996). Imported models of family structure are prevalent on television, and television may offer radically different ways of imagining sex and gender relations. The image of romantic love widely disseminated by television has profoundly modified representations of love in societies characterized by an arranged marriage system (Abu-Lughod, 1989; Davis & Davis, 1995; Locoh & Mouvagha-Sow, 2007). Individual autonomy, egalitarianism, and independence of thought, referred to as secular-rational or self-expression values (Inglehart, 1997; Inglehart & Baker, 2000; Inglehart & Welzel, 2005), are also frequently presented on television. These constructs may lead to changing conceptions of youth autonomy and may alter intergenerational and gender relationships. Television's commercial aspects may change consumption aspirations (Freedman, 1979). The Western/modern/cosmopolitan images and messages in television content worldwide illustrate and define what it is to be modern (Hornick, 2001). Television portrayals of family relationships, social roles, power relations, and societal norms shape the public consciousness (Gerbner, Gross, Morgan, & Signorielli, 1994), and these images are influential because social construction of reality depends heavily on what people see.

## *Impacts through Social Interaction*

Social interaction must also be taken into account when assessing the impacts of television (Katz & Lazarsfeld, 1955). Social interactions influence television's impact on attitudes and behavior via at least four mechanisms (Hornick & McAnany, 2001). (1) Information acquired from television can be passed from one person to the next. This is the simplest and most familiar form of interpersonal amplification of media exposure. (2) Television content may serve as a stimulus for the discussion of certain topics, with discussion leading to convergence on a shared response that would not have emerged otherwise. (3) Television exposure may create an opening for explicit discussion of formerly taboo topics, with the discussion leading to more legitimacy than would have emerged in the absence of explicit discussion. (4) Finally, media exposure may give people contemplating innovative behaviors that violate local norms a sense of belonging to another social network—a more distant and broad network—and this sense of belonging can serve to counteract their anxieties about expulsion from their existing localized network.

Note that mechanisms 2, 3, and 4 each concern normative responses to innovative attitudes and behaviors seen on television. Interpersonal dynamics undoubtedly contribute to the establishment and maintenance of social norms (Hechter & Opp, 2001). Several decades of research demonstrate that changes in knowledge/attitudes/behaviors are as much a function of who is known as what is known (Carley, 2001). That is, how a person responds to exposure to innovation is heavily influenced by what she/he thinks other relevant people support or oppose.

There is also the possibility of a fifth mechanism: (5) changes in media habits have a transforming effect on the social structure itself. Time spent watching television means time not spent on other activities; those watching television for several hours daily are unable to spend that time on a different activity. As boldly stated in Putman's *Bowling Alone* (Putnam, 2000), time spent watching television in the USA since its rapid diffusion in the 1950s has detracted from the vitality of various types of activities and social involvement. Community involvement declined not because of what people saw on television, but because they were home watching television rather than participating in community social activities. Alternatively, television could restructure social relationships by promoting family and community social integration (Kottak, 1990). For example, a community with a high degree of sex segregation in social activities may see this disappear as men and women watch television together. One ethnographic account of a rural Indian village found that before television's arrival, the men would spend their evenings out visiting with friends; after television's arrival, they stayed home and watched television with their wives and children (Johnson, 2000). One of the villagers described television's impact on relationships with nonfamily members: "Before television came, I did not talk much to my neighbor. We had nothing to talk about. But now I go to his house to watch TV at night and we see each other there. We have become close friends now, and they even sometimes come to my house for tea. My son is still quite young but I have been discussing it with my neighbor and we might arrange for my son to marry his daughter" (Johnson, 2000, p. 207).

Particularly important in family change theoretical frameworks is the extent to which this reorganization of activities alters the activity context from familial to nonfamilial. Most activities of daily living have been historically organized within the family (Ogburn & Nimkoff, 1955; Thornton & Fricke, 1987), but television watching may be a leisure activity that increasingly occurs outside the family context, changing interactions with both family and nonfamily members. Research has primarily emphasized the growth in nonfamily activities such as attending an educational institution and working in wage labor, finding that increases in nonfamily experiences result in greater youth independence, delayed marriage, increased contraceptive use, and reduced fertility (Axinn & Yabiku, 2001; Thornton & Lin, 1994). The reorganizing of leisure activities as a result of television's availability may produce similar changes.

To date, there has been little research on how mass media habits alter social relationships. Additionally, existing research has not been sensitive to the distinctions among the four mechanisms described previously. Some empirical support exists, however, for the simpler assertion that social interaction has a bearing on the nature and magnitude of television's impact. Examination of the impact of radio soap operas in Tanzania designed to encourage the adoption of family planning and reduce HIV/AIDS risk behaviors found that exposure to the soap opera stimulated discussions within informal social networks (Rogers et al., 1999), and that such discussions led to changes in risk behaviors (Vaughan, Rogers, Singhal, & Swalehe, 2000). In Peru, mass media exposure was found to stimulate informal, social network communication (Valente et al., 1996). In Bolivia, mass media exposure and interpersonal communication acted as substitutes for each other rather than reinforcing factors (Valente & Saba, 1998, 2001). This South American research underscores the point that indirect effects of mass media via social interaction are not necessarily straightforward, hence the importance of sound and comprehensive measurement of mass media exposure and social interaction.

## Data and Methods

In order to address problems with prior research—assessing the causal impacts of television and identifying possible mechanisms if impacts occurred—a randomized experiment was conducted in remote, rural areas of Vietnam inhabited by ethnic minority groups. First, 16 unelectrified villages that were similar economically, demographically, and culturally were selected. Next, baseline data collection, involving both qualitative (ethnographies, focus groups, intensive interviews, and oral histories) and quantitative (face-to-face survey interviews with all village residents 16 years of age and older; GIS data) strategies were conducted in all 16 villages. After baseline data collection, 8 villages were randomly assigned to the treatment group and 8 villages to the control group. Six months after random assignment, the treatment groups received televisions, generators, and deliveries of gasoline to operate the generators. The control villages did not receive televisions, generators, or gasoline. All 16 villages were observed for 3 years after random assignment to assess the causal impacts of television on individuals, families, and communities. The study took place from 2012 to 2017.

## *Field Sites*

Heavy television saturation in most world regions makes disentangling causation and establishing pathways of influence difficult. However, areas without television remain and provide valuable research opportunities. Additionally, these areas have the potential to experience substantial change as they generally continue to have high fertility rates, low school enrollment, and poorer health care access and utilization. Television has expanded rapidly in Vietnam, and 79% of urban households and 50% of rural households have television. Although cost remains a barrier to ownership—Vietnam's average per capita income is $638, television access is limited primarily by lack of electricity. Further expansion requires electricity provision to remote, mountainous areas not easily connected to the national grid (Malhotra, 2005).

Vietnam is a multiethnic society with substantial ethno-cultural diversity. The Kinh people are the majority ethnic group of Vietnam comprising 86% of Vietnam's 82 million population; the remaining 14% is made up of 52 different ethnic minority groups. Ethnic minorities are those who have Vietnamese nationality and reside in Vietnam, but who do not share the identity, language, and other cultural characteristics with the Kinh (World Health Organization, 2003). The Kinh primarily inhabit the fertile delta regions and coastal plains, and with few exceptions Kinh settlements are electrified. In contrast, Vietnam's minority groups mainly reside in mountainous areas lacking electricity. Substantial disparities between Kinh and ethnic minority groups are evident. Ethnic minorities account for 30% of Vietnam's poor and about 75% fall below the international poverty line compared to 31% of Kinh (United Nations, 2002). Estimates indicate that while 4% of Kinh have consumption that is so inadequate as to not meet even basic nutritional needs, this figure was 33% among ethnic minorities (Swinkles & Turk, 2006). Ethnic minorities are less well served by the health care system (Desai, 2000). They are far less likely to receive prenatal care, to be assisted by a doctor/nurse/midwife during birth, to consult a health care provider when a child is sick, or to vaccinate children (Baulch, Chuyen, Haughton, & Haughton, 2002). While assimilation, strongly endorsed by the government, occurs in some groups (e.g., ethnic groups such as the Tay, Muong, and Hoa), other groups, such as the Thai, remain culturally separate. I focus on the Thai, the second largest ethnic minority group in Vietnam.

Socioeconomic data gathered from commune records and spatial data were used to identify potential field sites using the following criteria: (1) the village was not located on or near a major road, (2) or within a short travel time from an electrified area, (3) there were no schools or health clinics, and (4) no current electrification plans exist. The resulting sample consists of 14 field sites in 12 communes. These villages have a young age structure: 30% of the population are under 15 years of age, about 25% are between 15 and 24, and less than 10% are more than 54 years old. The 14 villages were matched into 7 pairs, with one village in each pair randomly assigned to the treatment and the other to control status. Treatment sites received 1 television (and a generator, gasoline for its operation, and a safety enclosed fuel tank and other safety equipment) per 50 people in the field sites' population. Not every household received a television because financially it would have been cost prohibitive. Additionally, prior research (Johnson, 2000; Kottak, 1991) and our preliminary work indicated televisions were initially limited to a few households in villages. Those without television would go to a neighbor's house to watch. Therefore, television in a sample of households more accurately reflects the situation in many low-income settings. Televisions were located within existing households, with the specific household randomly selected.

## Ethnographic and Focus Group Findings

Ethnographers residing in all treatment villages described both the influence of television content and the influence of an alteration in social activities as potentially leading to family change. Although television was provided to only 1 household per 50 villagers, this did not limit viewing time. Villagers in households without television felt no hesitation in going to a neighbor's house who did have television. Discussions on television content were common following program viewing. Differences in family arrangements were a common point of discussion, and depictions of modern nuclear families in Hanoi, Ho Chi Minh City, and South Korea often provided a cautionary tale about too much youth autonomy or elder neglect.

Young people were eager consumers of programs, and frequently discussed content that reflected the experiences of those their same age. Differences between their experiences and youth in Hanoi centered on appearance—Hanoi youth were more stylish—and relationships with parents, but also education, career, and work opportunity differences. Ethnographers reported that treatment villages had far more frequent mixed sex group discussions and activities than in control villages.

The results from a series of focus group discussions highlight the influence of information from television, as well as the interaction between information and social activities. Focus groups were conducted with females in two age groupings: aged 15–19 and 20–26 in both treatment and control villages. Questions centered on sex education: what they learned, who they learned from, how they used that information, and what they felt they still did not know. Coding of themes revealed that there was substantial similarity between treatment village females in the older age group, aged 20–26, and both age groups in the control villages. In contrast, the responses of the treatment village younger age group, aged 15–19, were quite different. Keep in mind that the older age group received information about sex prior to television's introduction because most had already married and many already had children prior to television reaching their villages. This makes the experiences of the 15–19 year olds in the treatment group the same as the 15–19 year olds in the control villages. The younger age group in the control villages also lacked television as a source of information. Given the similarity of themes for the: (1) treatment village aged 20–26, (2) control village aged 20–26, and (3) control village aged 15–19, these three groups will be referred to as the No TV groups, while the treatment village aged 15–19 will be referred to as the TV group.

Women in the No TV group overwhelmingly cited family as the main source of information about sex: mothers, aunts, cousins, and older sisters. In sharp contrast, the TV group cited television as their primary source of information about sex, followed by mothers. The focus groups were conducted 6–8 months after television's introduction in the treatment villages. Clearly, some information about sex had been received prior to the arrival of television. Yet, when asked for the primary source of information, television was quickly cited.

In addition to differences in the source of information, there were also differences in what was taught. The following are some of the frequent responses given by the No TV group when asked what they were taught: "sex is a wife's duty," "sex is to have families," and "sex is with your husband only." While these themes were also mentioned in the TV group, other themes emerged that were unique to the TV group that were not mentioned in the No TV group: "you have sex with your boyfriend to show him you like him," and "sex is for fun."

While the preceding discussion highlights information provided by television, ethnographic data also highlights the importance of social interaction regarding the information learned. For the TV group, information from television was eagerly discussed with friends and opinions were exchanged. Focus group data reveals that these discussions often trivialized traditional views and endorsed more permissive views towards sex and sexual relations. These discussions may have given participants the impression that everyone had more permissive views and these permissive views were becoming the norm. The social interactions around the television content made it seem acceptable to have views on sex that were far less rigid than those held by the No TV group and may have given some young women permission to act on those more permissive views.

The reordering of social activities could have provided them the opportunity to act on those more permissive views. Prior to television, monitoring and supervision was easier for parents. With the arrival of television, especially since television was available only in a few households, parental monitoring became more challenging. Houses are small, one room structures on stilts. Usually occupied by 6–8 people, in the evenings houses with televisions were often bursting at the seams, fitting in as many as possible with others watching through the window on ladders. In this chaotic environment, parenting monitoring was challenging. Our TV group told us how they knew girls, not them of course, who would tell their parents they were going to so-and-so's household to watch a program but then sneak off after the program started to "do things with boys." This focus group data highlights the complexity of understanding the nature of television effects: information from television, the social interaction around that information, and the reordering of social activities that provide opportunities for behavioral change.

## Conclusion

The availability of television in the USA began in 1947 and spread rapidly throughout the 1950s. Although present in virtually all American homes since the late 1960s, we still know little about television's effects and its pathways of influence. Rather than being a "magic bullet" that imparts information leading to attitudinal and behavioral change, the potential impacts of television, if they do exist, are far more difficult to understand. As one of the older communication technologies, research on television offers other communication technologies both road maps and cautionary tales.

Examining the potential impacts of communication technology needs to pay careful attention to the direction of effects; is the technology causing the change or vice versa. Additionally, is it the communication technology that is leading to a change in behavior, or is there a third variable that is influencing both communication technology adoption and behavioral change? Can other settings, which may be slower to adopt new communication technologies, be used to test hypotheses?

## References

Abu-Lughod, L. (1989). Bedouins, cassettes, and technologies of popular culture. *Middle East Republic*, (159), 7–47 Retrieved from http://sites.psu.edu/cas204/wp-content/uploads/sites/4576/2013/10/Lila-AbuLughod-BedouinsCassettes.pdf

Axinn, W. G., & Yabiku, S. T. (2001). Social change, the social organization of families, and fertility limitation. *The American Journal of Sociology, 106*(5), 1219–1261.

Bandura, A. (1986). *Social foundations of thought and action: A social cognitive theory*. Englewood Cliffs, NJ: Prentice Hall.

Baulch, B., Chuyen, T. T. K., Haughton, D., & Haughton, J. (2002). Ethnic minority development in Vietnam: A socioeconomic perspective (Policy research working paper No. 2836). Washington, DC: World Bank. Retrieved from https://openknowledge.worldbank.org/handle/10986/14802

Boulay, M., Storey, J. D., & Sood, S. (2002). Indirect exposure to family planning mass media campaign in Nepal. *Journal of Health Communication, 7*(5), 379–399.

Brown, J. D., L'Engle, K. L., Pardun, C. J., Guo, G., Kenneavy, K., & Jackson, C. (2006). Sexy media matter: Exposure to sexual content in music, movies, television and magazines predicts black and white adolescent's sexual behavior. *Pediatrics, 117*(4), 1018–1027.

Brown, J. D., & Newcomer, S. F. (1991). Television viewing and adolescent sexual behavior. *Journal of Homosexuality, 21*(1–2), 77–91.

Bumpass, L. L. (1990). What's happening to the family? Interactions between demographic and institutional change. *Demography, 27*(4), 483–498.

Butcher, M. (2003). *Transnational television, cultural identity, and change: When STAR came to India*. New Delhi: Sage.

Caldwell, J. C. (1982). *Theory of fertility decline: Population and social structure.* London: Academic Press.
Cammack, M., & Heaton, T. B. (2001). Regional variation in acceptance of Indonesia's family planning program. *Population Research and Policy Review, 20*(6), 565–585.
Carley, K. M. (2001). Learning and using new ideas: A sociocognitive perspective. In J. B. Casterline (Ed.), *Diffusion processes and fertility transition: Selected perspectives* (pp. 197–207). Washington, DC: National Academies Press.
Chandra, A., Martino, S. C., Collins, R. L., Elliott, M. N., Berry, S. H., Kanouse, D. E., & Miu, A. (2007). Does watching sex on TV predict teen pregnancy? Findings from the National Longitudinal Survey of Youth. *Pediatrics, 122*(5), 1047–1054. https://doi.org/10.1542/peds.2007-3066
Chaterjee, N. (1999). AIDS-related information exposure in the mass media and discussion within social networks among married women in Bombay, India. *AIDS Care, 11*(4), 443–446.
Coale, A. J., & Watkins, S. C. (Eds.). (1986). *The decline of fertility in Europe. The revised proceedings of a conference on the Princeton European Fertility Project.* Princeton, NJ: Princeton University Press.
Collins, R. L. (2005). Sex on television and its impact on American youth: Background information on the RAND television and adolescent sexuality study. *Child and Adolescent Psychiatry Clinics in North America, 14*(3), 371–385.
Cornelius, D. L. (1997). *The broadcast media, reproductive preferences, and contraceptive knowledge and behavior: Evidence from Guatemala.* (Doctoral dissertation, University of Texas at Austin, Department of Sociology).
Das Gupta, M., Zhenghua, J., Bohua, L., Zhenming, X., Chung, W., & Hwa-Ok, B. (2003). Why is son preference so persistent in East and South Asia? A cross-country study of China, India and the Republic of Korea. *The Journal of Development Studies, 40*(2), 153–187.
Davis, S. S., & Davis, D. A. (1995). The mosque and the satellite: Media and adolescence in a Moroccan town. *Journal of Youth and Adolescence, 24*(5), 577–593.
Desai, J. (2000). *Vietnam through the lens of gender: Five years later—Results from the second Vietnam Living Standards Survey.* Retrieved from http://lnweb90.worldbank.org/ext/epic.nsf/ImportDocs/F3007CD13A7EDFF9852573BD005EC3B6?opendocument&query=VN
Doe, S. S. (2000). Cultural factors in child maltreatment and domestic violence in Korea. *Children and Youth Services Review, 22*, 231–236.
Easterlin, R. A. (1987). *Birth and fortune: The impact of numbers on personal welfare* (2nd ed.). Chicago: University of Chicago Press.
Faria, V. E., & Potter, J. E. (1999). Television, telenovelas, and fertility change in North-East Brazil. In R. Leete (Ed.), *Dynamics of values in fertility change* (pp. 252–274). New York: Oxford University Press.
Fishbein, M., & Ajzen, I. (1975). *Belief, attitude, intention, and behavior: An introduction to theory and research.* Redding, MA: Addison-Wesley.
Freedman, R. (1979). Theories of fertility decline: A reappraisal. *Social Forces, 58*(1), 1–17.
Galavotti, C., Pappas-DeLucca, K. A., & Lansky, A. (2001). Modeling and reinforcement to combat HIV: The MARCH approach to behavior change. *American Journal of Public Health, 91*(10), 1602–1607.
Gerbner, G., Gross, L., Morgan, M., & Signorielli, N. (1994). Growing up with television: The cultivation perspective. In J. Bryant & D. Zillerman (Eds.), *Media effects: Advances in theory and research* (pp. 17–41). Hillsdale, NJ: Erlbaum.
Guilkey, D. K., & Jayne, S. (1997). Fertility transition in Zimbabwe: Determinants of contraceptive use and methods choice. *Population Studies, 51*(2), 173–189.
Gupta, N. (2000). Sexual initiation and contraceptive use among adolescents in Northeast Brazil. *Studies in Family Planning, 31*(3), 228–238.
Gurman, T. A., & Underwood, C. (2008). Using media to address adolescent health: Lessons learned from abroad. In J. D. Brown (Ed.), *Managing the media monster: The influence of media (from television to text messages) on teen sexual behavior and attitudes* (pp. 40–83).

Washington, DC: The National Campaign to Prevent Teen Pregnancy and Unplanned Pregnancy Retrieved from http://www.stdhivtraining.org/x/Media_Monster1.pdf

Hechter, M., & Opp, K.-D. (Eds.). (2001). *Social norms*. New York: Russell Sage Foundation.

Hindustan Times. (2009, July 11). Village electrification can curb population growth. *Hindustan Times*. Retrieved from https://www.hindustantimes.com/delhi-news/village-electrification-can-curb-population-growth/story-Sgf9qgweZ5NOfDAFee6WeI.html

Hornick, R. C. (Ed.). (2001). *Public health communication: Evidence of behavior change*. Mahwah, NJ: Lawrence Erlbaum Associates.

Hornick, R. C., & McAnany, E. (2001). Mass media and fertility change. In J. B. Casterline (Ed.), *Diffusion process and fertility transition* (pp. 208–239). Washington, DC: National Academy Press.

Inglehart, R. (1997). *Modernization and postmodernization: Cultural, economic, and political change in 43 societies*. Princeton, NJ: Princeton University Press.

Inglehart, R., & Baker, W. E. (2000). Modernization, cultural change, and the persistence of traditional values. *American Sociological Review, 65*(1), 19–51.

Inglehart, R., & Welzel, C. (2005). *Modernization, cultural change, and democracy*. New York: Cambridge University Press.

Islam, M. A., Padmadas, S. S., & Smith, P. W. (2006). Men's approval of family planning in Bangladesh. *Journal of Biosocial Science, 38*(2), 247–259.

Islam, M. M., & Hasan, A. H. (2000). Mass media exposure and its impact on family planning in Bangladesh. *Journal of Biosocial Science, 32*(4), 513–526.

Johnson, K. (2000). *Television and social change in rural India*. New Delhi: Sage.

Kane, T. T., Gueye, M., Speizer, I., Pacque-Margolis, S., & Baron, D. (1998). The impact of a family planning multimedia campaign in Bamako, Mali. *Studies in Family Planning, 29*(3), 309–323.

Kattumuri, R. (2003). One-and-a-half decades of HIV/AIDS in Tamil Nadu: How much do patients know now? *International Journal of STD and AIDS, 14*(8), 552–559.

Katz, E., & Lazarsfeld, P. F. (1955). *Personal influence: The part played by people in the flow of mass communication*. New York: Free Press.

Kearney, M. S., & Levine, P. B. (2015, August). *Media influences on social outcomes: The impact of MTVs 16 and pregnant on teen childbearing* (Working Paper No. 19795). Cambridge, MA: National Bureau of Economic Research. Retrieved from http://www.nber.org/papers/w19795

Khawaja, N. P., Tayyeb, R., & Malik, N. (2004). Awareness and practices of contraception among Pakistani women attending a tertiary care hospital. *Journal of Obstetrics and Gynaecology, 24*(5), 564–567.

Kincaid, D. L., Merritt, A. P., Nickerson, L., De Castro Buffington, S., De Castro, M. P. R., & De Castro, B. M. (1996). Impact of a mass media vasectomy promotion campaign in Brazil. *International Family Planning Perspectives, 22*(4), 169–175.

Kiragu, K., Galiwango, M. K., Mulira, H. M., & Sekatawa, E. (1996). Promoting reproductive health in Uganda: Evaluation of a national IEC campaign (IEC field report No. 7). Baltimore, MD: Johns Hopkins School of Public Health, Center for Communication Programs.

Kottak, C. P. (1990). *Prime-time society: An anthropological analysis of television and culture*. Belmont, CA: Wadsworth Publishing Company.

Kottak, C. P. (1991). Television's impact on values and local life in Brazil. *Journal of Communication, 41*(1), 70–87.

Lesthaeghe, R., & Surkyn, J. (1988). Cultural dynamics and economic theories of fertility change. *Population and Development Review, 14*(1), 1–45.

Locoh, T., & Mouvagha-Sow, M. (2007). An uncertain future for African families. In R. Jayakody, A. Thornton, & W. G. Axinn (Eds.), *International family change: Ideational perspectives* (pp. 45–80). Mahwah, NJ: Lawrence Erlbaum.

Malhotra, A. K. (2005). Power to the people. *Vietnam Economic Times*, p. 154.

Martins, N., & Jensen, R. E. (2014). The relationship between "Teen Mom" reality programming and teenagers' beliefs about teen parenthood. *Mass Communications and Society, 17*(6), 830–852.

Mason, K. O. (1997). Explaining fertility transitions. *Demography, 34*(4), 443–454.
McQuail, D. (1994). *Mass communication theory: An introduction*. Thousand Oaks, CA: Sage.
National Research Council; Institute of Medicine. (2006). *Studying media effects on children and youth: Improving methods and measures* (Workshop summary). Washington, DC: The National Academies Press. Retrieved from https://doi.org/10.17226/11706
Nisbett, R., & Ross, L. (1980). *Human inferences: Strategies and shortcomings of human judgment*. Englewood Cliffs, NJ: Prentice Hall.
Ogburn, W. F., & Nimkoff, M. F. (1955). *Technology and the changing family*. Boston: Houghton Mifflin.
Potter, J. E., Cavenaghi, S. M., Caetano, A. J., & Assuncao, R. M. (1998, January). *The spread of television and fertility decline in Brazil: A spatial temporal analysis*. Paper presented at Workshop on Social Processes Underlying Fertility Change in Developing Countries, Washington, DC. Retrieved from https://www.popline.org/node/280962
Putnam, R. D. (2000). *Bowling alone: The collapse and revival of American community*. New York: Simon and Schuster.
Rogers, E. M., Vaughan, P. W., Swalehe, R. M., Rao, N., Svenkerud, P., & Sood, S. (1999). Effects of an entertainment-education radio soap opera on family planning behavior in Tanzania. *Studies in Family Planning, 30*(3), 193–211.
Sadik, N. (1995). Population information, communication, and education. *Asia-Pacific POPIN Bulletin, 7*(3), 6–10.
Schrum, L. J. (2002). Media consumption and perceptions of social reality: Effects and underlying processes. In J. Bryant & D. Zillman (Eds.), *Media effects: Advances in theory and research* (pp. 69–95). Mahwah, NJ: Lawrence Erlbaum Associates.
Singhal, A., & Rogers, E. M. (1999). *Entertainment-education: A communication strategy for social change*. Mahwah, NJ: Lawrence Erlbaum Associates.
Swinkles, R., & Turk, C. (2006, September 28). *Explaining ethnic minority poverty in Vietnam: A summary of recent trends and current challenges*. Paper prepared for World Bank Committee for Ethnic Minorities Meeting, Hanoi, Vietnam.
Thornton, A., & Fricke, T. (1987). Social change and the family: Comparative perspectives from the west, China, and South Asia. *Sociological Forum, 2*(4), 746–779.
Thornton, A., & Lin, H.-S. (1994). *Social change and the family in Taiwan*. Chicago: University of Chicago Press.
U.S. Bureau of the Census. (2006). *Statistical abstracts of the United States*. Washington, DC: U. S. Bureau of the Census.
United Nations. (2002). *Millennium development goals: Bringing the MDG's closer to the people*. Retrieved from http://www.un.org/millenniumgoals/2015_MDG_Report/pdf/MDG%20 2015%20rev%20(July%201).pdf
Valente, T. W., Poppe, P., & Merritt, A. (1996). Mass-media generated interpersonal communication as a source of information about family planning. *Journal of Health Communication, 1*(3), 247–265.
Valente, T. W., & Saba, W. P. (1998). Mass media and interpersonal influence in a reproductive health communication campaign in Bolivia. *Communication Research, 25*(1), 96–124.
Valente, T. W., & Saba, W. P. (2001). Campaign exposure and interpersonal communication as a factor in contraceptive use in Bolivia. *Journal of Health Communication, 6*(4), 303–322.
van de Kaa, D. J. (1996). Anchored narratives: The story and findings of a half century of research into the determinants of fertility. *Population Studies, 50*(3), 389–432.
Vaughan, P. W., Rogers, E. M., Singhal, A., & Swalehe, R. M. (2000). Entertainment-education and HIV/AIDS prevention: A field experiment in Tanzania. *Journal of Health Communication, 5*(Suppl 1), 81–100. https://doi.org/10.1080/10810730050019573
Vundule, C., Maforah, F., Jewkes, R., & Jordaan, E. (2001). Risk factors for teenage pregnancy among sexually active black adolescents in Cape Town. A case control study. *South African Medical Journal, 91*(1), 73–80.

Westoff, C. F. (1999). Mass communication and fertility. In R. Leete (Ed.), *Dynamics of values in fertility change* (pp. 237–251). New York: Oxford University Press.

Westoff, C. F., & Bankole, A. (1997). *Mass media and reproductive behavior in Africa (no. AR2), demographic and health surveys*. Calverton, MD: Macro International Retrieved from https://dhsprogram.com/publications/publication-ar2-analytical-studies.cfm

Westoff, C. F., & Bankole, A. (1999). *Mass* Media *and reproductive behavior in Pakistan, India, and Bangladesh* (No. AR10), Demographic and Health Surveys. Calverton, MD: Macro International. Retrieved from https://dhsprogram.com/publications/publication-ar10-analytical-studies.cfm

Williams, J. S., & Singh, B. K. (1976). The impact of mass media on fertility rates: An exploration. *Journal of Applied Communication Research, 4*(1), 19–24.

Wilson, J. (2014, January 13). Study: MTV's '16 and Pregnant' led to fewer teen births. *CNN*. Retrieved from https://www.cnn.com/2014/01/13/health/16-pregnant-teens-childbirth/index.html

World Bank, Independent Evaluation Group. (2008). *The welfare impact of rural electrification: A reassessment of costs and impacts*. Retrieved from https://siteresources.worldbank.org/EXTRURELECT/Resources/full_doc.pdf

World Health Organization. (2003). *Health and ethnic minorities in Vietnam* (Technical series No. 1). Hanoi, Vietnam: World Health Organization.

Wyer, R. S., Jr., & Srull, T. K. (1989). *Memory and cognition in its social context*. Hillsdale, NJ: Lawrence Erlbaum Associates.

# Chapter 8
# Did Mobile Phones Increase Adult Children's Maternal Contact?

**Judith Treas and Zoya Gubernskaya**

Mobile phones have become an indispensable and inescapable part of our lives. Social scientists interested in the family largely overlooked the arrival of this revolutionary consumer technology. At least initially, mobile phones seemed to be little more than an extension of the familiar landline or pager. Being too bulky and expensive for personal use, they were first marketed largely as business applications. Even compact handhelds were often overshadowed by the glamour of the internet and the novelty of social media. Because mobile phones diffused so rapidly however, everyone had one before most researchers could even begin to formulate important questions about the impact on family life and gather data about how mobile phones might change intimate relationships.

In the developing world where landlines and good roads were scarce, it was readily apparent that mobile phones were filling a significant need. For instance, mobile phones allowed parents to communicate much more frequently with their grown children who lived far away. Among older Thai parents, having daily or nearly daily phone contact with a non-coresident child rose from 12 to 18.5% between 2007 and 2011. Given the evidence, previous speculation that family solidarity between adult generations was in decline was rejected by some (Knodel, 2014).

With the advantages of hindsight, this chapter asks how the introduction and use of mobile phones in advanced Western societies has impacted intergenerational family relationships in adulthood. We situate our investigation in the broader social science debates about the past and future cohesion of kin networks, as well as the influence of new communication technology on social life more generally. Although family solidarity has several aspects (Bengtson & Roberts, 1991), we focus on the *associational* dimension using an outcome variable on frequency of contact between

J. Treas (✉)
Department of Sociology, University of California, Irvine, CA, USA
e-mail: jktreas@uci.edu

Z. Gubernskaya
Department of Sociology, University at Albany, SUNY, Albany, NY, USA



J. Van Hook et al. (eds.), *Families and Technology*, National Symposium on Family Issues 9, https://doi.org/10.1007/978-3-319-95540-7_8

mothers and their grown children. This maternal contact variable recognizes the lifelong strength of the mother–child bond (Rossi & Rossi, 1990). Frequency of maternal contact is not only linked to feelings of closeness but also facilitates concrete resource exchanges (Silverstein, Bengtson, & Lawton, 1997). Intergenerational contacts have many salutary effects, including promotion of the subjective well-being of older adults (Lowenstein, Katz, & Gur-Yaish, 2007; Silverstein & Bengtson, 1994).

Given repeated cross-sectional data for 1986 and 2001, the International Social Survey Program (ISSP) provides a serendipitous window on the neglected question of the family implications of the mobile phone rollout. Bracketing a critical 15-year period that captures the introduction and early diffusion of these phones in Western countries' consumer markets, the two survey years are a rare historical vantage on a natural quasi-experiment. Leveraging on the cross-national design of the ISSP, we exploit the differences between countries to evaluate the thesis that mobile phones increased the frequency of maternal contact. A series of analyses constitute an accumulation of support for a rise in intergenerational solidarity at the turn of the twenty-first century.

First, we lay out the 1986–2001 evidence showing an increase in the frequency with which adults had remote, but not in-person, contact with their mothers (Treas & Gubernskaya, 2012). Overall, compositional changes in populations were not found to account for increased contact. For several countries, there was a diminished influence of mother–child residential proximity on remote contacts. Strikingly, this is in line with the *end of geography* theorizing that new technology (e.g., mobile phones, and internet) makes distance less relevant for communication (Giddens, 1981; Graham, 1998; Harvey, 1990).

Second, we build on these results, which raised mobile phones as a possible driver of more frequent mother–child interaction at the start of the twenty-first century. We link 2001 ISSP maternal contact data for 24 developed nations with the country-level prevalence of mobile phones (Gubernskaya & Treas, 2016). There was substantial country-to-county variation in mobile phone saturation in 2001. As the analysis demonstrates, countries having a higher prevalence of mobile phones were also the ones where grown children had more frequent contacts with their mothers by letter, FAX, internet, or phone.

Third, we turn to the US data for further evidence regarding the role of new communication technology in promoting increased interaction between family members. Extending the analysis into the twenty-first century, we ask whether overall contact with kin increased. If so, was the increase in contact with kin linked to greater use of established means of communication or to the development of social media?

## Background

In the Western and developed world, the fate of family cohesion has long been a subject of debate. The French sociologist LePlay (1872/1982) was among the first to present a gloomy scenario for intergenerational support. He described aging parents left alone on the family farm by children who deserted the countryside for the greater economic opportunities of the cities. Later, the American sociologist Ernest Burgess (1926) ascribed to modernization the emergence of a small family liberated from the broad kin network. Indeed, Parsons (1949) described the nuclear family of parents and minor children as the only functional family type given industrial demand for mobile workers.

More recent thinking pushes back on the decline-of-the-extended-family thesis (Settersten, 2007), if only because there is a high level of exchange, affection, and contact between parents and grown children today (Swartz, 2009). Adults are more likely to have a surviving parent (Watkins, Menken, & Bongaarts, 1987). Parents are more likely to have a child nearby (Gillespie & Treas, 2017; Hank, 2007). Most Americans describe relationships with their parents as close (Lawton, Silverstein, & Bengtson, 1994). Fully 80–90% of adults in Europe and the USA report weekly contact with their mothers (Kalmijn & De Vries, 2009). Parents and grown children actively exchange support and services (Albertini, Kohli, & Vogel, 2007). Unfortunately, beyond demographic estimates of kin availability (Watkins et al., 1987) and historical trends in multigenerational households (Ruggles, 2007), longitudinal data are lacking to assess the relative vitality of contemporary family networks. Speculation that intergenerational cohesion is on the rise typically reasons from documented shifts in the composition of populations (Bengtson, 2001; Uhlenberg, 2005). To take one example, the growing numbers of singles is said to imply increased solidarity between the generations (Swartz, 2009), not only because the competing demands of marriage limit couples' engagement with the broader kin contact (Hank, 2007; Sarkisian & Gerstel, 2008) but also because single offspring may need more parental help.

Research results on trends in family solidarity have been mixed. A classic study found that working-class Londoners socialized often with family members (Bott, 1957/2001), but research on couples living in new housing estates outside London reported little traditional reliance on kin support (Young & Wilmott, 1954/1986). A 1962–1975 drop in the frequency that older Americans saw adult children was described (Crimmins & Ingegneri, 1990), but other research could not infer a trend for the UK in the 1980s and 1990s (Grundy & Shelton, 2001). Recent studies have offered more consistent support for increased kin contact. Recent Dutch cohorts of older adults interact more often with their children than earlier ones (van der Pas, van Tilburg, & Knipscheer, 2007). Between 1979 and 1994, repeated cross-sections showed that Swiss older adults also interacted more frequently with kin (Vollenwyder, Bickel, d'Epiney, & Maystre, 2002). Considering four European countries and the USA, no change in the frequency that adults visited their mothers between 1986 and 2001 was found, but remote contacts trended up (Kalmijn & De Vries, 2009). A later study analyzing seven countries confirmed that the increases were limited to mediated contacts via letter, phone, FAX, or internet (Treas & Gubernskaya, 2012).

## Did Maternal Contact Increase over Time?

Seven countries (Australia, Austria, West Germany, Great Britain, Hungary, Italy, and the USA) collected data on maternal contact in both the 1986 and 2001 ISSP. Pooling the two surveys, four countries saw significant ($p < 0.001$) increases in the frequency of remote contacts with mother (Treas & Gubernskaya, 2012). The four countries were notably diverse, including two market-oriented, individualistic cultures (Australia and Great Britain), a familistic society with more limited welfare provisions (Italy), and a country that was undergoing the transition from socialism (Hungary). Of the seven countries considered, Italians had the most frequent remote contacts and Hungarians the least. Italians averaged *at least once a week* in 1986 but edged up toward *at least several times a week* by 2001. Hungarians barely averaged *several times a year* in 1986; 15 years later, they reported between *several times a week* and *once a week*. The increase in interaction was limited to remote contacts. None of the seven countries saw a statistically significant change over the period in the mean frequency that adult children saw or visited mothers.

Figure 8.1 shows 1986–2001 net differences by country. They are based on multivariate, seemingly unrelated regressions (SUR) that simultaneously estimate frequencies of remote contacts and in-person visits. Even adjusting for a host of predictive covariates (gender, age, marital status, number of siblings, years of

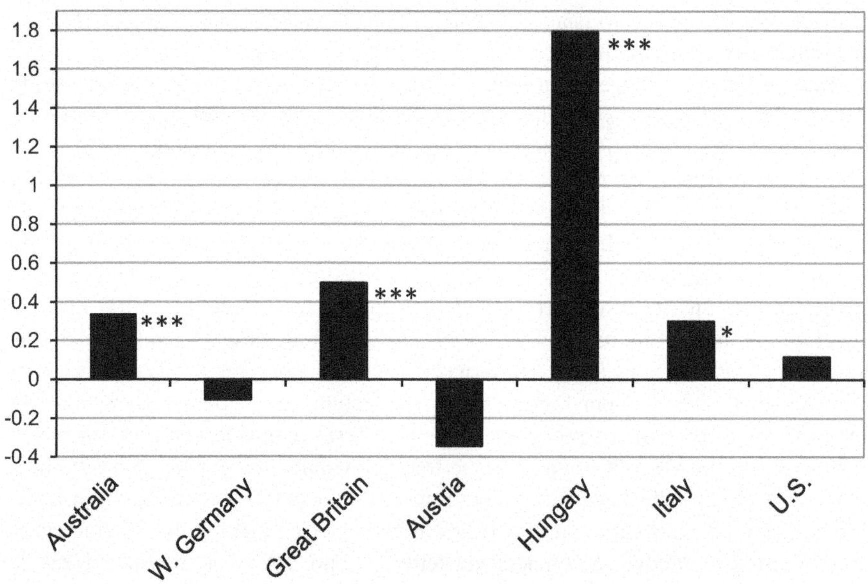


**Fig. 8.1** Difference in predicted contact with mother between 1986 and 2001 by country. $^{***}p < 0.001$, $^{**}p < 0.01$, $^{*}p < 0.05$. From the seemingly unrelated regression models (Treas & Gubernskaya, 2012, Table 2) adjusted for gender, age, marital status, number of siblings, years of education, family income, employment status, religiosity, and travel time

education, family income, employment status, religiosity, travel time to mother, and time squared), Australia, Great Britain, Hungary, and Italy still displayed statistically significant increases in remote contacts over the 15-year period. Thus, the results of the multivariate analysis inspire further confidence that there was an increase over time in contacts mediated by phone, internet, fax, or mail.

## *Did Population Changes Account for Increases in Maternal Contact?*

Changes over time in the composition of national populations are plausible explanations for trends in intergenerational relationships (Bengtson, 2001; Settersten, 2007; Treas, 1977). A number of individual-level factors, most of which have increased over time, are positively related to having more frequent maternal contact. These include being female (Hank, 2007; Treas & Cohen, 2006), having fewer siblings (Grundy & Shelton, 2001; Hank, 2007), being unmarried (Hank, 2007; Sarkisian & Gerstel, 2008), embracing secular values (Silverstein, Gans, & Yang, 2006), and being young or old rather than middle aged (Grundy & Shelton, 2001; Treas & Cohen, 2006). Theoretically, individuals with these characteristics might be expected to have increased maternal contact over time.

Of course, there are other factors that increased over time but are negatively related to contact, at least for visits. They include education (Kalmijn, 2006; Spitze & Logan, 1991) and residential distance between the generations (Hank, 2007; Mok, Wellman, & Carrasco, 2010). Evidence is inconclusive for income (Sarkisian & Gerstel, 2008; Waite & Harrison, 1992), perhaps because it both facilitates interaction and makes kin exchanges less essential. Nor has employment provided consistent results (Ikkink, van Tilburg, & Knipscheer, 1999; Waite & Harrison, 1992) despite arguments that the time demands of employment compete with extended kin (Treas, 1977).

Using the Blinder–Oaxaca method (Jann, 2008), the 1986–2001 increase in frequency of remote maternal contacts was algebraically decomposed into two components: (1) differences due to changing characteristics of the population (i.e., changes in means) and (2) differences due to changing weights for those characteristics (i.e., changes in coefficients; Treas & Gubernskaya, 2012). Population shifts registered in the changing means for sociodemographic characteristics of non-coresident adult children, including gender, age, marital status, number of siblings, years of education, family income, employment status, religiosity, and travel time. Following prior research and theorizing, these sociodemographic changes in population composition were hypothesized to account for the over-time increase in remote maternal contacts.

The results of the demographic decomposition exercise did not find compositional shifts to matter much for overall changes in the frequency of contact between mothers and grown children. Taken together, the various changes in population composition accounted for only 19% of the 1986–2001 increase in frequency of remote maternal contacts. Sociodemographic changes largely offset one another. Increased employment and declining religiosity depressed remote maternal contacts, but their effects were swamped by the positive influence on contact of increases in unmarried persons, education, and family income, as well as declines in numbers of siblings. Gender, age, and travel time did not register statistically significant contributions to the increased frequency of remote maternal contacts. Although many variables had predictable influences on remote intergenerational interaction, explanations based on overall changes in the demographic composition of populations were inadequate explanations of this change, if only because different trends worked against one another.

## *Are Mobile Phones a Plausible Explanation for Increased Maternal Contact?*

We find limited support for theorizing that links the increase in intergenerational solidarity to overall population shifts. Findings emerging from our prior analyses, however, do point to mobile phones as a neglected explanation for why Europeans in several diverse countries saw contact with their mothers increase at the end of the twentieth century.

First, due to the serendipity of the ISSP's 1986 and 2001 survey years, the observed increase in the frequency of maternal contact can be dated to the historical period that coincides with the growth of the mass market for mobile phones (Agar, 2013). The pervasiveness of mobile handheld devices rests on many innovations accomplished in a remarkably short period of time. These included the refinement of the underlying technology, the creation of cellular phone systems connected to existing public telephone systems, a build-out beyond big cities, and miniaturization transforming clunky cordless devices into genuinely mobile phones. On the road to transforming social relationships, there was the need for pricing that not only made cell phones attractive for business as well as personal use but also allowed handheld phones to compete with popular consumer technology such as pagers. Again, in much of the developed world, these innovations were largely accomplished between 1986 and 2001. In the Nordic countries that had introduced mobile cell phones to Europe, only about 2% of the population in 1987 had the devices, which were primarily for use on the job (Agar, 2013).

Second, recall that no country saw a statistically significant increase in the frequency of children seeing or visiting mothers. Increases in maternal contact were limited to *other* contacts that did not require face-to-face presence. This discounts the notion that contact frequency was driven by some unmeasured "taste" variable that increased grown children's desire to interact with mothers. Changing contact preferences would no doubt have registered on both in-person and remote contacts. Mobile phone technology was developed specifically to further remote communication. We would not expect mobile phones to have an impact on the frequency of visiting and seeing mothers. Although cheaper and more convenient phone calls make it easier to plan get-togethers, they also reduce the need for face-to-face visits to exchange information, for example. Thus, the decline or no change in in-person contacts is consistent with a unique role for handheld, cordless phones.

Third, *the end of geography* (Graham, 1998) and *time-space compression* (Harvey, 1990) have been central themes for new information and communication technologies. Together with developments in the faster movement of goods and people, the internet and mobile phones were argued to diminish the importance of distance. Remember that Austria and Hungary both demonstrated a 1986–2001 decline in the importance of proximity for the frequency of remote contacts between adult children and their mothers (Treas & Gubernskaya, 2012). This significant interaction between survey time and geographic space is what we would expect to see with new communication technologies that overcome the prior constraints of geography.

Figure 8.2 illustrates this interaction between survey year and mother–child residential distance, adjusted not only for the main effects of year and travel time, but also for gender, age, marital status, number of siblings, years of education, family income, employment status, and religiosity. The interaction terms for both countries were significant at the $p < 0.05$ level.

In the landline era of 1986, higher charges for long-distance calls discouraged remote contacts between those who lived far apart. In Fig. 8.2, the 1986 line for Austria shows just this pattern: The frequency of remote maternal contacts falls off from at least once a week for children living within 15 min of mother to once a month for those more than 12 h away. The 2001 line, however, is almost flat, indicating that distance had a considerably smaller effect on the frequency that Austrians contacted mothers remotely. In Hungary, the 2001 line was also notably flatter than in 1986. Although distance came to matter less for maternal contacts between the

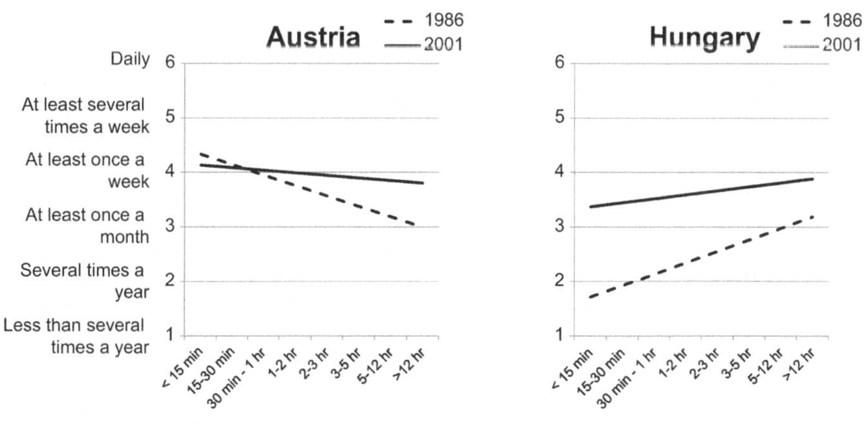


**Fig. 8.2** Predicted relationship between travel time and other contacts with mothers in 1986 and 2001. Source: Treas and Gubernskaya (2012)

two years, the Hungarian relationship between maternal contact and distance is paradoxically positive. This no doubt reflects the unique situation in socialist countries like Hungary where there were only seven landline phones per 100 persons in 1986 (The World Bank, n.d.-a). Grown children lived comparatively close to their mothers (results not shown), and public transportation was heavily subsidized. Hungarians most likely to call home were, therefore, likely to be those living far away. These two cases fall short of confirming that the diffusion of mobile phones led to the increases in remote contacts with mothers seen in 2001 versus 1986. Considering the time period observed and the lack of change in in-person visits, however, the evidence for the decline-of-geography thesis motivates a test of the notion that mobile phones had a positive effect on one key aspect of intergenerational solidarity.

Being so early in the diffusion process, the subscription variable can be thought of as measuring change from a zero baseline in the era of no mobile phones.

## *Did Mobile Phone Diffusion Account for Increased Maternal Contacts?*

Ideally, a researcher interested in adult intergenerational cohesion at the dawn of the mobile phone era would have followed individuals over time to observe changes in maternal contact as they adopted the new technology. Studying the implications of mobile phones for intergenerational contact is frustrated by the general lack of individual-level, longitudinal data for this historical period. Instead, we leveraged on cross-national variation in cell phone adoption. The pace and timing of the early diffusion of mobile phones in various countries probably owed less to demand than supply, namely, the speed with which the new phone systems were developed. Cell phone subscriptions give a clear idea of the countries that led or lagged in the adoption of mobile phones. The World Bank (n.d.-b) provides country-specific data on mobile phone subscriptions. Figure 8.3 illustrates not merely the rapid growth in access to mobile phones but also the extent to which people in various countries had access to mobile phones at different time points. For instance, in 2000 the number of mobile phone subscriptions varied from 30 per 100 persons in Hungary to over 75 per 100 persons in the UK, Switzerland, and Italy. With only 39 subscriptions per 100 persons in 2000, mobile phones were not as prevalent in the USA during the early 2000s compared to other developed countries (Stanley, 1999).

For 24 countries (Australia, Austria, Brazil, Canada, Chile, Czech Republic, Denmark, Finland, France, Germany, Great Britain, Hungary, Israel, Italy, Japan, Latvia, New Zealand, Norway, Poland, Russia, Slovenia, Spain, Switzerland, and the USA), we link country-specific data from the World Bank on 2001 mobile phone subscriptions per 100 persons and individual-level ISSP data for this year on grown children's maternal contact frequency. This permits a test of the hypothesis that countries where people had greater access to mobile phones were countries where grown children had more frequent remote contact with mothers.

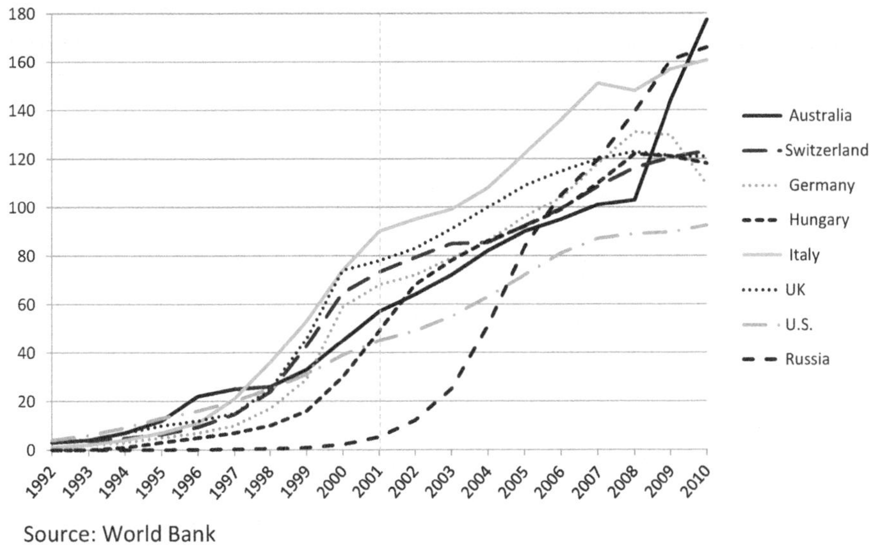


**Fig. 8.3** Mobile phone subscriptions per 100 persons. Source: World Bank

The hypothesis was tested using a random intercept two-level model (Gubernskaya & Treas, 2016). The model predicted frequency of remote contact in 2001 based on country-level mobile phone subscriptions and GNP per capita, a control for country wealth that might facilitate consumer uptake of the new phones. At the individual level, the model controlled for gender, age, marital status, numbers of children and siblings, education, employment status, religiosity, familistic attitudes, and proximity. All things considered, the results showed that mobile phone subscriptions in respondent's country were positively and significantly ($p < 0.05$) associated with the frequency of *other* remote contacts with mother. Given the newness of the mass consumer technology, each of the 24 countries studied had only recently had zero mobile phone subscribers. So, starting with this base, we can also think of the results as suggesting that the speed of mobile phone adoption was positively related to frequent maternal contacts.

The positive relationship was also seen (<0.001) even after cross-level interactions of mobile subscriptions with respondent's gender, age, and education were added to the model (Gubernskaya & Treas, 2016). The findings were consistent not only with the diffusion of mobile phones increasing the frequency of remote maternal contacts but also with impacting who called home more frequently. In keeping with traditional kin-keeping roles, women were significantly ($p < 0.001$) more responsive to the prevalence of these phones than were men. Perhaps indicative of a digital divide in mobile phone uptake, younger people's maternal contacts were more sensitive and older people less sensitive to mobile phones than were the middle aged. Predictably, given that mobile phones reduced cost barriers to calling, less educated respondents were more responsive to subscriptions than were more educated ones—so much so that there were no education differences for remote contacts where mobile phone access was very high.

## More Evidence from the US Data

Taken together, the analyses offer support for the hypothesis that the spread of mobile phone technology at the end of the twenty-first century resulted in greater remote contact between mothers and their adult children. The conclusion, of course, would be more persuasive if national surveys had longitudinal data on individuals' contacts and mobile phone adoption. We know of no such data for this time period. Lacking these data, we turn to a longitudinal US survey for additional evidence regarding the role of new communication media in promoting increased interaction between family members.

With three waves of individual data, Midlife in the United States (MIDUS) is a nationally representative, longitudinal survey of middle age adults. The first wave of data was collected in 1995–1996 on a representative sample of adults between ages 24 and 74 (Brim et al., 2016), followed by the second wave in 2004–2006 (Ryff et al., 2012). The third wave in 2013–2014 (Ryff et al., 2017) brought the analysis into the second decade of the twenty-first century when social media were ascendant. All three waves asked about the frequency of contact *through visits, phone calls, letters, or email* with family members who do not reside in respondent's household. The third wave also included a question about the frequency of contact with family members over *social media*, which included *Facebook*, *Twitter*, *MySpace*, *Skype*, *text messages*, *chat rooms*, etc. Although 23% of respondents were in touch daily with family members via social media in 2013–2014, these new platforms were not a factor in earlier waves. My Space did not launch until 2003, and Facebook was not available to the American public until 2006. Unlike mobile phones, not even country-specific rates for internet users were significant predictors of the frequency of maternal contact in 2001 (Gubernskaya & Treas, 2016).

MIDUS data are not directly comparable to the ISSP. They do not report visits and remote contacts separately. Nor do they distinguish mother–adult child contacts from contacts with other family members. The MIDUS data do offer insights on whether new communication media contributed to an increase in overall family contact over time, notably into the second decade of the twentieth century. And, importantly, they allow us to track changes in family contacts for individuals.

Using the three waves of MIDUS data, Table 8.1 presents the results from fixed effects regression models predicting the change in the mean frequency of contact with family members over time. The models estimate the average within-individual change between the waves while controlling for all *time-invariant* differences between the individuals, such as sex or education. The advantage of this MIDUS analysis is that we observe change in kin contact for individuals, rather than for populations whose members change across the repeated cross-sectional surveys of the ISSP. If the fixed effect results show an increase in the frequency of contact, we

**Table 8.1** Fixed effects models predicting changes in the mean frequency of contact with family members over time: MIDUS

| | Model 1 | Model 2 |
|---|---|---|
| Variables | Mean contact | Mean contact (+social media in W3) |
| Constant | 5.855*** | 5.854*** |
| | (0.016) | (0.016) |
| *(Ref.: Wave 1, 1995–1996)* | | |
| Wave 2, 2004–2006 | 0.125*** | 0.127*** |
| | (0.026) | (0.026) |
| Wave 3, 2013–2014 | 0.231*** | 0.418*** |
| | (0.031) | (0.031) |
| *N* | 12,873 | 12,874 |
| *n* | 6377 | 6377 |
| SD (u) | 1.802 | 1.796 |
| SD (e) | 1.168 | 1.161 |
| Rho | 0.580 | 0.582 |
| Corr | 0.007 | 0.006 |

***$p < 0.001$, $p < 0.01$, $p < 0.05$. Standard errors in parentheses

largely can discount the possibility that it occurred, because low-contact respondents died off and high-contact ones (e.g., young people) grew up to participate in later waves of the survey.

Asked in all three waves of MIDUS, the dependent variable in Model 1 is the mean frequency of contact with family members *through visits, phone calls, letters, or email*. Responses range from *never or hardly ever* (1) to *several times a day* (8); larger values correspond to higher frequency of contact. The dependent variable in Model 2 is the same for Wave 1 and Wave 2; in Wave 3, the mean frequency of contact was estimated based on the highest response on either contact *through visit, phone calls, letters, or email* or contact *over social media and text messages* measured on the same *1 to 8* scale (see Appendix for the exact wording of the questions and response categories).

The constant in the models is the mean contact in Wave 1 (1995–1996). On average, the respondents contacted their family members somewhat less that *several times a week* (5.855). A decade later (2004–2006), the average contact had increased by 0.125, approaching *several times a week*. Between the second wave and third wave (2013–2014), it increased 0.231, surpassing *several times a week*. On average, individuals increased kin contact by about 4% over the 20 years. As Model 2 shows, if contact over social media and text messages is taken into account, the average contact increased by 0.418 (that is, 7%) between the first and third wave.

The changes may seem modest. Over two decades, contacts went from slightly less than several times a week to slightly more. Adding social media, kin contacts bumped up a quarter of the distance to once a day. It is worth noting, however, that the average age at Wave 1 was 46. Because MIDUS oversampled middle age individuals, respondents in their 20s—those who reported the most frequent maternal contacts and who are often early adopters of new technology—constituted only 10% of the sample. As indicated by rho (the intra-class correlation coefficient), about 58% of the variation in the mean contact is due to the differences between the individuals. A very low correlation (0.007) between the intercept and the slope suggests that the change in the frequency of contact over time does not depend on the initial level of contact. This suggests that the changes were wide spread and not particularly localized to those already inclined to keep in touch with kin.

## Discussion

Cross-national analyses at the end of the twentieth century pointed to increases in remote contacts between mothers and their grown children. Because in-person visits did not increase and because the remote contact trend held even controlling for filial values, the cause does not appear to be a growing preference for maternal contact. Furthermore, decomposing the 1986–2001 difference in contact frequency into its demographic components did not find that the increase in remote contact was due to population changes. While some shifts in the composition of the populations promoted frequent contact, they were offset by shifts that discouraged it. Against a backdrop of classic theorizing on the decline of the extended family, an increase in the frequency of mother-and-adult-child contacts is striking. The puzzling failure of popular demographic explanations to account for this increase poses a challenge to our understanding.

In this chapter, we evaluate another plausible and seemingly obvious explanation: The diffusion of mobile phones is—at least in part—responsible for an increase in remote contact between kin. To the best of our knowledge, representative longitudinal data on individuals' mobile phone usage and frequency of kin contact are lacking for the critical period when mobile phones were diffusing rapidly through developed countries. This stands as a serious impediment to establishing definitively that the spread of mobile phones promoted family cohesion, as opposed to family cohesion stimulating the take-up of this new communication technology. Nonetheless, the contributions of communication technology to family solidarity is an important enough issue for us to exploit the existing, if piecemeal, data that can speak to the relation of kin communication and communication media.

The result is a set of findings, some significant and others not, that cumulatively bolster the argument that technology allowed us to realize a desire to stay in touch with family members. This argument no doubt resonates with individuals old enough to remember telephone landlines and the liberation offered by their first cell phone. Rather than withdrawing into virtual worlds, the evidence points to greater kin engagement at a distance for much of the developed world. If more recent results on social media and kin contact are any evidence, new forms of communication technology seem likely to continue to facilitate family solidarity.

## Appendix

MIDUS questions:

"This question asks about contact with family through visits, phone calls, letters, or email. How often are you in contact with any members of your family, that is, any of your brothers, sisters, parents, or children who do not live with you through visits, phone calls, letters, or email?" (asked in wave 1, 2, and 3).

"This question asks about social media, which includes Facebook, Twitter, MySpace, Skype, text messages, chat rooms, etc. How often are you in contact using social media with any members of your family, that is, any of your brothers, sisters, parents, or children who do not live with you?" (asked in wave 3 only).

Several times a day.
About once a day.
Several times a week.
About once a week.
Two or three times a month.
About once a month.
Less than once a month.
Never or hardly ever.

## References


Agar, J. (2013). *Constant touch. A global history of the mobile phone*. London, England: Icon.

Albertini, M., Kohli, M., & Vogel, C. (2007). Intergenerational transfers of time and money in European families: Common patterns – different regimes? *Journal of European Social Policy, 17*(4), 319–334.

Bengtson, V. L. (2001). The Burgess Award lecture: Beyond the nuclear family: The increasing importance of multigenerational bonds. *Journal of Marriage and Family, 63*(1), 1–16.

Bengtson, V. L., & Roberts, R. E. L. (1991). Intergenerational solidarity in aging families: An example of formal theory construction. *Journal of Marriage and Family, 53*(4), 856–870.

Bott, E. (2001). *Family and social network: Roles, norms, and external relationships in ordinary urban families* (2nd ed.). London, England: Routledge (Original work published 1957).

Brim, O. G., Baltes, P. B., Bumpass, L. L., Cleary, P. D., Featherman, D. L., Hazzard, W. R … Shweder, R. A. (2016). *Midlife in the United States (MIDUS 1), 1995-1996* (ICPSR 2760-V11). National Institute on Aging. Retrieved March 2016, from https://doi.org/10.3886/ICPSR02760.v11

Burgess, E. W. (1926). The family as a unit of interacting personalities. *The Family, 7*(1), 3–9 Retrieved from http://journals.sagepub.com/doi/pdf/10.1177/104438942600700101

Crimmins, E. M., & Ingegneri, D. G. (1990). Interaction and living arrangements of older parents and their children: Past trends, present determinants, future implications. *Research on Aging, 12*(1), 3–35. https://doi.org/10.1177/0164027590121001

Giddens, A. (1981). Time-space distanciation and the generation of power. In A. Giddens (Ed.), *A contemporary critique of historical materialism: Vol. 1. Power, property and the state* (pp. 90–108). Berkeley, CA: University of California Press.

Gillespie, B., & Treas, J. (2017). Adolescent intergenerational cohesiveness and young adult proximity to mothers. *Journal of Family Issues, 38*(6), 798–819. https://doi.org/10.1177/0192513X15598548

Graham, S. (1998). The end of geography or the explosion of place? Conceptualizing space, place and information technology. *Progress in Human Geography, 22*(2), 165–185. https://doi.org/10.1191/030913298671334137

Grundy, E., & Shelton, N. (2001). Contact between adult children and their parents in Great Britain 1986-1999. *Environment and Planning A, 33*(4), 685–697 Retrieved from http://journals.sagepub.com/doi/10.1068/a33165

Gubernskaya, Z., & Treas, J. (2016). Call home? Mobile phones and contacts with mother in 24 countries. *Journal of Marriage and Family, 78*(5), 1237–1249.

Hank, K. (2007). Proximity and contacts between older parents and their children: A European comparison. *Journal of Marriage and Family, 69*(1), 157–173.

Harvey, D. (1990). *The condition of postmodernity: An enquiry into the origins of cultural change*. Cambridge, MA: Blackwell.

Ikkink, K. K., van Tilburg, T., & Knipscheer, K. C. P. M. (1999). Perceived instrumental support exchanges in relationships between elderly parents and their adult children: Normative and structural explanations. *Journal of Marriage and Family, 61*(4), 831–844.

Jann, B. (2008). The Blinder–Oaxaca decomposition for linear regression models. *Stata Journal, 8*(4), 453–479.

Kalmijn, M. (2006). Educational inequality and family relationships: Influences on contact and proximity. *European Sociological Review, 22*(1), 1–16. https://doi.org/10.1093/esr/jci036

Kalmijn, M., & De Vries, J. (2009). Change and stability in parent–child contact in five western countries. *European Journal of Population, 25*(3), 257–276.

Knodel, J. (2014). Is intergenerational solidarity really on the decline? Cautionary evidence from Thailand. *Asian Population Studies, 10*(2), 176–194. https://doi.org/10.1080/17441730.2014.902160

Lawton, L., Silverstein, M., & Bengtson, V. (1994). Affection, social contact, and geographic distance between adult children and their parents. *Journal of Marriage and Family, 56*(1), 57–68.

Le Play, F. (1982). La Reforme sociale (Tours: Mame, 1872). In C. Bodard Silver (Ed.), *Frederic Le Play on family, work and social change*. Chicago, IL: The University of Chicago Press (Original work published 1872). Retrieved from https://www.amazon.com/Family-Social-Change-Heritage-sociology/dp/0226472663

Lowenstein, A., Katz, R., & Gur-Yaish, N. (2007). Reciprocity in parent-child exchange and life satisfaction among the elderly: A cross-national perspective. *Journal of Social Issues, 63*(4), 865–883.

Mok, D., Wellman, B., & Carrasco, J. (2010). Does distance matter in the age of the Internet? *Urban Studies, 47*(13), 2747–2783.

Parsons, T. (1949). The social structure of the family. In R. N. Anshen (Ed.), *The family: Its function and destiny*. New York, NY: Harper.

Rossi, A. S., & Rossi, P. H. (1990). *Of human bonding: Parent-child relations across the life course*. New York, NY: De Gruyter.

Ruggles, S. (2007). The decline of intergenerational coresidence in the United States, 1850 to 2000. *American Sociological Review, 72*(6), 964–989.

Ryff, C., Almeida, D. M., Ayanian, J., Binkley, N., Carr, D., Coe, C., … Williams, D. (2017, November). *Midlife in the United States (MIDUS 3), 2013-2014* (ICPSR 36346-V5). National Institute on Aging. https://doi.org/10.3886/ICPSR36346.v5

Ryff, C., Almeida, D. M., Ayanian, J., Carr, D. S., Cleary, P. D., Coe, C., … Williams, D. (2012, November). *Midlife in the United States (MIDUS 2), 2004-2006* [ICPSR 04652-V6]. National Institute on Aging. https://doi.org/10.3886/ICPSR04652.v6

Sarkisian, N., & Gerstel, N. (2008). Till marriage do us part: Adult children's relationships with their parents. *Journal of Marriage and Family, 70*(2), 360–376.

Settersten, R. A., Jr. (2007). Passages to adulthood: Linking demographic change and human development. *European Journal of Population/Revue européenne de Démographie, 23*(3–4), 251–272.

Silverstein, M., & Bengtson, V. L. (1994). Does intergenerational social support influence the psychological well-being of older parents? The contingencies of declining health and widowhood. *Social Science & Medicine, 38*(7), 943–957.

Silverstein, M., Bengtson, V. L., & Lawton, L. (1997). Intergenerational solidarity and the structure of adult child-parent relationships in American families. *American Journal of Sociology, 103*(2), 429–460.

Silverstein, M., Gans, D., & Yang, F. M. (2006). Intergenerational support to aging parents: The role of norms and needs. *Journal of Family Issues, 27*(8), 1068–1084.

Spitze, G., & Logan, J. R. (1991). Sibling structure and intergenerational relations. *Journal of Marriage and Family, 53*(4), 871–884.

Stanley, A. (1999, August 5). Cell phone craze has Italy humming. *New York Times*. Retrieved from http://www.nytimes.com/1999/08/05/world/cell-phone-craze-has-italy-humming.html

Swartz, T. T. (2009). Intergenerational family relations in adulthood: Patterns, variations, and implications in the contemporary United States. *Annual Review of Sociology, 35*, 191–212.

The World Bank (n.d.-a). *Fixed telephone subscriptions*. Retrieved June 1, 2011, from The World Bank, Data https://data.worldbank.org/indicator/IT.MLT.MAIN

The World Bank (n.d.-b). *Mobile cellular subscriptions (per 100 people)*. Retrieved September 1, 2017, from The World Bank, Data https://data.worldbank.org/indicator/IT.CEL.SETS.P2

Treas, J. (1977). Family support systems for the aged: Some social and demographic considerations. *The Gerontologist, 17*(6), 486–491. https://doi.org/10.1093/geront/17.6.486

Treas, J., & Cohen, P. (2006). Maternal co-residence and contact: Evidence from cross-national surveys. In A. H. Gauthier, C. Y. C. Chu, & S. Tuljapurkar (Eds.), *Allocating public and private resources across generations: Riding the age waves* (Vol. 2, pp. 117–137). Dordrecht, The Netherlands: Springer/Kluwer Academic Publishers.

Treas, J., & Gubernskaya, Z. (2012). Farewell to moms? Trends in maternal contact for seven countries in 1986 and 2001. *Journal of Marriage and Family, 74*, 297–311.

Uhlenberg, P. (2005). Demography of aging. In D. L. Poston & M. Micklin (Eds.), *Handbook of population* (pp. 143–167). New York, NY: Springer.

van der Pas, S., van Tilburg, T., & Knipscheer, K. (2007). Changes in contact and support in intergenerational relationships in the Netherlands: A cohort and time sequential perspective. *Advances in Life Course Research, 12*, 243–274.

Vollenwyder, N., Bickel, J.-F., d'Epiney, C. L., & Maystre, C. (2002). The elderly and their families, 1979-94: Changing networks and relationships. *Current Sociology, 50*(2), 263–280.

Waite, L. J., & Harrison, S. C. (1992). Keeping in touch: How women in mid-life allocate social contacts among kith and kin. *Social Forces, 70*(3), 637–654.

Watkins, S. C., Menken, J. A., & Bongaarts, J. (1987). Demographic foundations of family change. *American Sociological Review, 52*(3), 346–358.

Young, M. D., & Willmott, P. (1986). *Family and kinship in East London*. London, England: Penguin Books (Original work published 1957).

# Chapter 9
# Reducing Risk for Mental Health Conditions Associated with Social Media Use: Encouraging "REAL" Communication

**Brian A. Primack, Ariel Shensa, Jaime E. Sidani, Nicholas Bowman, Jennifer Knight, Sabrina A. Karim, Meghan Bisbey, Jason B. Colditz, Michelle S. Woods, and Cesar G. Escobar-Viera**

The most common mental health conditions, depression and anxiety, are increasing in prevalence and morbidity. For example, depression is now considered the leading cause of disability worldwide (World Health Organization, 2017). In the USA, the economic burden of depression is over $210 billion (Greenberg, Fournier, Sisitsky, Pike, & Kessler, 2015). Moreover, many individuals with depression also experience physical or psychiatric comorbidities—such as anxiety—that contribute to the overall disease burden (Greenberg et al., 2015). Only about half of individuals experiencing common mental health conditions receive treatment in the USA, and fewer than 10% receive treatment in many other countries (Center for Behavioral Health Statistics and Quality, 2015; World Health Organization, 2017). Depression is associated with a combination of biological, psychological, and social factors (World Health Organization, 2017). Prior research has identified media exposures, such as video games, television, movies, and the Internet, to be associated with the depression among adolescents (Bickham, Hswen, & Rich, 2015; Primack, Swanier, Georgiopoulos, Land, & Fine, 2009).

However, social media (SM) use has presented a puzzle in terms of its relationship with conditions such as depression and anxiety. SM use is rapidly increasing

B. A. Primack (✉)
University Honors College, University of Pittsburgh, Pittsburgh, PA, USA
e-mail: bprimack@pitt.edu

A. Shensa · J. E. Sidani · M. S. Woods · C. G. Escobar-Viera
Department of Medicine, University of Pittsburgh, Pittsburgh, PA, USA

N. Bowman · J. Knight
Department of Communication, University of West Virginia, Morgantown, WV, USA

S. A. Karim
University of Pittsburgh School of Medicine, Pittsburgh, PA, USA

M. Bisbey · J. B. Colditz
Center for Research on Media, Technology, and Health, University of Pittsburgh, Pittsburgh, PA, USA



J. Van Hook et al. (eds.), *Families and Technology*, National Symposium on Family Issues 9, https://doi.org/10.1007/978-3-319-95540-7_9

worldwide; for example, in the USA, the percentage of young adults using SM skyrocketed from 12% in 2005 to 90% in 2015 (Perrin, 2015). Among online adults in 2016, Facebook remains the most popular SM platform (79%, a 7% increase from 2015), followed by Instagram (32%), Pinterest (31%), LinkedIn (29%), and Twitter (24%; Greenwood, Perrin, & Duggan, 2016). Of note, as of 2016, a marked proportion of American adults (62%) reported getting their news from SM (Gottfried & Shearer, 2016).

Because the goal of SM platforms is to connect individuals, it is not surprising that some studies suggest the ability of SM to enhance emotional support, which would suggest the potential to alleviate conditions such as depression and/or anxiety. For example, Facebook use among college students may help maintain previously established relationships, and benefits seem to be particularly strong among users with low self-esteem and low life satisfaction (Ellison, Vitak, Gray, & Lampe, 2014). In addition to preserving existing social ties, SM facilitates the formation of new connections, which provides people with an alternative way to connect with others who share similar interests (Ellison, Heino, & Gibbs, 2006; Ellison, Steinfield, & Lampe, 2007). Furthermore, individuals with a greater number of SM connections report having greater social capital, which has also been associated with lower depression (Ellison, Steinfield, & Lampe, 2011; Ellison et al., 2014; Steinfield, Ellison, & Lampe, 2008). This may be because those with greater social capital are able to draw upon resources from other members of their networks, leading to useful information, new personal relationships, and employment opportunities (Granovetter, 1973; Paxton, 1999). Consistent with all of this information, having a larger Facebook audience has been associated with increased life satisfaction, perceived social support, and subjective well-being (Kim & Lee, 2011; Manago, Taylor, & Greenfield, 2012).

However, other studies suggest that increased SM exposure may counterintuitively be associated with *increased depression* among both adolescents (Lou, Yan, Nickerson, & McMorris, 2012; Pantic et al., 2012) and adults (Kross et al., 2013; Lin et al., 2016; McDougall et al., 2016; Shensa, Sidani, Lin, Bowman, & Primack, 2016). This may be because SM facilitates engagement in social comparison, giving users the impression that others tend to be happier and more meaningfully engaged than the users themselves (Acar, 2008; Chou & Edge, 2012; Lup, Trub, & Rosenthal, 2015). Frequency of social media use may lead to media multitasking—either between social media platforms or between social media and other tasks—which has been associated with depression, social anxiety, and declines in academic performance (Becker, Alzahabi, & Hopwood, 2013; Cain, Leonard, Gabrieli, & Finn, 2016; Xu, Wang, & David, 2016).

The primary purpose of this chapter is to review and summarize our recent studies that have explored this association between SM use and mental health. A secondary purpose is to propose a new paradigm through which to summarize the results. We developed this paradigm with attention toward informing future research and initial attempts at intervention in this area. The resulting mnemonic—REAL—suggests that, in order to reduce the risk of mental health problems related to SM, it may be useful to: (1) *R*enege negativity in SM interactions; (2) actively *E*ngage with

SM, but in a balanced *E*quilibrium; (3) focus SM attention on *A*ctual *A*llies—close "real-life" contacts as opposed to individuals with whom one has less direct interpersonal experience; and (4) *L*imit SM use not only in terms of time and frequency but also the number of platforms used.

# Methods

We conducted two overarching studies that form the basis for the data presented here. One was a 2014 survey of a nationally representative sample of about 1800 young adults, and the second was a more focused 2016 survey of a convenience sample of about 1200 young adults attending a large mid-Atlantic public university.

## *Study 1*

### Participants and Procedures

This study involved a nationally representative sample of the US young adults aged 19–32. We drew our sample from a large-scale web-based research panel developed and maintained by a survey research company called Growth from Knowledge (GfK; GfK KnowledgePanel®, 2013). Participants were recruited via random digit dialing and address-based sampling, reaching a sampling frame of over 97% of the US population (GfK KnowledgePanel®, 2013). The GfK Knowledge Panel® model has been shown to be a statistically valid method for surveying and analyzing health indicators from a nationally representative sample (Baker et al., 2010; Wagner, Baker, Bundorf, & Singer, 2004). From October to November 2014, the web-based survey was sent via email to a random sample of 3048 noninstitutionalized adults between the ages of 19 and 32 who had consented to participate in a previous study wave. The current data were collected during the 18-month follow-up of this study, which assessed multiple health behaviors among individuals ages 18–30 at baseline. We used only the 18-month follow-up data because the social media items were not asked at baseline. Responses were received from 1787 participants (59%). The median time for survey completion was 15 min and participants received $15 for their participation. This study was approved by the University of Pittsburgh Institutional Review Board and was granted a Certificate of Confidentiality from the National Institutes of Health.

**Measures** Participants completed online survey items including mental health outcomes (dependent variables), social media use (independent variable), and covariates. Mental health outcomes included depression, anxiety, and social isolation, which were all assessed using four-item scales developed by the Patient-Reported

Outcomes Measurement Information System (PROMIS). PROMIS is a National Institutes of Health Roadmap initiative whose aim is to provide precise, valid, reliable, and standardized questionnaires measuring patient-reported outcomes (PROs) across the domains of physical, mental, and social health (Cella et al., 2010).

The PROMIS depression scale was developed using item response theory to promote greater precision and decrease respondent burden (Cella, Gershon, Lai, & Choi, 2007). Specifically, the PROMIS depression scale has been correlated and validated with other commonly used depression instruments, including the Center for Epidemiological Studies Depression Scale (CES-D), the Beck Depression Inventory (BDI-II), and the Patient Health Questionnaire (PHQ-9; Choi, Schalet, Cook, & Cella, 2014; Pilkonis et al., 2014). The four-item PROMIS depression scale asked participants how frequently in the past 7 days they had experienced depression, including feeling hopeless, worthless, helpless, or depressed (Pilkonis et al., 2011). The PROMIS anxiety scale has been validated against the Mood and Anxiety Symptoms Questionnaire (MASQ), Generalized Anxiety Disorder Scale (GAD-7), and the Positive and Negative Affective Schedule (PANAS). Symptoms assessed included feeling fearful, anxious misery, and hyperarousal (Shensa et al., 2016).

We assessed participants' social media use in three complementary ways. First, participants were asked to estimate *total time per day* on social media for personal use. This item specifically instructed participants to not count any time spent on social media for work. Participants provided estimates in numerical fields for hours and minutes on an average day. Second, participants were asked to report their use of each of 11 widely used social media platforms, including Facebook, Twitter, Google+, YouTube, LinkedIn, Instagram, Pinterest, Tumblr, Vine, Snapchat, and Reddit (Duggan, Ellison, Lampe, Lenhart, & Madden, 2015; The Nielsen Company, 2012). Seven response choices ranged from "I do not use this platform" to "I use this platform 5 or more times a day." We based these items on the measures used by Pew Internet Research (Duggan et al., 2015). Using weighted averages based on the frequency responses, we computed social media site *visits per week*. Finally, we summed responses across platforms to obtain a total score without weighting values for frequency. Because there were seven response choices for each item which we coded as 0–6, the resulting *global frequency score* ranged from 0 to 66. In order to improve interpretability of results, we collapsed all independent variables into quartiles for primary analyses. To ensure robustness of results, we also conducted all analyses with independent variables as continuous.

We assessed multiple relevant covariates. For example, for analysis, we divided the sample into three age groups (19–23; 24–26; 27–32) and race/ethnicity into five mutually exclusive groups (White, non-Hispanic; Black, non-Hispanic; Hispanic; Biracial, multiracial; or Other, non-Hispanic). We also assessed other environmental and personal factors that may affect depression and social media use (Duggan et al., 2015; Kessler, Chiu, Demler, Merikangas, & Walters, 2005). These included relationship status (single or in a committed relationship), living situation (with a parent or guardian; with a significant other; or other situation), household income (under \$30,000; \$30,000–\$74,999; or \$75,000 or more), and education level (high school or less; some college; or bachelor's degree or higher).

**Analyses** To describe our sample, we computed percentages of the dependent variables, each of the independent variables, and the seven covariates. Next, we used chi-square tests to determine bivariable associations between each of the independent variables and covariates and the PROMIS outcomes. Because most outcome measures were ordered categorically (e.g., "low," "medium," or "high" risk for depression), after confirming that the proportional odds assumption was met, we used ordered logistic regression with appropriate sample weights to examine bivariable and multivariable associations between each social media variable and outcome. We decided a priori to include all covariates in our primary multivariable models. We also used regression analyses to examine whether there was an overall linear trend between each ordered categorical independent variable and the dependent variable. In order to take advantage of the nationally representative nature of the data, all primary analyses were conducted using survey weights which took into account sex, age, race/ethnicity, education, household income, census region, metropolitan area, and internet access.

Multiple sets of sensitivity analyses were conducted to examine the robustness of our results. For example, we conducted all analyses with the outcome variables as dichotomous instead of in tertiles. Second, we conducted all analyses with independent variables as continuous instead of ordered categorical variables. Third, we conducted all analyses using only covariates that had a bivariable association of $p < 0.15$ with the outcome (in order to avoid overcontrolling). Fourth, we conducted all analyses without survey weights. Results from all sensitivity analyses showed similar levels of significance and magnitude to those described here.

Statistical analyses were performed with Stata (Stata Corp, College Station, Texas), and two-tailed $p$-values $<0.05$ were considered to be significant.

## *Study 2*

**Participants and Setting** For this study, we conducted an online survey of adults 18 and above between July and August 2016. Participants were recruited in two ways. First, they were recruited from the social networking site Reddit, an online community of registered members, or "redditors." Registration on Reddit is anonymous and does not require an email address. Redditors may create posts, submit links to news and events, or upload pictures. Posts are organized and aggregated by topic, or "subreddits" (e.g., music, image sharing, news, location, or community). We identified 39 potential subreddits by conducting a search for "depression" on the main Reddit site. Because many subreddits require moderator approval to post surveys or research projects, we submitted requests to each subreddit for which a moderator could be identified. Of the 39 depression-related subreddits, seven granted us approval to post (/r/depression, /r/EOOD, /r/GFD, /r/depressionregimens,

/r/PostPartum_Depression, /r/trolldepression, and /r/mentalhealth). Additionally, we were granted permission to post on a local community subreddit (/r/ MorgantownWV). Because participation in surveys on Reddit increases if the researchers maintain a presence on the subreddit (Shatz, 2016), one of the authors was available on each subreddit to engage with the community and establish trust by answering questions.

A second method of recruiting for this study involved opening the survey questionnaire to students at the University of West Virginia. In August 2016, participants were recruited via an email distributed to all registered students, including both undergraduate and graduate students. The email invited recipients to participate in an online survey designed to understand both the positive and negative associations between SM use and well-being. Enrollment continued until about 1200 responses were received; this figure was based on power calculations that relied upon prior distributions and estimates for the independent and dependent variables.

Whether they were recruited via Reddit or West Virginia University (WVU), participants who clicked on the link were directed to an introduction explaining the study and an informed consent to participate in a 15-min survey. Those participants who consented were entered into a drawing for $50 gift cards (one card for every 25 participants who completed the survey). Data collection procedures were approved by the West Virginia University Institutional Review Board.

Importantly, we retained the ability to analyze data individually for either the Reddit population or the WVU population by including unique identifiers. We selected the appropriate population for each individual study based on the purpose of that particular study and the potential relevance to a more general population of college students and/or a population more specifically interested in mental health (as one would expect when recruiting via subreddits primarily focused on mental health).

**Measures** Participants completed a questionnaire that asked about depressive symptoms, social media use (SMU), and demographic variables. The dependent variables were the same as those described in Study 1. Similarly, the covariates used were the same as those described in Study 1. However, we leveraged this second data collection to capture a more nuanced and wider variety of data around SMU. For example, we measured both *passive and active SMU* with seven items originally developed by Pagani and colleagues for general Internet use (Pagani, Hofacker, & Goldsmith, 2011; Pagani & Mirabello, 2011) and later validated for research in the field of journalism and mass communications (Li, 2016). Participants were asked how often they usually engage in a number of behaviors while using any SM site (Li, 2016). Items associated with passive SMU included "read discussions," "read comments/reviews," and "watch videos or view pictures." Items associated with active SMU included "like/favorite/voting," "share others' content," "comment on or respond to someone else's content," and "post your own content." Response options were categorized as "never," "less than once a week," "once a week," "2-6 times a week," "once a day," and "several times a day."

We also assessed *positive and negative experiences on SM* by directly asking participants to estimate what percentage of their SM experiences involved positive and negative experiences, respectively. Participants interpreted the meaning of positive and negative experiences. This decision to allow participants to do so was made after focus groups suggested that offering various interpretations of positive and negative experiences would be counterproductive. We presented participants with sliders ranging from 0 to 100 as the response choice for each item. The resulting two scores served as independent variables. For logistic regression analyses, we transformed responses into a 10-point scale (1 point for every 10%), based on the natural distribution of responses around these anchors and to improve interpretability of results.

Finally, we assessed *real-life closeness* of participants' SM contacts using three items. These items asked individuals to approximate what proportion of their friends on the SM platform they use most they consider to be people with whom they have (1) no face-to-face (FTF) relationship, (2) a distant FTF relationship, and (3) a close FTF relationship. We adapted these items based upon prior work, which demonstrated the distinction in quality of friendships (McEwan & Guerrero, 2010, 2012). We presented participants with a slider ranging from 0 to 100 as the response choice for each item. The resulting three scores served as independent variables. For logistic regression analyses, we transformed responses into a 10-point scale (1 point for every 10%), based on the natural distribution of responses around these anchors and to improve interpretability of results.

In order to capture tendency toward "addictive" behaviors on SM, we assessed *problematic social media use (PSMU)* using a set of items adapted from the Bergen Facebook Addiction Scale (BFAS; Andreassen, Torsheim, Brunborg, & Pallesen, 2012). Each item represented one of six core elements of addiction (salience, mood modification, tolerance, withdrawal, conflict, and relapse). In the context of this study, we did not use this scale as a diagnostic tool, but instead sought to characterize a pattern of maladaptive SMU. We asked participants to respond based upon past year frequency using a Likert-type response scale with anchors of 0: *Very rarely* and 4: *Very often*. While original items specified "Facebook," we substituted "social media" to encompass more general SMU. The resulting composite scale ranged from 0 to 24 and served as the independent variable in our model.

**Analysis** Analyses were similar to those from Study 1. After describing our sample, we used chi-square tests to determine bivariable associations between each of the independent variables and covariates and the PROMIS outcomes. As in Study 1, the primary analytic methods were ordered logistic regression; however, we also used logistic regression when the outcome variable was dichotomous (e.g., during sensitivity analyses). Again, we decided a priori to include all covariates in our primary multivariable models. In this case, however, we did not use survey weights because this study involved a convenience sample. We again conducted multiple sets of sensitivity analyses to examine the robustness of our results. Statistical analyses were performed with Stata (Stata Corp, College Station, Texas), and two-tailed $p$-values <0.05 were considered to be significant.

## Results and Discussion

We present a summary of results and discussion from various analyses in four overarching categories, each of which corresponds to one of the components of the REAL mnemonic.

### *R: Renege Negativity*

The R in the REAL mnemonic reminds us to Renege negativity. This is because we found initial evidence that negativity experienced during SM exchanges is associated with poorer mental health outcomes, including both depression and social isolation.

All social media experiences are not the same in terms of positive or negative subjective experience. For example, an individual can spend 2 h engaging in experiences which feel highly positive to the user—such as supporting close friends with positive messages and "likes"—while another user might spend those same 2 h having highly negative experiences including vehement arguments on emotional topics such as politics. It would be valuable to determine if these distinct experiences may be differently associated with depression; if they are, that might open up a valuable direction for intervention.

For example, in our recent pilot study of college students ages 18–30 at one large mid-Atlantic University, we asked participants approximately what percentage of their social media interactions they would classify as negative. We found that, for every 10% increase in negativity they reported, there was an associated 14–20% increase in the odds of having depression or social isolation. The magnitude of the association differed depending on the specific operationalization of the mental health outcome. However, all models were statistically significant. We made a conscious choice in phrasing the R in the negative. In other words, we specifically chose not to phrase this in terms of emphasizing the positive. This is because our preliminary results related to *positivity* in SM interactions have been weaker and less conclusive. For example, we also asked participants about what percentage of their social media interactions were positive. In this case, however, for every 10% increase in positivity, there has only been a 2–6% reduction in mental health outcomes such as depression and social isolation. Furthermore, many of these results do not retain statistical significance.

It is interesting that the effect size for negative experiences seems to be higher than that for positive experiences. This may lead to the conclusion that negative SM experiences may be more "potent" than positive experiences as related to depression. This reasoning is consistent with the concept of *negativity bias*, which purports that there is a tendency for humans to give greater emphasis to negative entities (e.g., events, objects, and personal traits) compared with positive ones (Rozin & Royzman, 2001). This may be particularly relevant in the context of SM use.

For example, while positive experiences may be associated with fleeting positive reinforcement, negative experiences such as public SM arguments may rapidly escalate due to a need to shape or defend one's "digital identity" (Cover, 2015) and may in turn leave a lasting, potentially traumatic impression on the individual.

Because these data are cross-sectional, it may be that individuals with depression tend to subsequently have more negative experiences and fewer positive experiences on SM. This explanation is plausible, because depressed and/or anhedonic individuals may seek out SM relationships due to their tendency to shun in-person social opportunities (Caplan, 2003). Or, the association between SM experiences and depression could be bidirectional in nature.

## *E: Engage with Equilibrium*

This injunction encapsulates two components. First, it suggests that there may actually be value in engaging actively with social media. In fact, as we will see, preliminary analyses suggest that taking more of an active role in terms of participating in a social media community—versus taking a more passive role—seems to be more strongly associated with positive mental health outcomes. Second, however, this component of the mnemonic suggests that it is optimal for this active engagement not to pass over into an unbalanced state characterized by "addictive" patterns.

First, we will examine the issue of active versus passive experience on social media. While navigating SM sites, users may interact on different levels. Some users respond frequently to other users and actively share life experiences, create text, audio, or video content, exemplifying the "create and collaborate" traits common to other Web 2.0 technologies (O'Reilly & Battelle, 2009). However, passive users (also known as "lurkers") tend to primarily observe and maintain an overall low engagement level with the SM site activities (Pagani & Mirabello, 2011). Passive SMU has been associated with decreased well-being (Tromholt, 2016; Verduyn et al., 2015) and social anxiety (Shaw, Timpano, Tran, & Joormann, 2015).

Passive and active SMU might have differential associations with depression. To our knowledge, three prior studies have examined this association. One study suggested that increases in public, passive Facebook use was associated with a higher risk of depression (Frison & Eggermont, 2015). Another study suggested that the association between passive Facebook use and depression is mediated by feelings of envy (Tandoc, Ferrucci, & Duffy, 2015). Finally, one study found that active Facebook use was negatively associated with depression, but only among women with neurotic personality traits (Simoncic, Kuhlman, Vargas, Houchins, & Lopez-Duran, 2014).

These three studies focused on Facebook only. However, in our study we examined a broader range of SM platforms. We considered this valuable because use of multiple platforms is prevalent and increasing. For example, use of two or more SM platforms recently increased by 10% within a single year (Duggan et al., 2015). Although SM platforms differ according to primary intended purpose and functional features, passive and active SMU imply a similar set of behaviors across platforms. Moreover, individuals may engage more actively on one SM platform while being more passive on another. In addition, passive and active SMU may not be mutually exclusive of one another. For example, one most likely engages in passive SMU (e.g., reading others' posts) before engaging in active SMU (e.g., commenting on others' posts); however, one may engage in passive SMU without engaging in active SMU.

In our multivariable analyses that controlled for all covariates, each 1-point increase in passive SM use was associated with a 33% increase in odds of reporting severe depressive symptoms (AOR = 1.33, 95% CI = 1.17–1.51). In a second model, in which we included active SMU as the main independent variable, there were no significant results. When we included both passive and active SMU as main independent variables and all demographic covariates, each 1-point increase in passive SMU was associated with a 44% increase in odds of reporting severe depressive symptoms (AOR = 1.44, 95% CI = 1.25–1.66). Additionally, each 1-point increase in active SMU was associated with a 15% decrease in odds of reporting severe depressive symptoms (AOR = 0.85, 95% CI = 0.75–0.96). Therefore, there did seem to be an association between passivity and depression; however, the association between active engagement and depression was less clear. For example, in one model there was an association between active use and less depression, while another model did not show a significant difference. Still, taken as a whole, these results suggest that a more active pattern—as compared with a passive one—may be associated with overall well-being.

However, the "E" in this case should remind us also that it may be important to keep a balance or "Equilibrium" in one's active use of SM in order to avoid problematic social media use (PSMU), which has emerged as a maladaptive pattern of SMU. While the clinical meaning of PSMU is still under study, research on the topic has been very active in recent years (Andreassen, 2015; Andreassen, Pallesen, & Griffiths, 2016; Durak & Senol-Durak, 2014; Meena, Mittal, & Solanki, 2012; Wang, Lee, & Hua, 2015). Initial measurement of PSMU focused on Facebook only (Andreassen et al., 2012; Muench, Hayes, Kuerbis, & Shao, 2015), coining the phrase "Facebook addiction." Subsequent studies found that Facebook addiction was indeed associated with depression among both high school (Hanprathet, Manwong, Khumsri, Yingyeun, & Phanasathit, 2015) and college students (Koc & Gulyagci, 2013). Furthermore, researchers have since addressed addictive characteristics of SMU more broadly, assessing addictive or problematic use of multiple social networking sites or across social media in general (Andreassen, 2015; Kuss & Griffiths, 2011; Meena et al., 2012). Thus, PSMU has been characterized as being overly concerned about and driven by a strong motivation to log on to or use social media, devoting so much time and effort to SMU that it impairs other social activities, studies/job, interpersonal relationships, and/or psychological health and well-being (Andreassen & Pallesen, 2014).

Research on the US and international populations has shown that the association between PSMU and depression is complex. For example, a study of teenagers in urban India concluded that excessive time spent on social media leads to PSMU, which subsequently and negatively impacts relationships, community involvement, and academic achievement (Meena et al., 2012). Furthermore, results from a sample of German adolescents and young adults indicate that PSMU may be linked to depression via mediators such as self-regulation and use expectation (Wegmann, Stodt, & Brand, 2015). In contrast, a recent large-scale Norwegian study of adults found that PSMU was associated with decreases in depressive symptoms (Andreassen et al., 2016).

Our analyses demonstrated that individuals in the highest quartile of PSMU had significantly increased odds of depressive symptoms compared to individuals who reported no PSMU in bivariable and multivariable models (OR = 3.66; 95% CI = 2.38–5.65; AOR = 3.13; 95% CI = 1.94–5.05, respectively). Among covariates, SMU time was also significantly associated with increased odds of depressive symptoms in the bivariable model but not in the multivariable model (OR = 1.75; 95% CI = 1.22–2.51; AOR = 0.62; 95% CI = 0.38–1.01, respectively). SMU frequency was associated with significantly increased odds of depressive symptoms in both bivariable and multivariable models (OR = 2.69; 95% CI = 1.84–3.92; AOR = 2.51; 95% CI = 1.56–4.03, respectively). Additionally, PSMU demonstrated a dose–trend relationship with depressive symptoms in bivariable and multivariable models (both significant at $p < 0.001$).

## *A: Actual Allies*

Given that SM provides the opportunity to contact people with or without any previous real-life contact, there has been increased interest in the potential importance of the "actual closeness" of SM contacts. For example, one study focused on the specific value of Facebook to maintain formerly established relationships (as opposed to creating relationships with new individuals) (Ellison et al., 2007). This study also found that there were particularly strong benefits among users with low self-esteem and low life satisfaction in this regard (Ellison et al., 2007). Similarly, studies have demonstrated that individuals with a greater number of SM "actual friends"—relationships rooted in an FTF connection—have reported greater social capital, which may enhance well-being (Ellison et al., 2011, 2014).

However, other evidence suggests that when there is no real-life closeness, SM relationships may be associated with declines in emotional well-being. For example, studies of young adult SM users found that frequency of use and inclusion of a greater number of people who participants did not know was associated with negative self-perceptions and depression (Lin et al., 2016; Shensa et al., 2016).

Therefore, having more close "real-life friends" in one's SM milieu may be associated with lower risk of depressive symptoms, while having more "strangers" (i.e., individuals never met face-to-face) in one's SM milieu may be associated with a higher risk of mental health symptoms. This pattern would be consistent with social network theory, which suggests that strong ties (i.e., real-life friends) are based on trust and affection and are likely to offer emotional support in uncertain situations

(Krackhardt, 1992). Conversely, weak ties (i.e., non-face-to-face friends) are helpful for finding new information and resources, but they may provide low levels of intimacy and relationship intensity (Granovetter, 1973).

In our study of college students ages 18–30, participants reported having *no FTF relationship* with a mean of 38.7% (SD = 30.1%) and median of 30% (IQR = 10–61%) of their SM contacts. Participants reported having a "distant" *FTF relationship* with a mean of 37.7% (SD = 25.2%) and a median of 32% (IQR = 20–55%) of their SM contacts. Finally, they reported having a "close" *FTF relationship* with a mean of 34.5% (SD = 26.7%) and a median of 27% (IQR = 12–50%) of their SM contacts. Therefore, it is not uncommon to maintain connections with a variety of individuals—some known outside of SM and some not.

Multivariable results demonstrated that the proportion of SM contacts with which one had *no FTF relationship* was significantly associated with depressive symptoms (AOR = 1.09; 95% CI = 1.05–1.13; $p < 0.001$), after controlling for age, sex, race/ethnicity, relationship status, and living situation. The proportion of individuals with which one had a *distant FTF relationship* was *not* significantly associated with depressive symptoms in multivariable models. Finally, the proportion of SM contacts with which one had a *close FTF relationship* was significantly associated with *decreased* odds of depressive symptoms (AOR = 0.93; 95% CI = 0.89–0.97; $p = 0.001$), after controlling for age, sex, race/ethnicity, relationship status, and living situation.

This study extended prior studies by: (1) assessing SM as a general construct instead of focusing on one platform, (2) examining real-life closeness of SM contacts across a spectrum (no FTF, distant FTF, and close FTF relationship), and (3) assessing risk of depression using a reliable and valid scale. The results were interesting; they suggested that SM relationships may actually be detrimental if they include individuals with whom the users have no real-life closeness. One explanation for this may be that, compared with real-life relationships, SM-only relationships may be characterized by lower reciprocity (Almaatouq, Radaelli, Pentland, & Shmueli, 2016; Greitemeyer, Mügge, & Bollermann, 2014). For example, it is common on platforms such as Instagram or Twitter to have relationship asymmetry, in which an individual follows a contact but is not followed back, and prior research on tie strength has noted the importance of mutually acknowledged relationships (Friedkin, 1980). Thus, SM-only contacts may offer little substantive support. Another plausible explanation for the association between having no FTF relationship with SM contacts and depressive symptoms is the exposure to potentially detrimental content. This phenomenon is supported by social comparison theory (Chou & Edge, 2012; Krasnova, Widjaja, Buxmann, Wenninger, & Benbasat, 2015). For example, on SM users often present an idealized, highly curated version of themselves. Increased exposure to this content may lead to harmful social comparisons, envy, and subsequent depressive feelings (Chou & Edge, 2012; Krasnova et al., 2015; Tandoc et al., 2015). Finally, individuals with a greater proportion of SM-only contacts may also engage in contentious interactions that they would otherwise avoid given the inherent accountability of a future FTF encounter. These negative SM experiences may then lead to negative affect, rumination, and depression (Davila et al., 2012; Feinstein, Bhatia, Hershenberg, & Davila, 2012).

Because these data are cross-sectional, it may also be that individuals with more severe depressive symptoms tend to have a greater proportion of SM-only contacts. This explanation is plausible because social anxiety, social isolation, and poor self-image—conditions that often accompany depression—may make SM-only relationships more appealing (Caplan, 2003). For example, SM relationships can be accessed from home and do not require the spontaneity of FTF interactions. To that end, individuals who suffer from depression may perceive online social interaction as less threatening and believe themselves to be more effective in this environment than FTF (Caplan, 2003). Additionally, individuals who have chronic recurrent depression may have less established FTF relationships perhaps due to unemployment, lack of social affiliation, or failed relationships (Crabtree, 2014; Vujeva & Furman, 2011). Thus, the proportion of SM-only friendships would naturally be greater. Alternatively, the association between composition of SM contacts and depressive symptoms is bidirectional in nature.

This study also found that having a greater proportion of SM contacts with whom participants had close FTF relationships was associated with decreased depressive symptoms. This finding reflects the body of research that demonstrates the benefits of SM use (Ellison et al., 2007; Manago et al., 2012) and suggests that using SM to supplement or maintain established FTF relationships may be associated with less depression. For example, the ease and accessibility of SM can facilitate more consistent and frequent communication that would otherwise be challenging to maintain due to factors such as geographic separation, lack of privacy, and busy schedules (Ellison et al., 2007; Manago et al., 2012). It is also plausible that happier individuals simply have greater overlap between FTF and SM relationships, and thus a smaller proportion of SM-only contacts. For example, happier individuals may have more real-life social affiliations and connections—jobs, extended families, sports, or religious affiliations—and use SM to extend relationships established in FTF contexts. This is also suggested by research around strength of ties demonstrating the importance of relationships between people that have overlapping affiliations (Alba & Kadushin, 1976; Breiger, 1974). Lastly, as mentioned above, the association between having a greater proportion of SM contacts with whom individuals have a close FTF relationship and decreased depressive symptoms could be bidirectional.

In summary, there is preliminary evidence that there may be value in focusing one's SM contacts on individuals who are "Actual Allies"—individuals with whom one has had prior FTF experience, and particularly those one considers to be "close" friends.

## *L: Limit Time, Frequency, and the Number of Platforms Used*

The final component of the REAL mnemonic suggests that there may be potential value in simply limiting the overall exposure to social media. Three different aspects of SMU appear to be important: time, frequency, and number of platforms used.

For example, in the weighted sample of our national study, compared to those in the lowest quartile of total time per day spent on social media, participants in the highest quartile had significantly increased odds of depression (AOR = 1.66, 95% CI = 1.14–2.42), even after controlling for all covariates. Similarly, in multivariable models, compared with those in the lowest quartile, depression was more common among those in the highest quartiles of social media site visits per week (AOR = 2.74, 95% CI = 1.86–4.04). All associations between independent variables and depression demonstrated strong dose–response relationships ($p < 0.001$), and results were robust to all sensitivity analyses. Therefore, both time and frequency seemed to be important.

Again, because these data were cross-sectional, the directionality of this association is not clear. It may be that individuals with depression tend to use more social media. For example, depressed individuals with a diminished sense of self-worth may turn to social media-based interactions for validation (Caplan, 2002; Sanders, Field, Diego, & Kaplan, 2000). Subsequently, individuals may suffer from continuous rumination and guilt surrounding Internet use, while feeling compelled to continue the cycle due to low self-efficacy and negative self-appraisal (Caplan, 2002; Davis, 2001). Due to the high accessibility of social media and the possibility of socialization in a controlled setting, individuals with underlying depression and anhedonia may be more drawn to social media than to FTF interactions (Morahan-Martin & Schumacher, 2003; Young & Rogers, 1998).

It may also be that those who use increased amounts of social media subsequently develop increased depression. Multiple studies have linked social media use with declines in subjective mood, sense of well-being, and life satisfaction (Chou & Edge, 2012; Kross et al., 2013; Sagioglou & Greitemeyer, 2014). For example, passive consumption of social media content—as opposed to active communication—has been associated with a decrease in bonding and bridging social capital and an increase in loneliness (Burke, Marlow, & Lento, 2010). One explanation may be that exposure to highly idealized representations of peers on social media elicits feelings of envy and the distorted belief that others lead happier and/or more successful lives (Krasnova, Wenninger, Widjaja, & Buxmann, 2013; Tandoc et al., 2015). Consequently, these envious feelings may lead to a sense of self-inferiority and depression over time (Smith & Kim, 2007). It is also possible that the feeling of "time wasted" by engaging in activities of little meaning on social media negatively influences mood (Sagioglou & Greitemeyer, 2014). Additionally, the substantial rise in the amount of time young individuals spend on the Internet—particularly on social media—has led some to call for the recognition of "Internet addiction" as a distinct psychiatric condition that is closely associated with depression (Block, 2008; Morrison & Gore, 2010). Finally, it is possible that increased social media exposure may increase the risk of cyberbullying, which may also increase feelings of depression (Lenhart, 2007; O'Keeffe & Clarke-Pearson, 2011).

Regardless of the direction of association between social media use and depression, these findings should be of interest to clinicians and public health practitioners. For example, it may be valuable for clinicians to assess social media use among depressed individuals to probe for maladaptive patterns of use which may be contributing to mood dysregulation. Additionally, there may be useful ways of leveraging social media to decrease stigma of depression and identify individuals at risk, such as detecting self-disclosures of depression on social media (Moreno et al., 2011). Because social media has become an integrated component of human interaction, it is important for clinicians interacting with young adults to recognize the important balance to be struck in encouraging potential positive use but redirecting from problematic use. With regard to public health practitioners, these findings suggest that social media may provide valuable venues to screen for depression or to disseminate targeted educational messages regarding depression. Such messages could promote awareness regarding maladaptive use and its association with mood disorders.

In addition, we have found evidence suggesting that social media "diffusion" (SMD, or the use of multiple different platforms) may also play a role. In our study, we asked about 11 different SM platforms by name. Interestingly, only 3% of individuals reported using none of the 11 social media platforms, and 52 (3%) reported using all of them. SMD was normally distributed, with a mean of 4.2 and a standard deviation of 2.5 on a scale ranging from 0 to 11. Thus, the average individual uses more than four different platforms. To improve interpretability of results, SMD was classified as 0–2, 3–4, 5–6, or 7–11. However, SMD was also treated as continuous in sensitivity analyses.

In a fully adjusted multivariable model that controlled for all covariates and SMU, compared with those who used 0–2 platforms, those who used 7–11 platforms had about three times the odds of reporting high levels of *depressive symptoms* (OR = 3.1, 95% CI = 1.9, 5.0). There was a linear association between SMD and depression in this multivariable analysis; for increasing quartiles of SMD, odds ratios for increased level of depressive symptomology were 1.0 (reference), 1.6, 2.2, and 3.1, respectively ($p < 0.001$ for overall linear association).

Similarly, in a fully adjusted multivariable model that controlled for all covariates and SMU, compared with those who used 0–2 platforms, those who used 7–11 platforms had more than three times the odds of reporting high levels of *anxiety symptoms* (OR = 3.3, 95% CI = 2.0, 5.3). Again, there was a linear association between SMD and anxiety in the multivariable analyses; for increasing quartiles of SMD, odds ratios for increased level of anxiety symptomology were 1.0 (reference), 1.4, 1.9, and 3.3, respectively ($p < 0.001$ for overall linear association).

These results are broadly consistent with the previous research that has suggested associations between overall SMU and both depression and anxiety (Chou & Edge, 2012; Kross et al., 2013; Lin et al., 2016; Sagioglou & Greitemeyer, 2014; Shensa et al., 2016). However, our analyses make an important contribution to the literature suggesting that the overall association between SMU and symptoms of depression and anxiety may be driven less by the total amount of SMU and more by the number of different platforms used.

Because our data were cross-sectional, the directionality of this association is unclear. It may be that individuals who suffer from depressive and/or anxiety symptoms tend to subsequently use a broader range of social media outlets. This may be because these individuals tend to search multiple different avenues for a setting that feels most comfortable and in which they feel most accepted (Lin & Lu, 2011).

Taken together, these results suggest that more SM use seems to be associated with mental health concerns, not only when "more" SM is defined in terms of time or frequency but also when SM is defined in terms of the number of different platforms used.

## Conclusion

This review and summary of our recent studies exploring associations between SMU and mental health suggest that many different specific aspects of SMU may be differentially associated with mental health outcomes. In particular, in order to reduce the risk of mental health problems related to SM, it may be useful to: (1) *R*enege negativity in SM interactions; (2) actively *E*ngage with SM, but in a balanced *E*quilibrium; (3) focus SM attention on *A*ctual *A*llies—close "real-life" contacts as opposed to individuals with whom one has less direct interpersonal experience; and (4) *L*imit SMU not only in terms of time and frequency but also the number of platforms used.

As previously discussed, the major limitation of the studies we present is that they were cross-sectional, which precludes our ability to determine directionality. Therefore, a highly important next step will be to conduct longitudinal studies that may help disentangle cause and effect. In the meantime, it is worth noting that there are often good conceptual reasons that we might expect the association between social media use and mental health conditions to be bidirectional. For example, increased overall use of social media may indeed increase exposure to content that may exacerbate depression or anxiety. However, it is also reasonable to conclude that conditions such as depression and anxiety might lead an individual to engage with more social media. This may result in a concerning vicious cycle. As we explore directionality via longitudinal studies, it will be important not to think of this as an either/or phenomenon.

Another important caveat of these findings is that they have focused on young adults. We considered this appropriate for initial research in this area because young adults are at a developmental time that has been associated with the development of mental health conditions such as depression and anxiety. They are also at risk for suicide. In addition, they are known to commonly use social media. However, it will be useful for future studies to branch out in terms of the study population. One clear direction of potential value will be to examine younger individuals. While there are age limitations for certain social media platforms, others can be, and indeed commonly are, used by grade school youth. Therefore, it would be interesting to revisit many of the questions described in this manuscript among individuals ages 11–17.

It will also be useful to examine these issues among older individuals. Adults ages 65 and older are experiencing the most rapid increases in social media use. This population is also at risk for mental health conditions. In addition, they are likely, because of their different developmental concerns, to manifest unique associations between social media use and mental health issues. For example, while among young adults there has been an association between social media use and increased mental health concerns, this may not be the case among older adults, for whom social media may be more important as a vehicle for retaining connections.

Another direction for future study will be qualitative research. This type of assessment can also help determine cause and effect. For example, by hearing in-depth accounts around social media use and mental health conditions directly from individuals, we can begin to make more general inferences. In developing qualitative studies such as these, it will be important to consider the study population. For example, it may be specifically useful to focus on individuals who have substantial, diagnosed mental health concerns. One reason this population would be valuable to study is because they are at high risk for the sequelae of mental health conditions such as disability and suicide. However, this population represents a small overall cohort of society. Therefore, it may also be useful to conduct qualitative studies with members of the general population. Although they may not be as much at risk for significant morbidity and mortality, we cannot escape the fact that social media, because it is so widespread throughout developed and developing societies, represents an important overall exposure.

Despite the limitations noted above, we maintain that there is value in beginning to consider best practices for using social media while optimizing mental health and that the REAL mnemonic may help that process. We acknowledge that this body of research is early and inconclusive. However, amid substantially increasing global concerns around mental health and rapidly growing reliance upon social media, caution and forethought are warranted. The components of the REAL mnemonic are not extreme. Suggestions such as limiting social media use to fewer platforms, focusing on real-life friends, and exercising caution at signs of addiction to social media have face value and are unlikely to have untoward negative effects.

## References


Acar, A. (2008). Antecedents and consequences of online social networking behavior: The case of Facebook. *Journal of Website Promotion, 3*(1–2), 62–83. https://doi.org/10.1080/15533610802052654

Alba, R. D., & Kadushin, C. (1976). The intersection of social circles. *Sociological Methods & Research, 5*(1), 77–102. https://doi.org/10.1177/004912417600500103

Almaatouq, A., Radaelli, L., Pentland, A., & Shmueli, E. (2016). Are you your friends' friend? Poor perception of friendship ties limits the ability to promote behavioral change. *PLoS One, 11*(3), e0151588. https://doi.org/10.1371/journal.pone.0151588

Andreassen, C. S. (2015). Online social network site addiction: A comprehensive review. *Current Addiction Reports, 2*(2), 175–184. https://doi.org/10.1007/s40429-015-0056-9

Andreassen, C. S., Billieux, J., Griffiths, M. D., Kuss, D. J., Demetrovics, Z., Mazzoni, E., & Pallesen, S. (2016). The relationship between addictive use of social media and video games and symptoms of psychiatric disorders: A large-scale cross-sectional study. *Psychology of Addictive Behaviors, 30*(2), 252–262. https://doi.org/10.1037/adb0000160

Andreassen, C. S., & Pallesen, S. S. (2014). Social network site addiction—an overview. *Current Pharmaceutical Design, 20*(25), 4053–4061. https://doi.org/10.2174/13816128113199990616
Andreassen, C. S., Pallesen, S., & Griffiths, M. D. (2016). The relationship between addictive use of social media, narcissism, and self-esteem: Findings from a large national survey. *Addictive Behaviors, 64*, 287–293. https://doi.org/10.1016/j.addbeh.2016.03.006
Andreassen, C. S., Torsheim, T., Brunborg, G. S., & Pallesen, S. (2012). Development of a Facebook addiction scale. *Psychological Reports, 110*(2), 501–517. https://doi.org/10.2466/02.09.18.PR0.110.2.501-517
Baker, R., Blumberg, S. J., Brick, J. M., Couper, M. P., Courtright, M., Dennis, J. M., ... Zahs, D. (2010). Research synthesis. *Public Opinion Quarterly, 74*(4), 711–781. https://doi.org/10.1093/poq/nfq048
Becker, M. W., Alzahabi, R., & Hopwood, C. J. (2013). Media multitasking is associated with symptoms of depression and social anxiety. *Cyberpsychology, Behavior, and Social Networking, 16*(2), 132–135. https://doi.org/10.1089/cyber.2012.0291
Bickham, D. S., Hswen, Y., & Rich, M. (2015). Media use and depression: Exposure, household rules, and symptoms among young adolescents in the USA. *International Journal of Public Health, 60*(2), 147–155. https://doi.org/10.1007/s00038-014-0647-6
Block, J. J. (2008). Issues for DSM-V: Internet addiction. *The American Journal of Psychiatry, 165*(3), 306–307. https://doi.org/10.1176/appi.ajp.2007.07101556
Breiger, R. L. (1974). The duality of persons and groups. *Social Forces, 53*(2), 181. https://doi.org/10.2307/2576011
Burke, M., Marlow, C., & Lento, T. (2010). Social network activity and social well-being. In *Proceedings of the SIGCHI Conference on Human Factors in Computing Systems* (pp. 1909–1912). New York, NY: ACM. https://doi.org/10.1145/1753326.1753613
Cain, M. S., Leonard, J. A., Gabrieli, J. D. E., & Finn, A. S. (2016). Media multitasking in adolescence. *Psychonomic Bulletin & Review, 23*(6), 1932–1941. https://doi.org/10.3758/s13423-016-1036-3
Caplan, S. E. (2002). Problematic internet use and psychosocial well-being: Development of a theory-based cognitive-behavioral measurement instrument. *Computers in Human Behavior, 18*(5), 553–575. https://doi.org/10.1016/S0747-5632(02)00004-3
Caplan, S. E. (2003). Preference for online social interaction: A theory of problematic Internet use and psychosocial well-being. *Communication Research, 30*(6), 625–648. https://doi.org/10.1177/0093650203257842
Cella, D., Gershon, R., Lai, J.-S., & Choi, S. (2007). The future of outcomes measurement: Item banking, tailored short-forms, and computerized adaptive assessment. *Quality of Life Research, 16*(Suppl. 1), 133–141. https://doi.org/10.1007/s11136-007-9204-6
Cella, D., Riley, W., Stone, A., Rothrock, N., Reeve, B., Yount, S., ... Hays, R. (2010). The Patient-Reported Outcomes Measurement Information System (PROMIS) developed and tested its first wave of adult self-reported health outcome item banks: 2005-2008. *Journal of Clinical Epidemiology, 63*(11), 1179–1194. https://doi.org/10.1016/j.jclinepi.2010.04.011
Center for Behavioral Health Statistics and Quality. (2015). *Behavioral health trends in the United States: Results from the 2014 National Survey on Drug Use and Health* (HHS Publication No. SMA 15-4927, NSDUH Series H-50). Retrieved from http://www.samhsa.gov/data/
Choi, S. W., Schalet, B., Cook, K. F., & Cella, D. (2014). Establishing a common metric for depressive symptoms: Linking the BDI-II, CES-D, and PHQ-9 to PROMIS depression. *Psychological Assessment, 26*(2), 513–527. https://doi.org/10.1037/a0035768
Chou, H. T. G., & Edge, N. (2012). "They are happier and having better lives than I am": The impact of using Facebook on perceptions of others' lives. *Cyberpsychology, Behavior and Social Networking, 15*(2), 117–121. https://doi.org/10.1089/cyber.2011.0324
Cover, R. (2015). *Digital identities: Creating and communicating the online self.* Cambridge, MA: Academic Press.
Crabtree, S. (2014, June 9). In U.S., depression rates higher for long-term unemployed. *Gallup-Healthways Well-Being Index.* Retrieved from http://www.gallup.com/poll/171044/depression-rates-higher-among-long-term-unemployed.aspx

Davila, J., Hershenberg, R., Feinstein, B. A., Gorman, K., Bhatia, V., & Starr, L. R. (2012). Frequency and quality of social networking among young adults: Associations with depressive symptoms, rumination, and corumination. *Psychology of Popular Media Culture, 1*(2), 72–86. https://doi.org/10.1037/a0027512

Davis, R. A. (2001). Cognitive-behavioral model of pathological Internet use. *Computers in Human Behavior, 17*(2), 187–195. https://doi.org/10.1016/S0747-5632(00)00041-8

Duggan, M., Ellison, N. B., Lampe, C., Lenhart, A., & Madden, M. (2015). *Social media update 2014*. Pew Research Center, Internet and Technology. Retrieved from http://www.pewinternet.org/files/2015/01/PI_SocialMediaUpdate20141.pdf

Durak, M., & Senol-Durak, E. (2014). Which personality traits are associated with cognitions related to problematic Internet use? *Asian Journal of Social Psychology, 17*(3), 206–218. https://doi.org/10.1111/ajsp.12056

Ellison, N. B., Heino, R., & Gibbs, J. (2006). Managing impressions online: Self-presentation processes in the online dating environment. *Journal of Computer-Mediated Communication, 11*(2), 415–441. https://doi.org/10.1111/j.1083-6101.2006.00020.x

Ellison, N. B., Steinfield, C., & Lampe, C. (2007). The benefits of Facebook "friends": Social capital and college students' use of online social network sites. *Journal of Computer-Mediated Communication, 12*(4), 1143–1168. https://doi.org/10.1111/j.1083-6101.2007.00367.x

Ellison, N. B., Steinfield, C., & Lampe, C. (2011). Connection strategies: Social capital implications of Facebook-enabled communication practices. *New Media & Society, 13*(6), 873–892. https://doi.org/10.1177/1461444810385389

Ellison, N. B., Vitak, J., Gray, R., & Lampe, C. (2014). Cultivating social resources on social network sites: Facebook relationship maintenance behaviors and their role in social capital processes. *Journal of Computer-Mediated Communication, 19*(4), 855–870. https://doi.org/10.1111/jcc4.12078

Feinstein, B. A., Bhatia, V., Hershenberg, R., & Davila, J. (2012). Another venue for problematic interpersonal behavior: The effects of depressive and anxious symptoms on social networking experiences. *Journal of Social and Clinical Psychology, 31*(4), 356–382. https://doi.org/10.1521/jscp.2012.31.4.356

Friedkin, N. (1980). A test of structural features of Granovetter's strength of weak ties theory. *Social Networks, 2*(4), 411–422. https://doi.org/10.1016/0378-8733(80)90006-4

Frison, E., & Eggermont, S. (2015). Exploring the relationships between different types of Facebook use, perceived online social support, and adolescents' depressed mood. *Social Science Computer Review, 45*(2), 1–19. https://doi.org/10.1177/0894439314567449

GfK KnowledgePanel®. (2013). *KnowledgePanel design summary*. Retrieved from http://www.knowledgenetworks.com/ganp/docs/KnowledgePanel%28R%29-Design-Summary.pdf

Gottfried, J., & Shearer, E. (2016). *News use across social media platforms 2016*. Pew Research Center, Internet and Technology. Retrieved from http://www.journalism.org/2016/05/26/news-use-across-social-media-platforms-2016/

Granovetter, M. S. (1973). The strength of weak ties. *American Journal of Sociology, 78*(6), 1360–1380. https://doi.org/10.1086/225469

Greenberg, P. E., Fournier, A.-A., Sisitsky, T., Pike, C. T., & Kessler, R. C. (2015). The economic burden of adults with major depressive disorder in the United States (2005 and 2010). *The Journal of Clinical Psychiatry, 76*(2), 155–162. https://doi.org/10.4088/JCP.14m09298

Greenwood, S., Perrin, A., & Duggan, M. (2016). *Social media update 2016*. Washington, DC. Retrieved from http://www.webcitation.org/6r4NbntGd

Greitemeyer, T., Mügge, D. O., & Bollermann, I. (2014). Having responsive Facebook friends affects the satisfaction of psychological needs more than having many Facebook friends. *Basic and Applied Social Psychology, 36*(3), 252–258. https://doi.org/10.1080/01973533.2014.900619

Hanprathet, N., Manwong, M., Khumsri, J., Yingyeun, R., & Phanasathit, M. (2015). Facebook addiction and its relationship with mental health among Thai high school students. *Journal of the Medical Association of Thailand, 98*(Suppl 3), S81–S90 Retrieved from http://www.ncbi.nlm.nih.gov/pubmed/26387393

Kessler, R. C., Chiu, W. T., Demler, O., Merikangas, K. R., & Walters, E. E. (2005). Prevalence, severity, and comorbidity of 12-month DSM-IV disorders in the National Comorbidity Survey Replication. *Archives of General Psychiatry, 62*(6), 617–627. https://doi.org/10.1001/archpsyc.62.6.617

Kim, J., & Lee, J. R. (2011). The Facebook paths to happiness: Effects of the number of Facebook friends and self-presentation on subjective well-being. *Cyberpsychology, Behavior and Social Networking, 14*(6), 359–364. https://doi.org/10.1089/cyber.2010.0374

Koc, M., & Gulyagci, S. (2013). Facebook addiction among Turkish college students: The role of psychological health, demographic, and usage characteristics. *Cyberpsychology, Behavior, and Social Networking, 16*(4), 279–284. https://doi.org/10.1089/cyber.2012.0249

Krackhardt, D. (1992). The strength of strong ties: The importance of Philos in organizations. In N. Nohria & R. Eccles (Eds.), *Networks and organizations: Structure, form, and action*. Cambridge, MA: Harvard Business School Press.

Krasnova, H., Wenninger, H., Widjaja, T., & Buxmann, P. (2013). *Envy on Facebook: A hidden threat to users' life satisfaction?* Paper presented at International Conference on Wirtschaftsinformatik, Leipzig, Germany. Retrieved from https://www.ara.cat/2013/01/28/855594433.pdf

Krasnova, H., Widjaja, T., Buxmann, P., Wenninger, H., & Benbasat, I. (2015). Why following friends can hurt you: An exploratory investigation of the effects of envy on social networking sites among college-age users. *Information Systems Research, 26*(3), 585. https://doi.org/10.1287/isre.2015.0588

Kross, E., Verduyn, P., Demiralp, E., Park, J., Lee, D. S., Lin, N., … Ybarra, O. (2013). Facebook use predicts declines in subjective well-being in young adults. *PLoS One, 8*(8), e69841. https://doi.org/10.1371/journal.pone.0069841

Kuss, D. J., & Griffiths, M. D. (2011). Online social networking and addiction—a review of the psychological literature. *International Journal of Environmental Research & Public Health, 8*(9), 3528–3552. https://doi.org/10.3390/ijerph8093528

Lenhart, A. (2007). *Cyberbullying*. Pew Research Center, Internet and Technology. Retrieved from http://www.webcitation.org/6eVgbqVbe

Li, Z. (2016). Psychological empowerment on social media: Who are the empowered users? *Public Relations Review, 42*(1), 49–59. https://doi.org/10.1016/j.pubrev.2015.09.001

Lin, K., & Lu, H. (2011). Why people use social networking sites: An empirical study integrating network externalities and motivation theory. *Computers in Human Behavior, 27*(3), 1152–1161. https://doi.org/10.1016/j.chb.2010.12.009

Lin, L. Y., Sidani, J. E., Shensa, A., Radovic, A., Miller, E., Colditz, J. B., … Primack, B. A. (2016). Association between social media use and depression among U.S. young adults. *Depression and Anxiety, 33*(4), 323–331. https://doi.org/10.1002/da.22466

Lou, L. L., Yan, Z., Nickerson, A., & McMorris, R. (2012). An examination of the reciprocal relationship of loneliness and Facebook use among first-year college students. *Journal of Educational Computing Research, 46*(1), 105–117. https://doi.org/10.2190/EC.46.1.e

Lup, K., Trub, L., & Rosenthal, L. (2015). Instagram #instasad?: Exploring associations among instagram use, depressive symptoms, negative social comparison, and strangers followed. *Cyberpsychology, Behavior and Social Networking, 18*(5), 247–252. https://doi.org/10.1089/cyber.2014.0560

Manago, A. M., Taylor, T., & Greenfield, P. M. (2012). Me and my 400 friends: The anatomy of college students' Facebook networks, their communication patterns, and well-being. *Developmental Psychology, 48*(2), 369–380. https://doi.org/10.1037/a0026338

McDougall, M. A., Walsh, M., Wattier, K., Knigge, R., Miller, L., Stevermer, M., & Fogas, B. S. (2016). The effect of social networking sites on the relationship between perceived social support and depression. *Psychiatry Research, 246*, 223–229. https://doi.org/10.1016/j.psychres.2016.09.018

McEwan, B., & Guerrero, L. K. (2010). Freshmen engagement through communication: Predicting friendship formation strategies and perceived availability of network resources from communication skills. *Communication Studies, 61*(4), 445–463. https://doi.org/10.1080/10510974.2010.493762

McEwan, B., & Guerrero, L. K. (2012). Maintenance behavior and relationship quality as predictors of perceived availability of resources in newly formed college friendship networks. *Communication Studies, 63*(4), 421–440. https://doi.org/10.1080/10510974.2011.639433

Meena, P. S., Mittal, P. K., & Solanki, R. K. (2012). Problematic use of social networking sites among urban school going teenagers. *Industrial Psychiatry Journal, 21*(2), 94–97. https://doi.org/10.4103/0972-6748.119589

Morahan-Martin, J., & Schumacher, P. (2003). Loneliness and social uses of the Internet. *Computers in Human Behavior, 19*(6), 659–671. https://doi.org/10.1016/S0747-5632(03)00040-2

Moreno, M. A., Jelenchick, L. A., Egan, K. G., Cox, E., Young, H., Gannon, K. E., & Becker, T. (2011). Feeling bad on Facebook: Depression disclosures by college students on a social networking site. *Depression and Anxiety, 28*(6), 447–455. https://doi.org/10.1002/da.20805

Morrison, C. M., & Gore, H. (2010). The relationship between excessive Internet use and depression: A questionnaire-based study of 1,319 young people and adults. *Psychopathology, 43*(2), 121–126. https://doi.org/10.1159/000277001

Muench, F., Hayes, M., Kuerbis, A., & Shao, S. (2015). The independent relationship between trouble controlling Facebook use, time spent on the site and distress. *Journal of Behavioral Addictions, 4*(3), 163–169. https://doi.org/10.1556/2006.4.2015.013

O'Keeffe, G. S., & Clarke-Pearson, K. (2011). The impact of social media on children, adolescents, and families. *Pediatrics, 127*(4), 800–804. https://doi.org/10.1542/peds.2011-0054

O'Reilly, T., & Battelle, J. (2009). *Web squared: Web 2.0 five years on*. Web 2.0 Summit. Sebastopol, CA. Retrieved from http://www.web2summit.com/web2009/public/schedule/detail/10194

Pagani, M., Hofacker, C. F., & Goldsmith, R. E. (2011). The influence of personality on active and passive use of social networking sites. *Psychology and Marketing, 28*(5), 441–456. https://doi.org/10.1002/mar.20395

Pagani, M., & Mirabello, A. (2011). The influence of personal and social-interactive engagement in social TV web sites. *International Journal of Electronic Commerce, 16*(2), 41–68. https://doi.org/10.2753/JEC1086-4415160203

Pantic, I., Damjanovic, A., Todorovic, J., Topalovic, D., Bojovic-Jovic, D., Ristic, S., & Pantic, S. (2012). Association between online social networking and depression in high school students: Behavioral physiology viewpoint. *Psychiatria Danubina, 24*(1), 90–93.

Paxton, P. (1999). Is social capital declining in the United States? A multiple indicator assessment. *American Journal of Sociology, 105*(1), 88–127. https://doi.org/10.1086/210268

Perrin, A. (2015). *Social media usage: 2005-2015*. Pew Research Center, Internet and Technology. Retrieved from http://www.pewinternet.org/2015/10/08/social-networking-usage-2005-2015/#

Pilkonis, P. A., Choi, S. W., Reise, S. P., Stover, A. M., Riley, W. T., & Cella, D. (2011). Item banks for measuring emotional distress from the Patient-Reported Outcomes Measurement Information System (PROMIS®): Depression, anxiety, and anger. *Assessment, 18*(3), 263–283. https://doi.org/10.1177/1073191111411667

Pilkonis, P. A., Yu, L., Dodds, N. E., Johnston, K. L., Maihoefer, C. C., & Lawrence, S. M. (2014). Validation of the depression item bank from the Patient-Reported Outcomes Measurement Information System (PROMIS) in a three-month observational study. *Journal of Psychiatric Research, 56*, 112–119. https://doi.org/10.1016/j.jpsychires.2014.05.010

Primack, B. A., Swanier, B., Georgiopoulos, A. M., Land, S. R., & Fine, M. J. (2009). Association between media use in adolescence and depression in young adulthood: A longitudinal study. *Archives of General Psychiatry, 66*(2), 181–188. https://doi.org/10.1001/archgenpsychiatry.2008.532

Rozin, P., & Royzman, E. B. (2001). Negativity bias, negativity dominance, and contagion. *Personality and Social Psychology Review, 5*(4), 296–320. https://doi.org/10.1207/S15327957PSPR0504

Sagioglou, C., & Greitemeyer, T. (2014). Facebook's emotional consequences: Why Facebook causes a decrease in mood and why people still use it. *Computers in Human Behavior, 35*, 359–363. https://doi.org/10.1016/j.chb.2014.03.003

Sanders, C. E., Field, T. M., Diego, M., & Kaplan, M. (2000). The relationship of Internet use to depression and social isolation among adolescents. *Adolescence, 35*(138), 237–242.

Shatz, I. (2016). Fast, free, and targeted: Reddit as a source for recruiting participants online. *Social Science Computer Review, 35*(4), 537–549. https://doi.org/10.1177/0894439316650163

Shaw, A. M., Timpano, K. R., Tran, T. B., & Joormann, J. (2015). Correlates of Facebook usage patterns: The relationship between passive Facebook use, social anxiety symptoms, and brooding. *Computers in Human Behavior, 48*, 575–580. https://doi.org/10.1016/j.chb.2015.02.003

Shensa, A., Sidani, J. E., Lin, L., Bowman, N., & Primack, B. A. (2016). Social media use and perceived emotional support among US young adults. *Journal of Community Health, 41*(3), 541–549. https://doi.org/10.1007/s10900-015-0128-8

Simoncic, T. E., Kuhlman, K. R., Vargas, I., Houchins, S., & Lopez-Duran, N. L. (2014). Facebook use and depressive symptomatology: Investigating the role of neuroticism and extraversion in youth. *Computers in Human Behavior, 40*, 1–5. https://doi.org/10.1016/j.chb.2014.07.039

Smith, R. H., & Kim, S. H. (2007). Comprehending envy. *Psychological Bulletin, 133*(1), 46–64. https://doi.org/10.1037/0033-2909.133.1.46

Steinfield, C., Ellison, N. B., & Lampe, C. (2008). Social capital, self-esteem, and use of online social network sites: A longitudinal analysis. *Journal of Applied Developmental Psychology, 29*(6), 434–445. https://doi.org/10.1016/j.appdev.2008.07.002

Tandoc, E. C., Ferrucci, P., & Duffy, M. (2015). Facebook use, envy, and depression among college students: Is facebooking depressing? *Computers in Human Behavior, 43*, 139–146. https://doi.org/10.1016/j.chb.2014.10.053

The Nielsen Company. (2012). *State of the media: The social media report 2012*. Retrieved from http://www.nielsen.com/us/en/insights/news/2012/social-media-report-2012-social-media-comes-of-age.html

Tromholt, M. (2016). The Facebook experiment: Quitting Facebook leads to higher levels of well-being. *Cyberpsychology, Behavior, and Social Networking, 19*(11), 661–666. https://doi.org/10.1089/cyber.2016.0259

Verduyn, P., Lee, D. S., Park, J., Shablack, H., Orvell, A., Bayer, J., … Kross, E. (2015). Passive Facebook usage undermines affective well-being: Experimental and longitudinal evidence. *Journal of Experimental Psychology: General, 144*(2), 480–488. https://doi.org/10.1037/xge0000057

Vujeva, H. M., & Furman, W. (2011). Depressive symptoms and romantic relationship qualities from adolescence through emerging adulthood: A longitudinal examination of influences. *Journal of Clinical Child & Adolescent Psychology, 40*(1), 123–135. https://doi.org/10.1080/15374416.2011.533414

Wagner, T. H., Baker, L. C., Bundorf, M. K., & Singer, S. (2004). Use of the Internet for health information by the chronically ill. *Preventing Chronic Disease, 1*(4), A13.

Wang, C., Lee, M. K. O., & Hua, Z. (2015). A theory of social media dependence: Evidence from microblog users. *Decision Support Systems, 69*, 40–49. https://doi.org/10.1016/j.dss.2014.11.002

Wegmann, E., Stodt, B., & Brand, M. (2015). Addictive use of social networking sites can be explained by the interaction of Internet use expectancies, Internet literacy, and psychopathological symptoms. *Journal of Behavioral Addictions, 4*(3), 155–162. https://doi.org/10.1556/2006.4.2015.021

World Health Organization. (2017). *Depression* (Fact sheet). Retrieved from http://www.who.int/mediacentre/factsheets/fs369/en/

Xu, S., Wang, Z., & David, P. (2016). Media multitasking and well-being of university students. *Computers in Human Behavior, 55*(Part A), 242–250. https://doi.org/10.1016/j.chb.2015.08.040

Young, K. S., & Rogers, R. C. (1998). The relationship between depression and Internet addiction. *CyberPsychology and Behavior, 1*(1), 25–28. https://doi.org/10.1089/cpb.1998.1.25

# Chapter 10
# Interplay Between Families and Technology: Future Investigations

**Xiaoran Sun and Cassie McMillan**

Technology has become increasingly pervasive in American society, leading researchers, journalists, parents, teachers, and popular culture alike to question how technology has shaped our daily lives. The influx of technology raises a variety of new issues, many of which are specifically of interest to family scholars. For instance, it remains unclear whether technology is changing the way we form, maintain, and understand families—and the conditions under which these changes are for better or worse.

The chapters presented in this volume provide critical insight to help us better understand the relations between families and technology. In this final chapter, we bring specific attention to three themes that resonate throughout the volume: (1) how technology has shaped power dynamics in families, (2) the role technology has played in redefining and adjusting boundaries between family members and around the family, and (3) the relation between technology, family, and inequality. We conclude with suggestions for future research on family and technology by pointing to the need to integrate more theory and novel methods. Overall, we think that there is much promise in studying how families and technology are interconnected and believe that this line of research will continue to influence family scholarship.

---

Authors contributed equally.

X. Sun
Department of Human Development and Family Studies, Penn State, University Park, PA, USA
e-mail: xiaoran.sun@psu.edu

C. McMillan (✉)
Department of Sociology and Criminology, Penn State, University Park, PA, USA
e-mail: mcmillan@psu.edu



J. Van Hook et al. (eds.), *Families and Technology*, National Symposium on Family Issues 9, https://doi.org/10.1007/978-3-319-95540-7_10

## Technology and Power Dynamics in Families

Technology can profoundly influence the power dynamics in modern families. Family members gain and maintain their power based on the structural hierarchy in family systems and their own resources, and those with more power have a greater capacity to make decisions and influence others' behaviors (Cox & Paley, 1997; Dunbar, 2004; Minuchin, 1985; Safilios-Rothschild, 1976). Technology challenges traditional family hierarchy and shifts power structures by bringing unique resources, especially knowledge and information, to family members who historically held limited power within the family unit (e.g., children, and women). Several chapters in this volume consider whether and how technology impacts the power structures within parent–youth and couple relationships.

### *Parent–Child Power Structures*

In the traditional parent–child subsystem, determined role structures and resources via expertise knowledge and information allow parents to hold more power over their children. With the swift development of technology, however, parent–youth power dynamics have begun to change in at least three ways as technology is becoming increasingly intertwined with family life. First, youth increasingly act as technology brokers and/or innovators who guide and teach their parents about how to use technology. From enacting this role, children may *gain* power in the family due to their greater access to resources such as technology-related knowledge and information. Meanwhile, parents often assimilate to technological change at a slower rate, leading them to depend on their children to assist them in navigating new technological landscapes (Dworkin, Chap. 2; Nathanson, Chap. 1). This phenomenon may be more salient in immigrant families or families of low socioeconomic status since parents in these families are even less likely to have access to new technologies (Clark, Chap. 3; Nathanson, Chap. 1).

Second, new technologies can alter parents' ability to monitor their children's behaviors. Technology brings new challenges to parental monitoring that can *reduce* parents' power. Parental monitoring of youth's technology use has become increasingly challenging as a result of recent transition in families from using shared stationary forms of technology, such as televisions and desktops, to private mobile devices including smartphones and laptops (Nathanson, Chap. 1). Private technology use, in combination with anonymity on the internet (Hertlein, Chap. 5) and the swift development in new technologies (Dworkin, Chap. 2), enables youth to covertly violate family rules, and as a result, parent's authority and control over their children decreases. Nonetheless, technology can simultaneously provide tools that facilitate parental monitoring and assist parents to *maintain*, or even *enhance*, control over the actions of their children. When youth or adult children leave home, mobile phones and the internet can increase parent's contact with their children and provide more opportunities for parental involvement in their personal lives (Treas & Gubernskaya, Chap. 8). At the extreme, these opportunities may even lead to helicopter parenting, by which parents maintain undue influence over their geographically distant children.

A third way that technology changes parent–youth power dynamics is by providing children with access to information that may contradict the traditions and values held by their parents, especially for families in non-Western, developing countries. After the introduction of television into rural villages in Vietnam, parents were no longer children's only channel to information that originates outside of family (Jayakody, Chap 7). Instead, children were able to gain knowledge via television, and these new perspectives often challenged what their parents had previously taught. This influx of new information may reduce parents' authority over their children's attitudes and behaviors, particularly those relating to dating and sexuality.

In sum, new technologies may reduce hierarchy in parent–child power structures by empowering children and decreasing parents' authority. This brings new challenges to parenting and may reduce the effectiveness of parental control, not only with regard to children's technology use but also over other behavioral domains, as these changes in the power structure can be extended to general parent–child interactions and family life. Nevertheless, the extent of this impact depends on the context surrounding the family's technology use, including socioeconomic status, immigration status, race and ethnicity, and parents' levels of familiarity with new technologies. Researchers should be cautious when generalizing findings to different sociocultural contexts.

## *Power Dynamics in Dating and Couple Relationships*

The chapters also provide timely and innovative insights into how technology may impact couple relationships. Technology is shifting the power dynamics between partners, though scholars are still debating whether this shift is reducing or expanding inequality between men and women. First, men have traditionally monopolized opportunities to initiate romantic relationships, whereas dating apps and websites may empower women to take more initiative in this process and have more control when selecting potential partners, holding conversations, and planning dates (Rosenfeld, Chap. 6; Schwartz &Velotta, Chap. 4). Nevertheless, questions need to be answered about whether this shift in the power dynamic continues as the relationship further develops, particularly within those aspects of the relationships that occur offline. Moreover, if dating apps show too many potential partners, the objectification of women may intensify and in turn reduce women's power in dating (Schwartz & Velotta, Chap. 4).

Within formed couple relationships, it is also unclear if the conditions under which technology is implemented negatively impact or strengthen the relationship. According to investment and exchange theories, when commitment levels are inconsistent between partners, the individual who is more committed, and thus more attached and dependent, is likely to hold less power (Drigotas, Safstrom, & Gentilia, 1999; Rusbult, 1980; Safilios-Rothschild, 1976). Dating apps may undermine relationship commitment by providing users with alternative partners (Schwartz & Velotta, Chap. 4). Partners with low relationship commitment are more likely to engage in infidelity, and online tools provide them with more opportunities to do so. For instance, niche online dating sites specifically market themselves as products to connect users looking for extramarital relationships (Hertlein, Chap. 5; Schwartz & Velotta, Chap. 4). However, it is unclear whether technology has actually increased the likelihood of infidelity. Only a small proportion of married heterosexual individuals who have extramarital relationships arranged their affairs through apps (16% for men, 12% for women, Rosenfeld, Chap. 6). In a panel discussion during the symposium, Hertlein, Schwartz, and Diane Felmlee stated that it is also debatable whether technology makes infidelity easier or more difficult to expose. On one hand, evidence of infidelity, such as pictures, phone numbers, and browsing history, can be easily uncovered by partners who share access to each other's devices; on the other hand, infidelity can be hidden with evidence easily deleted. Furthermore, technologies may help increase relationship commitment by providing online platforms for the public announcement of one's relationship status (e.g., Facebook official) and by facilitating couples' communication and conflict resolution (Hertlein, Chap. 5).

In sum, answers to whether and how technology has changed the power dynamics and quality in dating and couple relationships remain unclear. It is likely that technology differentially impacts couple relationships depending on other dimensions of the relationship. For example, couples with high levels of relationship commitment may be less influenced by the number of potential partners displayed online, whereas those with low commitment may be more vulnerable. Likewise, individuals with a tendency towards infidelity may always be able to find ways to form extramarital relationships, despite whether technologies provide such opportunities. Nevertheless, technology may bring benefits to couples whose communication and commitment are more challenging to maintain offline. Thus, we need both macrolevel population research to describe changes on the societal level in dating processes and couple relationships and microlevel research on interactions among technology, individuals' relationship attitudes, and relationship dynamics.

## Technology and Boundaries Between and Around Family Systems

Chapters in this volume collectively address the implications of technology for boundaries both within families and between families and the social world beyond. According to family systems theory, boundaries are implicit lines drawn between different (sub)systems regarding privacy, control, responsibilities, and communication; they are governed by family rules and interaction patterns and play a significant role in family functioning by defining and differentiating family (sub) systems (Minuchin, 1985). Boundaries regulate the interactions between subsystems (e.g., individuals, and dyads), as well as between entire family units and the outside world. These boundaries should be firm enough to maintain the integrity and organization of each (sub)system so that it is insulated from external risks, yet permeable and adjustable to allow healthy communication across boundaries and to maintain the adaptability of family systems. Boundaries that are too diffuse or rigid can be a manifestation of or lead to family dysfunction (Kerig, 2005; Minuchin, 1985). Family members' technology use may challenge the regulation, maintenance, and adjustment of family boundaries, and in turn, these processes may shape technology use. This interplay is likely to have important implications for family well-being.

Discussions of the role of technology in boundaries within the family system have focused on those between parents and children (Dworkin, Chap. 2; Hertlein, Chap. 5; Nathanson, Chap. 1) and between partners in couple relationships (Hertlein, Chap. 5). To explain the parent–youth boundary for technology use, Dworkin and Nathanson applied social domain theory to argue that adolescents often strive to define acceptable technology use, especially their online behaviors such as social media use, as part of the personal domain over which they own privacy rights and their parents have limited or no access. Parents may push back against these efforts and retain youth's technology use in the shared, conventional domain that they have power to control (Hessel, He, & Dworkin, 2017; Smetana, Crean, & Campione-Barr, 2005). If parent's definition of the domain of technology use is inconsistent with that of their children, youth may perceive that boundaries have been violated and their privacy invaded, which may lead to family conflict and ultimately to behavioral problems (Hessel et al., 2017). Previous research on the use of family-shared technologies (e.g., televisions) has found positive effects of parental active mediation (i.e., communication with youth about media content), especially their evaluative comments on media content, in shaping children's attitudes and socio-emotional outcomes (Nathanson, Chap. 1).

We know less about the effects of parental mediation and monitoring on the use of personal technologies (e.g., smartphones) that youth tend to define as being in their personal domains. Parents' long-term monitoring may reduce trust and introduce more conflicts between parents and youth, as well as interfere with youth's autonomy development (Hertlein, Chap. 5). By applying the concept of healthy boundaries, we could conclude that, although there may be benefits to parental monitoring and involvement in youth's technology use, it is also important to prevent both intrusive parenting and disengagement from regulation of youth's technology use. Intrusive parenting can hinder autonomy development, whereas disengagement and permissiveness may expose youth to risky technology use, especially online behaviors and content that are harmful to their well-being. Instead, because firm yet flexible boundaries are valuable for family functioning, it should benefit the family unit to formulate well-defined, transparent rules regarding children's technology access that are adjustable based on youth's developmental needs (Hertlein, Chap. 5). This means it is important that parents formulate clear rules governing youth's technology use. More research is needed to test the effect of rule setting on defining family boundaries and encouraging youth well-being. Future work is also needed to examine the effectiveness of technology-related rules when there are inconsistencies between partners.

Likewise, inconsistencies between partners in their domain definitions of technology use may introduce conflict. Partners may have different expectations about what online behaviors are acceptable (Hertlein, Chap. 5) and the extent of access they should have to each other's private electronic devices. Partners may also have inconsistent expectations about how much they allow technology to permeate their family life. If one partner has a more permeable boundary between technology use and family life, the other may interpret this behaviors as technoference (i.e., interference of technology devices with family interactions), which can result in more couple conflicts and lower satisfaction (Hertlein, Chap. 5). Complementing the family systems tenet on the necessity of clear boundaries, Hertlein's Couple and Family Technology Framework holds that ambiguity in the rules surrounding technology use can create couple discord. In addition to better regulating couples' expectations for technology use, rules can increase relationship commitment and reduce exposure to potential opportunities for infidelity. However, despite these potential benefits, Hertlein finds that few couples actually establish such rules in their relationships. Further qualitative and quantitative research needs to provide a better understanding of barriers to couples' rule setting on technology use and provide information to guide interventions and therapy for helping couples establish healthier boundaries.

Technology not only permeates family life and influences within-family functioning but can also shape boundaries between the family and other social institutions, such as larger social networks and communities, media, and workplaces. Modern technology can increase the permeability of boundaries between the family and other institutions, which may provide families with more access to supportive networks and information. Online forums and videos are new and effective ways for parents to obtain information about child rearing, particularly for low-income parents who have had limited access to these resources (Dworkin, Chap. 2). The advent of television provided couples with more accessible information about HIV and safe sex practices (Jayakody, Chap.7). Still, technology can blur boundaries between the family and the social world beyond, which may result in negative consequences for family life. For example, technology challenges work–family balance as it makes it more normative for employees to bring work home (Hertlein, Chap. 5). One way to address this issue is for institutions to establish clear policies that limit technology-related work interference at home.

In sum, technology brings new opportunities and challenges to family functioning by its implications for family boundaries. Existing theories, including family systems theory, social domain theory, and the Couple and Family Technology Framework, emphasize the importance of establishing clear yet permeable boundaries that take developmental and contextual factors into account. There is a lack of evidence for these theories though, and limited work has considered how boundaries around technology are formed, maintained, and adjusted. More research is needed to provide evidence to support these theories and provide guidance for therapy, interventions, and policy.

## Technology and Family Inequality

The authors of this volume address how technology interacts with family at a broader societal level by discussing whether technology challenges or reinforces traditional structures of inequality. On the one hand, there is evidence that technology may *reduce* socioeconomic inequalities that have historically shaped the way families form and interact. For instance, online dating websites provide singles with new opportunities to meet potential partners and have proved to be a useful resource to those in tight dating markets (Rosenfeld, Chap. 6; Schwartz & Velotta, Chap. 4). Sexual minorities, singles over fifty, and racial and religious minorities have traditionally had limited opportunities to meet potential partners. Online dating has evened the playing field by providing these demographic groups with increased odds of forming romantic partnerships and families (Rosenfeld, Chap. 6). Similarly, technology may help foster equality among families coming from different socioeconomic backgrounds. Following the introduction of television in rural Vietnamese communities, young people gained access to new information that had previously only been available to those in wealthy Western countries (Jayakody, Chap. 7). Television can introduce populations to new ideas surrounding HIV prevention, gender norms, and the role of sex in intimate relationships (Gerbner, Gross, Morgan, & Signorielli, 1986), and this exposure has consequences for how individuals interact with family members. For instance, new information about sexually transmitted diseases is likely to have improved health and fertility outcomes for the couples who participated in Jayakody's study (Chap. 7).

On the other hand, several chapters in this volume suggest that there are multiple avenues through which technology can replicate, or even exacerbate, inequalities that have traditionally structured family relations. First, when new technologies are introduced, they often preserve structures of inequality that undermine children from underprivileged families. While excess social media use is correlated with several adverse health outcomes for all children and adolescents (Primack, Chap. 9), there is evidence that social media may have additional negative ramifications for youth from disadvantaged backgrounds. For example, previous work has shown that children from immigrant families and sexual minority youth are more likely to be victims of cyberbullying and are at greater risk of privacy violations (Clark, Chap. 3; Felmlee & Faris, 2016). Future work is needed to better understand how the effects of technology use vary according to race, nativity, socioeconomic status, sexuality, and family structure. In particular, scholars should consider whether these effects further disadvantage children and families from minority groups.

Additionally, the chapters in this volume point to several examples of how new technologies are encouraging the replication of traditional gender roles when individuals form and maintain their families. Traditional gender norms have delegated responsibilities for caregiving and providing emotional support to female family members and these standards may help account for women's economically disadvantaged positions in the labor market (Budig & England, 2001; Correll, Benard, & Paik, 2007). While new technologies, such as cell phones, have resulted in positive outcomes, including increased intergenerational contact, much of this contact is maintained through female family members (Treas & Gubernskaya, Chap. 8). As a result, technology is likely to represent another avenue through which mothers and daughters assume caretaking and kin-keeper roles. This pattern is likely to have long-lasting implications for gender inequality. For instance, female family members may make sacrifices to their educational aspirations and careers, while male family members are disconnected from intimacy that supports psychological well-being.

Relatedly, it remains unclear whether online dating is empowering women in the relationship formation process or if it is maintaining traditional gender roles and inequalities (Rosenfeld, Chap. 6; Schwartz & Velotta, Chap. 4). While online dating may provide women with increased autonomy, recent empirical work has shown that men are significantly more likely to initiate contact on online dating sites (Kreager, Cavanagh, Yen, & Yu, 2014). Additionally, research suggests that women tend to receive as much gender-based harassment from potential male partners when they date online versus offline (Whitty & Carr, 2006). Overall, these findings suggest that the same gender norms which guide offline dating may apply to online dating. Women continue to lack autonomy in the relationship formation process and it remains unclear if new technologies have done much to challenge this. Future research should further consider how technology can empower those from disadvantaged positions and combat social inequalities.

## Directions for Future Work on Families and Technology

Building on the three themes discussed above, we conclude by offering suggestions for future work investigating the implications of technology for families. First, the authors in this volume originate from a diverse array of scientific disciplines, which all carry their own set of rich, well-developed theories. We believe that in order for research on family life and technology to make the most meaningful impact, scholars need to further integrate social, psychological, and developmental theories into their empirical work. For example, social exchange theory and the investment model have long been applied to understand marital stability and decision-making processes (Drigotas et al., 1999; Luke, Goldberg, Mberu, & Zulu, 2011; Rusbult, 1980; Safilios-Rothschild, 1976). Future research should consider how new technologies are likely to both complement and challenge these traditional frameworks. Online dating websites, for instance, have made it increasingly easier for individuals to meet potential partners (Schwartz & Velotta, Chap. 4). By applying the investment model to online dating, scholars could test whether the existence of these new alternative partners poses a credible threat to the commitment levels of existing couples.

We also think that scholars should continue to apply family systems theory (Minuchin, 1974) to understand how technology has influenced family dynamics and to guide families on how to cope with challenges brought by technology. As new technology continues to permeate family systems, we foresee the need to update and reinvigorate aspects of family systems theory by incorporating technology as a component in family dynamics. Finally, we see promise in applying tenets of life course theory, particularly Elder's (Elder Jr., 1994) concept of "linked lives," to the study of family and technology. Elder's theory posits that the experiences of individuals are interdependent because they are embedded in particular social relationships throughout their life span, such as that of parent and child or husband and wife. We know that children are increasingly playing the role of brokers between new technological information and their families (Dworkin, Chap. 2), yet we have little idea as to how this role change will shape children's development and affect the way they form and maintain their own families. As technology continues to advance and new questions emerge, integrating and building upon established theoretical frameworks will prove to be a crucial task for family researchers.

Second, in order to answer novel research questions about family and technology, scholars need to collect new types of data and incorporate cutting-edge methods into their research. For instance, to better understand the role technology plays in shaping outcomes of interest, scholars need to begin collecting longitudinal and panel survey data that include questions about both family functioning and individuals' technology use (Primack, Chap. 9). We also see promise in creative experimental approaches for making causal inferences. The controlled experiment described by Jayakody (Chap. 7) allowed researchers to study a population both before and after the introduction of television. As technologies, such as the internet and smartphones, are introduced to new communities throughout the world, we encourage scholars to apply similar research designs to test key theoretically grounded questions regarding the relation between families and technology. Moreover, researchers need to be aware of the diversity of the populations they study and consider how the sociocultural and economic contexts in which families are situated may shape the family–technology interplay.

As technology continues to advance at increasingly rapid rates, family researchers should incorporate sources of big data to continue answering questions that are both innovative and whose answers are impactful. Traditional methods of data collection (e.g., surveys, experiments, and interviews) will always play an invaluable role in the study of families, but there is much to be learned from data that are already being collected from the technologies families use on a daily basis. Websites and mobile devices gather data that are detailed, dynamic, and often freely available to the public (e.g., Twitter data). In order for family scholars to make meaningful substantive conclusions from these new sources of big data, we see promise in integrating statistical and computational techniques from text, network, and spatial analyses. Through the implementation of text analysis, scholars can better understand the sentiment and content of messages that family members send to one another through the internet or mobile devices (Tausczik & Pennebaker, 2010). Techniques from network analysis can provide insight as to how technology encourages the formation and dissolution of social relationships. Recent work on online dating has conceptualized the web of connections between users as a social network, to make novel observations about the structures that guide opportunities for couple formation (Felmlee & Kreager, 2017; Lewis, 2013). Finally, spatial analysis offers tools that researchers can utilize to test whether technology is breaking down the boundaries of geography when it comes to decisions involving family formation and family planning. Spatial analysis has been used to show that social diffusion, or the spread of new ideas, norms, and technologies, accounts for a substantial portion of fertility decline in Eastern Europe (Goldstein & Klüsener, 2014). While there is much to be learned from integrating big data into research on families and technology, we also believe that scholars should critically consider the ethical dilemmas that may arise from this type of research. Family researchers should take particular care to protect the privacy of those individuals whose data they are analyzing.

Finally, we believe that family scholars should take an active role in advocating for policies that enable families to make choices about technology use that promote family well-being and for policies that hold companies accountable for detrimental effects of their products. On January 11, 2018, Mark Zuckerberg, the CEO of Facebook, posted on his Facebook account that his company would make major modifications to the social media website to maximize its ability to bring people together and benefit their well-being (Zuckerberg, 2018). When changes like these are made, sociologists, psychologists, and family scholars should critically consider what positive and/or negative implications there may be for family life. Of course, there is still much to be learned as to whether technology changes power structures, draws new boundaries, and challenges systems of inequality within the context of the family. As the field progresses, family scholars should engage with policy makers and offer their expertise when controversies arise over the role technology should play in shaping family life.

## Conclusion

In sum, the 2017 Penn State Symposium on Family Issues revealed many avenues through which technology has and will continue to impact family functioning, the well-being of family members, and the social world that surrounds families. Although the conditions under which technology has positive, negative, and/or neutral impacts on families have not yet been delineated, we can conclude that the introduction and development of new technologies has changed family life in many ways—some for better and some perhaps for worse. We encourage family scholars to conduct further theoretical and empirical work, including that which uses new data sources and innovative methods, to better understand and explain the impacts of technology. There is still much to be learned on how families can enjoy the benefits of technology, while overcoming the new challenges that it introduces.

## References


Budig, M. J., & England, P. (2001). The wage penalty for motherhood. *American Sociological Review, 66*(2), 204–225.

Correll, S. J., Benard, S., & Paik, I. (2007). Getting a job: Is there a motherhood penalty? *American Journal of Sociology, 112*(5), 1297–1339.

Cox, M. J., & Paley, B. (1997). Families as systems. *Annual Review of Psychology, 48*, 243–267.

Drigotas, S. M., Safstrom, C. A., & Gentilia, T. (1999). An investment model prediction of dating infidelity. *Journal of Personality and Social Psychology, 77*(3), 509–524.

Dunbar, N. E. (2004). Dyadic power theory: Constructing a communication-based theory of relational power. *Journal of Family Communication, 4*(3&4), 235–248.

Elder, G. H., Jr. (1994). Time, human agency, and social change: Perspectives on the life course. *Social Psychology Quarterly, 57*(1), 4–15.

Felmlee, D. H., & Faris, R. (2016). Toxic ties: Networks of friendship, dating, and cyber victimization. *Social Psychology Quarterly, 79*(3), 243–262.

Felmlee, D. H., & Kreager, D. A. (2017). The invisible contours of online dating communities: A social networks perspective. *Journal of Social Structure, 18*(1), 1–27.

Gerbner, G., Gross, L., Morgan, M., & Signorielli, N. (1986). Living with television: The dynamics of the cultivation process. In J. Bryant & D. Zillmann (Eds.), *Perspectives on media effects* (pp. 17–40). Hillsdale, NJ: Erlbaum.

Goldstein, J. R., & Klüsener, S. (2014). Spatial analysis of the causes of fertility decline in Prussia. *Population and Development Review, 40*(3), 497–525.

Hessel, H., He, Y., & Dworkin, J. (2017). Paternal monitoring: The relationship between online and in-person solicitation and youth outcomes. *Journal of Youth and Adolescence, 46*(2), 288–299.

Kerig, P. K. (2005). Revisiting the construct of boundary dissolution: A multidimensional perspective. *Journal of Emotional Abuse, 5*(2–3), 5–42.

Kreager, D. A., Cavanagh, S. E., Yen, J., & Yu, M. (2014). "Where have all the good men gone?" gendered interactions in online dating. *Journal of Marriage and Family, 76*(2), 387–410.

Lewis, K. (2013). The limits of racial prejudice. *Proceedings of the National Academy of Sciences, 110*(47), 18814–18819.

Luke, N., Goldberg, R. E., Mberu, B. U., & Zulu, E. M. (2011). Social exchange and sexual behavior in young women's premarital relationships in Kenya. *Journal of Marriage and Family, 73*(5), 1048–1064.

Minuchin, P. (1985). Families and individual development: Provocations from the field of family therapy. *Child Development, 56*(2), 289–302.

Minuchin, S. (1974). *Families and family therapy*. Cambridge, MA: Harvard University Press.

Rusbult, C. E. (1980). Commitment and satisfaction in romantic associations: A test of the investment model. *Journal of Experimental Social Psychology, 16*(2), 172–186.

Safilios-Rothschild, C. (1976). A macro-and micro-examination of family power and love: An exchange model. *Journal of Marriage and Family, 38*(2), 355–362.

Smetana, J., Crean, H. F., & Campione-Barr, N. (2005). Adolescents' and parents' changing conceptions of parental authority. *New Directions for Child and Adolescent Development, 108*, 31–46.

Tausczik, Y. R., & Pennebaker, J. W. (2010). The psychological meaning of words: LIWC and computerized text analysis methods. *Journal of Language and Social Psychology, 29*(1), 24–54.

Whitty, M. T., & Carr, A. N. (2006). *Cyberspace romance: The psychology of online relationships*. New York: Palgrave Macmillan.

Zuckerberg, M. (2018, January 11). [Facebook post]. Retrieved from https://www.facebook.com/zuck/posts/10104413015393571

# Index





J. Van Hook et al. (eds.), *Families and Technology*, National Symposium on Family Issues 9, https://doi.org/10.1007/978-3-319-95540-7

The manufacturer's authorised representative in the EU is Springer Nature Customer Service Centre GmbH, Europaplatz 3, 69115 Heidelberg, Germany. If you have any concerns regarding our products, please contact ProductSafety@springernature.com

Printed and bound by CPI Group (UK) Ltd, Croydon, CR0 4YY
28/11/2025
02007706-0006